PSI WARS: TED, WIKIPEDIA AND THE BATTLE FOR THE INTERNET

PSI WARS: TED, WIKIPEDIA AND THE BATTLE FOR THE INTERNET

Craig Weiler

www.whitecrowbooks.com

CONTENTS

FOREWORD VII

PREFACE... XV

CHAPTER ONE: IS THIS REALLY HAPPENING? 1

CHAPTER TWO: YES, IT'S REALLY HAPPENING 9

CHAPTER THREE: THEY LIKE ME!
   THEY REALLY . . . UH, NEVERMIND 17

CHAPTER FOUR: CONTROVERSY THE OLD FASHIONED WAY:
   SLANDER AND INSULTS 23

CHAPTER FIVE: YUP, IT'S A REAL SCIENCE 35

CHAPTER SIX: EVERY GOOD CONTROVERSY NEEDS A
   RABBLEROUSER 49

CHAPTER SEVEN: MEET THE IDEOLOGUES, ER, SKEPTICS.......... 55

CHAPTER EIGHT: TED THROWS DOWN WITH
   SHELDRAKE AND HANCOCK 69

CHAPTER NINE: WHEN SKEPTICS ATTACK:
   SKEPTICAL ORGANIZATIONS AND WEBSITES 75

CHAPTER TEN: SHELDRAKE AND HANCOCK DELIVER
THE SMACKDOWN 101

CHAPTER ELEVEN: THE UNIVERSE JUST GOT WEIRDER:
NONLOCAL CONSCIOUSNESS 111

CHAPTER TWELVE: TED DOUBLES DOWN ON THE CRAZY 123

CHAPTER THIRTEEN: WIKIPEDIA: THE RESOURCE FROM HELL.... 133

CHAPTER FOURTEEN: MESSY DIVORCE:
A TEDX BECOMES AN EX... 163

CHAPTER FIFTEEN: PARAPSYCHOLOGY: THE RODNEY
DANGERFIELD OF SCIENCE 183

CHAPTER SIXTEEN: THE ANTI-CLIMACTIC CLIMAX......................... 189

CHAPTER SEVENTEEN: THE ARGUING MACHINE 201

CHAPTER EIGHTEEN: EXTEDXWESTHOLLYWOOD ...
THERE'S NO BUSINESS LIKE SHOW BUSINESS....................... 211

CHAPTER NINETEEN: DEEPAK CHOPRA JOINS THE FUN.................. 217

CHAPTER TWENTY: ONCE MORE INTO THE BREECH........................ 225

CHAPTER TWENTY-ONE: WHENCEFORTH FROM HERE?................ 231

ENDNOTES 237

ABOUT THE AUTHOR.. 247

INDEX 249

FOREWORD

A REPORT FROM

THE BATTLE GROUND

"Controversies in science, like wars, are wasteful procedures and seldom the best way to settle issues. But they are not entirely fruitless, and the battle over ESP is such an instance."

JOURNAL OF PARAPSYCHOLOGY EDITORIAL, 1942
J.B. RHINE, CHARLES STUART & J.G. PRATT

Ever since I considered pursuing a career in parapsychology, I remember feedback from some of my peers advising caution. They offered this caution not because of their awareness of the typical criticisms placed on parapsychology, but for the lack of research positions and jobs. Criticism comes with the territory for all manner of professions. Dealing with claims of psychic abilities such as telepathy, precognition and phenomena suggestive of survival of the mind/personality beyond death, were going to carry with them a wide array of potential conventional explanations. All these phenomena are typically referred to as 'psi' (ψ), the initial letter in Greek for the word psyche or "mind" which serves as a blanket term for all parapsychological phenomena.

Explaining such phenomena away becomes harder when they are examined in the controlled and stringent conditions of the laboratory. Even here, there is a good overall case for psi. Statistically, the effects reported from experiments are comparable to other areas of psychology and the social sciences. Discounting this mountain of evidence is a real challenge to some skeptics, who see these claims as directly contradicting basic principles of the current materialist worldview. And yet, general surveys of psi find that the majority of the public can relate to having these experiences at some point in their lives, with some also finding them to be a regular occurrence.

Systematic research of these phenomena began in the late 19th century with significant contributions by the Society for Psychical Research and its American counterpart. But parapsychology gradually earned itself a place amongst the sciences from the 1920s thanks to the work of Drs. Joseph Banks (J.B.) Rhine and Louisa Rhine, along with their colleagues at Duke University (Durham, NC). Not only were formal methods for testing extra-sensory perception (ESP) and psychokinesis (PK) developed, but they were refined, as replications began to be carried out by scientists from other disciplines who saw the potential in parapsychology, or wanted to exercise their own skepticism about the reality of psi in controlled conditions. J. B. Rhine established the *Journal of Parapsychology* in 1937 as a platform for controlled studies to be critically debated and further refined. Some would argue that the only reason that parapsychology has produced good evidence for the reality of ESP and PK is due to the 'file drawer effect' in that only successful studies see publication and the failures are hidden away. But from the beginning, the *Journal of Parapsychology* has welcomed experimental 'failures' as well as 'successes' so that the published record is as balanced and representative as possible. From my own experience, there are not enough research funds nor person-power (those in employment or working independently in parapsychology) to be able repeatedly to conduct studies and discard them if nothing is found; every study counts and provides us with something to learn from. All cards are on the table.

By 1957 the Rhines established the Parapsychological Association (PA), and in 1969 it became an affiliate of the American Association for the Advancement of Science (AAAS) – with noted resistance from a few individuals who did not want the PA to have such recognition. The PA remains an affiliate of the AAAS today, and, despite a small minority of individuals unjustly believing parapsychology to be a pseudoscience, it seems that perhaps some of those people would fall into the category of "dogmatic skeptics" or, indeed, "pseudo-skeptics" to whom Mr. Craig Weiler refers throughout *Psi Wars*.

Noted skeptic, Professor Chris French, presented a clear-cut case in recent times to the Centre for Inquiry, London, for why parapsychology is a science. The simple answer is that it conforms to known methods and analyses of the sciences within which it is placed – that being among the social sciences (i.e. psychology). In fact, several methodological protocols have worked their way into the social sciences because of the pioneering work of parapsychology. For example, as Professor Caroline Watt explained in her 2005 presidential address to the PA, it can be demonstrated that parapsychology is responsible for the development of several methodical advances in mainstream science. These include: blind methods (early screening in card guessing), randomization, and meta-analyses to assess the outcome of groups of studies. Professor Watt stated:

> I believe that the quality of parapsychologists' methodology is as good as, and often better than, that of psychologists.

We cannot 'out' a science and call it a pseudoscience on the grounds that we object to the very topics it aims to explore if it is conducted within the constraints of generally accepted scientific methods – otherwise, those objections are literally no more than prejudice. The processes by which reports of psi seem to occur need to be scrutinised, this requires good methods and a skeptical mind, much as it does with any other exploration in science. The key thing to remember is that all sciences explore anomalies, in that they are trying to advance knowledge and our understanding of various systems, from space exploration (astrophysics), to weather systems (meteorology), diseases (medicine), and brain function (neuroscience). Much of what we think we know still has an unmapped boundary area, and this is where new research can often be most fruitful. It is the duty of any scientist to approach their given topic with a skeptical mind and charter new territory; separating what is known from what is seemingly unknown – and from there attempt to control and understand seemingly new mechanisms and systems (e.g. the cognitive process of ESP and PK).

In the United Kingdom there are around a dozen universities delivering taught modules on parapsychology, usually within psychology curricula. A key objective of these modules is to provide students with the means to think critically and adopt a healthy level of skepticism that they can apply to all areas of psychology, which they deal with. Wikipedia is a useful subject through which to explore how that process can go awry. I cannot remember when I personally noticed that Wikipedia grossly misrepresented the nature and findings of parapsychology – it seems as if it has always been the case. However, it has certainly become more noticeable in recent times as students come to rely on the Internet as a source of information, and who are now part of a technology driven culture. In hearing of something new in class – or when it comes to personal study – turning to mobile phones to research information in an attempt to find out more has become typical behavior. This will often bring up a Wiki page as the first source, which, for many, is never given a second thought as to whether it is reliable or not. And yet, this clearly becomes a problem when students would speak in class of things they've read about online and believed they'd learnt correctly, only to find the lecturers (specialists working in the field) give a completely different picture. And, by this, I do not mean that university-based academics are presenting evidence only in favor of psi; rather, the aim is to provide a fair balance of positive and negative findings, to praise and criticise as appropriate. All the pieces of the jigsaw are provided, not just a selection of pieces or personal preference for how the final picture should look.

Students of this generation also appreciate TED talks, given that they are so easy to access online with many topics to choose from in bite size twenty-minute presentations. The fact that those with a focus on parapsychology, such as talks by biologist Dr. Rupert Sheldrake and physicist Dr. Russell Targ, were banned for a period of time – owing to petty arguments centred around science taking investigations of psi seriously – has only led to an increase in views for these videos. But such arguments and knee-jerk banning without honestly considering the content of such talks, with an informed skeptical mind, defeated the very point of TED talks and the freedom to discuss science and the efforts made in our progression of knowledge. It is here, in particular, that Mr. Weiler made a positive difference. He became involved in the discussions, he followed them intricately, and he became an activist in order to bring the dispute down to Earth – voicing the case and strength of parapsychological research. Order and balance was required to bring resolution and a productive way forward for how information is received and disseminated by TED talks. Lessons were learned.

New students of science, and indeed parapsychology, are unlikely to be aware of these controversies. When we have discussed them in class, the reaction is often one of shock that information would be distorted or even purposely withheld so as to sway the public view. For example, when they have seen and read various studies on telepathy, and the overall evidence for its reality, it is then odd – indeed frustrating – for the students and others to see many basic Internet searches on telepathy saying, "there is no evidence for telepathy". To add to this, on BBC Radio 4's *Today* programme, in October 2001, magician and proclaimed skeptic James Randi stated in a recorded interview:

> There is no firm evidence for the existence of telepathy, ESP or whatever you wish to call it ...

As Dr. Sheldrake has said, "it is a typical dogmatic skeptical mantra"; it becomes meaningless in light of the known evidence that can be gleaned from very basic reading. Professor Etzel Cardeña gave a concise review of the evidence for psi from parapsychological research that was published in the *American Psychologist* in 2018, which demonstrates a strong scientific case for psi. For the scientifically literate, the paper presents a perfect review for the strength of the experimental evidence gathered to date, especially for those simply uninformed in this area or skeptical and keen to know more. This paper led to a response from Professor Arthur Reber, and noted critic of parapsychology Professor James Alcock, who chose not to challenge the empirical evidence, or to present data of their own that might contradict it but instead opted for the tactic of arguing on theoretical grounds that psi must be false as it contradicts known physicalist-materialist frameworks. In an article for the Society for Psychical Research entitled 'the egregious state of skepticism', Professor Chris Roe criticised the strategy for relying on little more than "weak rhetorical strategies and vague allusions to problems or inadequacies". Further to this, an entire issue of the *Journal of Scientific Exploration* in 2019 dedicated an editorial and several commentaries on the response to Cardeña by Reber and Alcock, and was similarly scathing of this rather embarrassing example of skepticism.

My own training as a psychologist and skeptical activist, has assisted me in exploring how what we already know can explain away many assumed instances of psi, especially from real-world accounts – but I have also learned that what we seemingly know does not help explain everything. Taking a critical stance is highly important for any scientist and also learning how to weigh up the given evidence. In 1984, Dr. Michael Hough, former editor of the *Bulletin of the Australian Institute for Parapsychological Research* (AIPR), made a clear distinction between those labelling themselves as skeptics:

> Skeptics can be categorised into two gradational types:
>
> (a)   The person who only forms opinion after properly examining the evidence for and against.
>
> (b)   The person who merely debunks the paranormal ("we battle irrationality"), because of fear of the unknown, or negative childhood religious experiences [for example]. Typical is: cynicism, overstatement, preoccupation with trickery, a smug attitude, ("we are best at using reason; we might be right"). Debate is stifled with reams of questions (impossible to answer in the time available).

Within this book, full focus is on those who would label themselves as 'skeptics' but fall into 'type b' outlined by Dr. Hough. Mr. Weiler makes this distinction clear from the outset, before taking you on an in-depth and personal journey of conflict and exposure of improper uses of skepticism. And for the public and others, how this can have an unjustified damaging impact on what 'evidence' for psi has been presented on the Internet to date.

The *Psi Wars* are indeed a reality, but are not necessarily a direct battle between those researching psi and those who appear to have a personal dislike of the research and its implications. The latter tend to select evidence, or more often, quotes they can find from popular critics to fit their world-view. Science does not operate this way. Science is based on data, and we should move in the direction it points and attempt to interpret it based on what we know. If the data begins to go beyond the known, then we have the potential for making new discoveries. There is an ever-increasing body of knowledge and data in support of psi; some of which may be explained by anomalistic psychological processes, which produce the illusion of an anomalous experience or ability. However, there are so many case reports and studies, which seem to go beyond these confines. Thus, parapsychology continues to explore such claims, and is steadily progressing with the modest funds it receives, and the small number of parapsychologists actively engaged world-wide.

Mr. Weiler has done a great service to the field as a journalist well-read in the research. He has spent a considerable amount of time exposing and debunking how information can be manipulated or withheld from the public in this technological age of communication and learning. Many people already know of such controversies in a general sense due to their own backgrounds, and therefore know not to trust every word of the media and public platforms of information. But certainly, for all, aware of the controversies or not, the depth of detail and exposure of the truth of such issues within *Psi Wars* is eye-opening!

As Professor Roe stated in his 2017 presidential address to the PA on 'Withering Skepticism' it may seem tempting just to ignore "dyed in the wool skeptics" but on the contrary:

> [J]ust as a government in office needs a discerning opposition to call it to task to ensure good governance, so parapsychology needs a strong capable counter-advocate movement to ensure our methods are fit for purpose and our findings valid and meaningful.

Being skeptical, and engaging with skeptical debate, is extremely important. The information contained within this book is a direct hit of counter argument and exposure, highlighting when skepticism is misused and beliefs and personal biases take over rational debate and science communication. Craig Weiler has compiled a compelling case that is presented to you, here, as a concise personal report, which delivers the evidence and certainly makes no apologies. The more people are aware of the controversies, the easier the fight will become for fair and balanced science communication. *Psi Wars* is certainly not fruitless – this book bears many fruits!

Callum E. Cooper, Ph.D.
10, April, 2020

University of Northampton
Exceptional Experiences & Consciousness Studies
(EECS) research group

PREFACE

I t is now 2020 and seven years have passed since the science controversy at TED happened. After achieving a very minor level of fame for participating in the controversy, my life went back to normal.

I'd had close to nothing to do with TED before this began. (TED is a nonprofit company that puts on conferences, with interesting speakers, which they film, edit and put up on the web. They are called "TED talks" and they're very popular.) I don't particularly like watching video on the web and most of the talks were about subjects that didn't really interest me. But in a very short order I found my fortunes intertwined with theirs for a while as our paths intersected.

The TED controversy was a milestone of sorts in the sciences and deserved a good telling. But it is a story that needs updating. The controversy that TED staff jumped into is not over and still rages within the sciences. There is a shift happening that is achingly slow, but it is there and needs to be documented. The German physicist Max Planck once observed "Science advances one funeral at a time." He stated:

> A new scientific truth does not triumph by convincing its opponents and making them see the light, but rather because its opponents eventually die, and a new generation grows up that is familiar with it.

That is as good a definition of the TED controversy as you're likely to get. The slow change of a major scientific paradigm occurs in an environment that is nothing like the shining example of objectivity that we make science out to be. It is messy, often nasty and full of open hostility.

The TED controversy was such a perfect example of this that it was of historical significance in the sciences. A great deal of this change normally occurs beyond the view of anyone but academics and they risk their careers if they advocate for a new paradigm. But the TED controversy was open war in the sciences and gave a rare glimpse into the sheer power of inertia and cognitive dissonance in this battle of scientific theories.

There may never be anything like this controversy again. It was a science unicorn. The way it all slowly unfolded and worked itself into a crescendo was a one-off. The new developments that kept coming and coming, over a period of about a month and a half, gave an enormous number of people time to learn about it and contribute.

It was serendipitous for me because it allowed me to collect years of research on organized skepticism and dogma in the academic scientific world and show how it all laid the groundwork for this controversy to take place exactly the way it did. It was the Internet that made this all possible and it is the same Internet that is moving us less slowly in the direction of an inevitable scientific shift.

The ground is moving underneath the feet of media companies like TED and will continue to do so. They are falling behind in understanding the sciences because they cling to a presumably safe, skeptical position. So much has changed about how we get our information that it's not reasonable to expect everyone to quickly adapt. Decades of bad habits will be difficult to overcome. But it must happen. When your audience knows more than you do about a subject, which you profess to be an expert on, that's a recipe for trouble. That is what happened to TED.

It's not the science itself, which has changed much, but rather the public access to it; particularly the areas commonly referred to as "fringe."

This controversy had all the kicking and screaming that goes along with scientific change and this is what I want readers to see and understand for what it is. The science part of the science controversy is basically over, but the change in perception is the battle that really matters. The TED controversy is a demonstration of just how intense that battle can get and how hard people will fight to avoid changing. TED closed ranks with the skeptical old guard and paid dearly for it.

In that sense, the TED controversy is a warning of things to come. The genie is not going back in the bottle. Similar decisions will yield similar results in the future and things will never really go back to being the way they were. The massive shift in scientific theoretical thinking is coming and no one can stop it.

CHAPTER ONE

IS THIS REALLY

HAPPENING?

A Very Vivid Moment . . .

The house lights dimmed, the music died down and the host came out. Above me was the inside of a beautiful geodesic dome that acted like an immersive movie screen, displaying all kinds of awesome graphics and in front of me was a small stage. It was a full house and you could feel the excitement. In less than a minute I would be walking on stage to give a twenty-minute speech.

Only two weeks prior, this entire elaborate production had been thrown into complete disarray. It was supposed to be a TED talk, but it had all gone terribly wrong. The original venue had been lost, the sponsors had vanished and several speakers bowed out because of the enormous controversy. Somehow, though, in completely amazing fashion, it had all come together with the majority of the original speakers.

I would never have been invited if the controversy had not taken place. But it had and here I was. I heard my name and I walked up onto the platform and into the bright lights in front of the crowd. There was no podium and I had no idea what to do with my hands. I tried not to move them too much while the presenter, Suzanne Taylor, was talking.

That was the least of my worries. Having only learned that I was going to be speaking on very short notice, all of my attempts to plan a speech had failed. I had never done this speech before; I'd not rehearsed it at all and had no notes. On top of that I had almost lost my voice.

Now, here I was, up on the stage and about to speak in mere seconds. All too quickly the presenter stepped down. I stood for a moment, quietly, in front of the audience, gathering my courage. At least I knew what I was going to talk about. I began to tell a story of change and how the controversy that had tossed this conference into complete uncertainty was just the beginning of a vast intellectual sea change that was happening right before our eyes.

There was a huge controversy at TED, which took place between early March and mid-April of 2013 that was confusing and perplexing. TED is well known and was quite a big deal at the time when I first wrote this book. The question I found myself asking over and over again was "why?" It was a controversy that seemed pointless because it would have been so easy to handle if the TED leadership had just had their wits about them. Yet, time and again, they made choices that dug their hole deeper and deeper until, finally, they were buried under a sea of criticism. What happened was completely unnecessary, yet also inevitable given the current cultural conditions surrounding our sciences.

The controversy cannot be understood by itself; it has to be seen within the context of a larger cultural picture, so this book is about both. It wasn't about people doing outrageous things or behaving like jerks (although that did happen), but rather the controversy is a significant milestone on the road to a fundamental cultural change.

It gives a hint of things to come. Deep within this kerfuffle lurks a much more significant point of contention: the nature of consciousness itself.

The controversy took place entirely on the Internet with people around the globe connected only through their computers. That fact alone still seems remarkable to me as someone who grew up with a rotary phone and a black and white television with three channels and no remote control. Communication has come a very long way in a very short time.

Yet, the kind of controversy that occurred at TED could easily have taken place over a hundred years ago. That part hasn't changed much. The squabble over the nature of consciousness predates the Internet, the computer and even the car. Its origins date back to the year in which the very first district (in New York) was lit by electricity and the very first World Series was played.

2

The year was 1882 and quite a lot happened that year. P.T. Barnum bought his famous elephant, "Jumbo;" the last bare knuckle boxing championship took place; Britain ran its first electric trains and the Red Cross was formally established. It was the year that the outlaw Jesse James was killed by Robert Ford and the first Labor Day parade was held. The world saw its very first string of Christmas tree lights and the germ that causes tuberculosis was discovered. The automobile would not be invented for another four years.

1882 is also the year that the Society for Psychical Research (SPR) was founded in London, England, to investigate as they put it: "that large body of debatable phenomena designated by such terms as mesmeric, psychical and spiritualistic", and to do so "in the same spirit of exact and unimpassioned enquiry, which has enabled science to solve so many problems."

Had these psychical researchers not found anything of interest in their investigations or had their investigations been badly done and easily refuted, that might have put an end to the matter right then and there, but that's not what happened. They did find a fair share of frauds, charlatans and wishful thinking, but they also found anomalies that were clearly not explainable by any normal means.

These anomalies remain largely unexplained today, partly due to the ephemeral nature of the phenomena but also because of the sheer weight of disbelief by the larger scientific community.

It is not possible scientifically to discover psychic ability directly. It is not a thing. In order to determine its existence, you have to rule out all other possibilities so that whatever is left, however improbable, is psychic ability. The problem with this is that for some skeptics this is never enough. You can never answer every single maybe-you-missed-something speculation. Although the reputations of the scientists involved in these investigations was beyond reproach and although they went over everything in excruciating detail, it did not prevent people from second guessing them. They could do the work and publish it fully, and openly, but they could not make people believe it and struggled even to get it read.

At the same time, psychology was in its infancy and working to get respectability. The introduction of psychical research was as unwelcome in that field as a roach in a glass of milk. It introduced an element of uncertainty into psychological research that is still avoided to this day. To allow psychic ability was to allow ghosts, poltergeists, spiritualism, spells, witchcraft and all manner of unsavory things that scientists were working to avoid. Magic is not supposed to be real. A concerted effort was made to disparage and ridicule this field of research.

And with that began the scientific controversy whose fires have never really died down. As early as 1886 the criticism began with many of the same characteristics that can be seen today: skeptical attacks on the credibility of researchers; skeptical explanations that did not conform to the evidence—vague straw man arguments[1] and a lack of interest in understanding or doing a thorough reading of what they were criticizing.

Most of the attacks came from the newly created *Psychological Review*, the first scientific psychology Journal. Parapsychology historian Carlos Alvarado noted:

> The contents of the *Psychological Review* reflect the hostile position many psychologists took towards psychical research during the 19th century. As argued elsewhere (e.g., Alvarado, 2006; Coon, 1992), psychical research was generally rejected by psychologists of the time for a variety of reasons, one of which involved psychology's own struggle to be recognized as a science.[2]

When you explore the fringes of science it is possible to see its frayed ends. Gone is the myth of the rational, objective scientist and in its place can be found a simple human being, subject to prejudices, biases, politics and irrationality, all of which can be found in this assessment of SPR field research by Joseph Jastrow:

> It seems probable that when a number of these cases have been collected, that their general nature and law-abiding character will be understood, that a rational group of associations may be clustered about the term 'mediumistic,' (*sic*) and that the temptation to magnify the doings of some of this class into a bundle of miracles will gradually pass away—all of which would be welcome consummations for the progress of Psychology.[3]

If you come back to this statement from the 1900's after reading some other skeptical comments from present day, you'll find that they're remarkably similar in nature. F.W.H. Myers, whose work was an early influence on Carl Jung, complained even then of the irrational skepticism he encountered.

It was in this atmosphere that the Society for Psychical Research conducted its studies into poltergeists and mediums as well as other anomalous phenomena. A thorough analysis of some exceptional case studies from that era and the skepticism that surrounds them even to this day can be found in the book *Randi's Prize*, by Robert McLuhan (2010).

Fast-forward to the 1930's and the collected works of Joseph Banks Rhine. Often referred to as the father of modern parapsychology, Rhine brought an end to the field work associated with mediums, psychics and séances. In its place he used controlled laboratory experiments and statistics to determine the existence of psychic ability. He is credited with being the first person to make use of statistical meta analyses, but he is best known for creating Zener cards for use in simple telepathy experiments. The Parapsychological Association provides this summary of his work:

> What conclusions can we draw about Rhine's overall research program? By 1940, 33 experiments had accumulated, involving almost a million trials, with protocols which rigorously excluded possible sensory clues (e.g., by introducing distance and/or barriers between sender and receiver, or by employing precognition protocols i.e., where the target has not yet been selected at the time subjects make their responses).

> Twenty-seven (27 of the 33 studies produced statistically significant results—an exceptional record, even today. Furthermore, positive results were not restricted to Rhine's lab. In the five years following Rhine's first publication of his results, 33 independent replication experiments were conducted at different laboratories. Twenty (20) of these (or 61%) were statistically significant (where 5% would be expected by chance alone).

> A meta-analysis was done specifically for precognition experiments conducted between the years 1935 - 1987. (Honorton, C., & Ferrari, D. [1989]. Meta-analysis of forced-choice precognition experiments 1935 - 1987. *Journal of Parapsychology*, vol 53, 281 - 308). This included 309 studies, conducted by 62 experimenters. The cumulative probability associated with the overall results was p = 10-24 (that is equivalent to .000000000000000000000001 where .05 is considered statistically significant). The scientific evidence for precognition, the most provocative of all parapsychological phenomena, stands on firm statistical grounds. [4]

If all of that sounds confusing, think of it this way: the odds that Rhine's life work doing parapsychology experiments was all for naught is a billion trillion to one. In other words, it's a very safe bet that he was doing valid research.

Rhine's work demonstrated very decisively that psychic ability is real and that should have closed the door on parapsychology skepticism, but that's not what happened.

He was accused of sloppy research, poor methodology, bad math and a variety of other slurs too numerous to mention. Seventy years after the formation of the SPR the basic problem remained the same. No matter how much research someone did and no matter how good it was or how convincing the accumulation of evidence, it was still impossible to get the scientific community to believe it. In 1951 psychologist Donald Hebb wrote this:

> Why do we not accept ESP [extrasensory perception] as a psychological fact? [The Rhine Research Center] has offered enough evidence to have convinced us on almost any other issue ... Personally, I do not accept ESP for a moment, because it does not make sense. My external criteria, both of physics and of physiology, say that ESP is not a fact despite the behavioral evidence that has been reported. I cannot see what other basis my colleagues have for rejecting it ... Rhine may still turn out to be right, improbable as I think that is, and my own rejection of his view is—in the literal sense—prejudice.[5]

In 1957 the Parapsychological Association was established and through much persistence, became a member of the American Association for the Advancement of Science in 1969. The difficulty wasn't in getting voted in, rather, the difficulty was to even get to that point. The screening committee refused to even examine their case until some serious back room wrangling forced the issue on the fourth try. At that point the committee conceded that the procedures were scientific, and the matter was put to the vote where the PA was overwhelmingly accepted by a vote of 170 to 30.[6]

More researchers have followed Rhine since then, but all their research has met the same irrational skepticism. No matter how good the work is, someone, somewhere will attack it and the mainstream scientific community will have its new reasons, however flimsy, for ignoring the results.

Nevertheless, parapsychology has progressed slowly through the years in fits and starts whenever enough money becomes available. Relatively low-cost experiments have racked up over the years with the result that there is a fairly impressive body of research that has been conducted.

Throughout all this time the skepticism has been pretty much the same dance to successively different tunes. One hundred and thirty years after the founding of the Society for Psychical Research, the research is still demonstrating the existence of psychic ability and mainstream scientists are still ignoring it. I'll be going into more detail about the social milieu of skepticism and parapsychology, but this brief summary should provide a basic understanding of the nature of the controversy that TED was wading into. It is socially acceptable to dismiss all parapsychological research as pseudoscience and to call parapsychologists quacks, but, at the same time, the facts don't support this claim.

And that's pretty much where things stood right up until about 2004, which is when the Internet provided a radically new battlefield, which has been used as a cultural force for change by both sides. On the one hand, skeptics have used the Internet very much to their advantage in spreading their point of view, but, on the other hand, it has also provided an unstoppable venue for opposing points of view to be heard. The science of parapsychology has slowly made its way onto the Internet and it is circumnavigating skeptical interference and forcing a sharing of facts. As a result, more people have become aware of the enormous gap between the facts of parapsychology and the skeptical mainstream viewpoint supported by mainstream science and mainstream media. This is creating a cultural storm that could not have taken place at any other time in history. If you take away the highly politicized subjects of evolution and global warming that split along political and/or religious lines, this is the largest scientific controversy going.

The TED controversy is a snapshot of a massive cultural and scientific change happening right smack in the middle of it.

The ghosts, the ghoulies and gypsies with their crystal balls are pushing their way into the scientific lab and forcing a real scientific examination of things that go bump in the night. The safe and secure imaginary world where the universe is a giant machine that can be figured out with math, where all that paranormal stuff can be explained away as delusion or fraud, is slowly breaking apart.

If this were just a scientific controversy and nothing else, it would have been over long ago after enough evidence had been accumulated. Science is not the issue here. Something else is in play that is causing this controversy to take place. All of western society is having to face its ultimate heart of darkness.

CHAPTER TWO

YES, IT'S REALLY
HAPPENING

The TED controversy traces its roots to reddit, a kind of enormous sharing and commenting website. It has a subcategory for TED where various TED conferences and videos are shared and commented upon.

TED, which stands for Technology, Entertainment and Design, has branched out in recent years and covers a wide variety of topics. It was started in 1984 by Richard Saul Wurman who wanted to show the powerful convergence of tech, entertainment and design, but his first conference lost money. He tried again, this time in 1990, with a partner, Harry Marks. It was successful, and the TED conference soon became a regular event in Monterey, California. At the time, it was invitation-only, but it drew big names:

> Over the years, TED speakers have included Bill Gates, Frank Gehry, Jane Goodall, Al Gore, Billy Graham, Annie Lennox, Peter Gabriel, Quincy Jones and Bono.[7]

In 2001, Wurman turned over the company to Chris Anderson's Sapling Foundation and Anderson became TED's curator. In 2006, TED started putting up videos of the talks, which became so popular that

TED built up a website around them. By 2009, TED talks surpassed 100 million views, and brought fame to people such as Jill Bolte Taylor and Sir Ken Robinson. Shortly thereafter, the TEDx program was initiated, which opened the TED program to independent organizers. TED has grown so popular that in 2012 they celebrated their one billionth view.

The reddit commenting was about a TEDx (independently produced) event in Spain in 2012. It was the sort of hysterical overreaction that can be found virtually everywhere on the Internet.

> The TED name is being dragged through the mud in Valencia, Spain, where a TEDx-approved event is promoting pseudoscientific stuff like (and I quote): crystal therapy, Egyptian psychoaromatherapy, healing through the Earth, homeopathy and even "basic mind control" (...)

> (...) Seeing the TED name associated with this freak show in a country where science and education have already been cornered and budget-cut by its own government is extremely sad. TED should react and examine its own standards in order to avoid being ashamed by these hordes of rain-makers and mystic scam artists in the future.[8]

An anonymous redditor and his buddies thought that the Spain event was too New Agey. Really, that's all there was to it. It was, however, just the sort of hyped up outrage that could catch the imagination of skeptics and they quickly voted it up. It had over 300 up votes, a very high number. Not only that, they set about to down vote comments, which they didn't like, to make them disappear.

Almost all of the comments on that thread agreed with the original post critiquing the event. I almost missed seeing that some comments had been suppressed by negative voting, so that they were under the threshold needed to be seen without additional clicking to open them. I opened the supposedly inferior comments and, lo and behold, all of them were in support of the TEDx event. This is very typical of how the skeptics handle debate. They try to shut out ideas that they don't like. (I will be dealing with who-is-a-skeptic in another chapter.)

But, at this point, it was just another skeptical reddit thread.

The conference was an easy target and it had all the necessary elements to drive skeptical outrage to 11. Reiki, crystal therapy, aroma therapy and the favorite skeptical punching bag, homeopathy. The tendency of skeptics to gang up and attack things as a group tends to make their numbers look larger than they actually are. In any case, it was probably the large discussion and the high approval rating of the original comment that caught the attention of the TED staff.

Lara Stein, the director of the whole TEDx program division, responded on that thread:

> (...) In the past we have handled most of these issues as one-offs and dealt with the organizers individually. Thanks to this discussion we decided to take on the "bad science" issue directly and openly.

On December 7 2012, Lara Stein sent a warning to the TEDx organizers, cautioning them about what would be considered unacceptable programming:

1. What is bad science/pseudoscience?

There is no bright and shining line between pseudoscience and real science, and purveyors of false wisdom typically share their theories with as much sincerity and earnestness as legitimate researchers (Michael Gordin's recent book, *The Pseudoscience Wars,* is a great overview). Needless to say, this makes it all terribly hard to detect and define.

Marks of bad science:

- Has failed to convince many mainstream scientists of its truth
- Is not based on experiments that can be reproduced by others
- Contains experimental flaws or is based on data that does not convincingly corroborate the experimenter's theoretical claims
- Comes from overconfident fringe experts
- Uses over-simplified interpretations of legitimate studies and may combine with imprecise, spiritual or new age vocabulary, to form new, completely untested theories.
- Speaks dismissively of mainstream science
- Includes some of the red flags listed in the two sections below

2. Red flag topics

These are not "banned" topics by any means—but they are topics that tend to attract pseudo-scientists. If your speaker proposes a topic like this, use extra scrutiny. An expanding, depressing list follows:

Food science, including:

- GMO food and anti-GMO foodists
- Food as medicine, especially to treat a specific condition: Autism and ADHD, especially causes of and cures for autism

Because of the sad history of hoaxes with deadly consequences in the field of autism research, really look into the background of any autism-related talk. If you hear anything that sounds remotely like, "Vaccines are related to autism,"—RUN AWAY. Another non-legitimate argument: "We don't know what works, so we have to try everything." Pretty much all the time, this argument is designed to cause guilt in suffering parents so they'll spend money on unproven treatments.

More:

- "Healing," including Reiki, energy fields, alternative health and placebos, crystals, pyramid power
- "Free energy" and perpetual motion machines, alchemy, time travel
- The neuroscience of [fill in the blank]—not saying this will all be non-legitimate, but that it's a field where a lot of goofballs are right now
- The fusion of science and spirituality. Be especially careful of anyone trying to prove the validity of their religious beliefs and practices by using science

Look carefully at talks on these topics: ask to see published data, and find a second source, unrelated to the speaker and a recognized expert in the field, who can validate the research.

This directive would be very confusing to anyone who knows how science really works. Experiments get done, they pass peer review, they get published in the appropriate journals and, voilà, *science*. All of this rambling post should be reduced to this: "All scientific claims must be backed by peer reviewed scientific research. Do not overstate or otherwise exaggerate this research." There, done.

TED's approach was very problematic. Who is a purveyor of false wisdom? How many researchers do you need to convince before you are mainstream? (This isn't as straightforward as it seems. Does this include only experts in your field, or do you include any scientist who has an opinion regardless of how well informed they are?) How do you define an "overconfident fringe expert?" What if someone speaks dismissively of mainstream science, but they are right? (This happens more often than you might think.)

Perhaps the most difficult part of this is that TED's motto is "Ideas Worth Spreading." But if the only ideas that are allowed are already mainstream, what exactly is the point of spreading them?

A far more serious issue with this directive is that it was so completely at odds with the facts. Questioning whether genetically modified (GMO) food is good for you is certainly a legitimate scientific topic. As most medicine is plant based, the idea that food is not medicine is quite radical. The question of autism and vaccines is actually still open despite what gets reported in the mainstream media. *The British Medical Journal* is facing charges of libel and fraud from Dr. Wakefield, whose work was independently replicated.[9] And the supposed pseudoscience of Reiki is backed by 42 peer reviewed studies and scientific papers and five systematic reviews published in 25 different scientific journals.[10]

TED's guidelines for science weren't very scientific. They were, instead, a collection of values and beliefs about science based on a reactionary point of view that is commonly associated with the skeptical community.

TEDxWhiteChapel Controversy

Now that TED had reacted to the reddit thread and assumed an ultra-conservative approach to scientific topics, the stage was set for a full-blown controversy. This came in the form of an independently produced conference (signified by the "x" in TEDx) named TEDxWhitechapel, which was held at Artsadmin's Toynbee Studios in London England.

The new science policy was quickly put to the test. On January 12, 2012, the event: *Visions for Transition. Challenging existing paradigms and redefining values (for a more beautiful world)* took place. This event featured, among others, a speech by Rupert Sheldrake titled "The Science Delusion" and a speech by Graham Hancock titled "The War on Consciousness." Both speeches were short, about twenty minutes long, and were questioning many of the assumptions that underlie modern science.

The talks at TEDxWhitechapel were duly filmed, edited and put on the main video website for TED with all the other videos. It was at this point that the controversy got rolling.

On March 6, PZ Myers, associate professor of Biology at the University of Minnesota Morris, and longtime skeptic, posted a short blurb condemning Sheldrake's talk.[11] On the same day, skeptic Kylie Sturgess also posted a quick piece slamming it.[12] And skeptic Jerry Coyne, a Professor in the Department of Ecology and Evolution at the University of Chicago, adds his opinion.[13] His alarming title: *TEDx talks completely discredited: Rupert Sheldrake speaks, argues that speed of light is dropping!* The main part of Sheldrake's speech, which questioned the materialistic dogmas of modern science, was not addressed by Coyne. Coyne's article focused on just one part of Sheldrake's speech that brought up the possibility that the speed of light might fluctuate. To Sheldrake, this was a *possibility* worth exploring. Coyne, however, treated this as if Sheldrake claimed that the speed of light was changing.

Jerry Coyne sent an email to Emily McManus, an atheist who was an editor at TED. Coyne published the McManus reply in which she referred to his "thoughtful blog post." I found that to be remarkably poor judgment. In his blog post were these statements:

"... They've started incorporating substandard speakers, including woomeisters"

"... Reached their nadir with a TEDx talk at Whitechapel by Rupert Sheldrake, who gives Deepak Chopra a run for the title of World's Biggest Woomeister"

"... Proves Jesus; his weakness for telepathy and other bizarre mental phenomena; and his general attitude that science is DOING IT RONG" *(sic)*

"It's all on view in this dreadful talk (...)"

"What the crackpots don't understand (...)"

This name calling, ridicule and overgeneralization cannot possibly be characterized as "thoughtful." It was like the reddit thread, a hysterical overreaction. Yet the TED staff seemed blind to this hyperbole. The hostile insulting language did not seem to raise any red flags for them about the quality of the complaint.

This was a slippery slope. TED was relying on an obviously biased point of view. Rupert Sheldrake had been invited as a speaker to give a talk at TEDxWhitechapel and did so free of charge. To have him speak and then turn around and accuse him of being a bad scientist and then remove his talk was morally wrong. A proper course of action would have been to contact him and begin a dialog to go over what they thought was wrong with the speech in order to give him a chance to address their concerns.

It should have happened behind the scenes to avoid any embarrassment to anyone. Instead, the TED staff rushed the process of evaluation and soon found themselves in the middle of a budding controversy.

CHAPTER THREE

THEY LIKE ME!
THEY REALLY . . . UH,
NEVERMIND

I'm a parapsychology journalist. It's a title that would not have been possible a few short years ago and, even now, is quite new. Previously, I would not have had any way to get published outside of the occasional New Age magazines that were 95% ads, and my writing doesn't really fit into that category. But now, thanks to the Internet and blogging software, I have been able simply to put my writing out there and let people find me. Over the years I've built an audience and a reputation solely based on what I've posted on my own blog.

I have been able to write about whatever struck me as interesting rather than try to cater to the views of editors or slant my writing to match the style of a newspaper or magazine. This has allowed me to draw readers from around the world who share my particular set of interests.

I had been writing for five years when the controversy started and had already made a name for myself by straddling the line between being psychic and following the research.

I did not just start up a blog, wade into the middle of the TED controversy, and suddenly become an important part of it. My initial foray into blogging started in 2007. At first it was about politics. But, although I was popular, I found it unrewarding. Mostly, I was just another talking head among many and I didn't feel that I could make much of a difference.

I soon began writing about psychic stuff, which I find quite interesting. In 2008, I started blogging on The *Daily Kos* under the heading, "A Well Kept Secret." And I was blasted by skeptics immediately. This, in turn, led me to start doing some serious investigating.

I did not set out to write about science but ended up getting pushed into it by the intense skepticism that I faced. I discovered, the hard way, that this was a very deep rabbit hole I was going down. I had to force myself to read scientific papers, their rebuttals and the rebuttals to the rebuttals in order to grasp what was going on. The problem was that while we can generally learn all we care to know about a particular science by reading popular articles, the same is not true of controversial subjects. With parapsychology it's possible to read two completely conflicting articles, both written by scientists on exactly the same thing. One of them is wrong and there is only one way to find out. Go deeper and find out what really happened. It was exhausting. I don't do statistics and I don't do physics calculations and these are both part of the source material. When I ran into these things, I had to find a source that explained their meaning without getting into the math. It was difficult, but with persistence I managed it.

Writing about a controversial subject means that you have to cover all your bases (if you can) because any errors you make are going to be paraded around under your nose and used as an excuse to dismiss everything else you might say. It's very important to be thorough.

So rather than simply read a couple of articles about quantum physics, I read beginner textbooks to get an understanding of what that field of science says about reality. It involved learning about some of the ground-breaking experiments that demonstrated entanglement and the experimenter effect, among other things.

I'm glad I did it because it opened up a view of science that I'd never had before. Quantum physics is something that a lot of people misunderstand.

Because I was writing about science, I had to familiarize myself with parapsychology and learn some of the ways in which ideas are expressed in that field. Opinions are more cautious, and care must be taken not to overstate what you know. There is no room for ideological pontificating in a good scientific paper; and with the science came more and more research so that I really understood what I was talking about.

I used to hate doing research, but, over the years of doing my blog and getting acquainted with using the Internet, I gradually came to accept it. Of course, the Internet made research a thousand times easier than it used to be. When I first started seriously researching and blogging about parapsychology in 2008, there wasn't a lot of literature online. There still isn't very much, but, back then, most of what you could find was an echo chamber of ridiculous skeptical sites that referred to one another as references.

The most popular skeptical approach was to use Randi's Million Dollar Challenge as proof that psychic ability didn't exist. (A non profit foundation offers people who claim psychic ability a million dollars if they can prove that their psychic abilities are legitimate. The thinking of some skeptics is that since no one has passed the challenge, it must mean that no one is psychic. I'll be covering the foundation and its contest in another chapter.)

Many people who start researching parapsychology seriously notice, almost immediately, that there is a rather pronounced difference in quality between skeptical and parapsychology-favorable literature. Non peer reviewed skeptical literature in general tends to be openly critical and dismissive of all parapsychological subject matter and tends either to omit or misrepresent data favorable to parapsychology.

By contrast, parapsychology-favorable literature tends to deal honestly with unfavorable data and overall tends to be straightforward and matter-of-fact.

Studying parapsychology turned my view of scientists upside down. The popular image of parapsychologists as sloppy pseudoscientists living in their own world of make believe was quickly shot down. They were not only doing real science, they were doing it better than practically anyone else. And, if you think about it, it makes sense. They live under a constant shadow of criticism where every error will be discovered and touted as a failure of the entire science. They HAVE to be careful.

Parapsychologists are brave. Those who commit themselves to that field are in for a lifetime of controversy, lies, deception and back stabbing. They have to defend themselves at every turn and will never have much status as a scientist.

They routinely discourage people from following them in their footsteps because they know how damaging that can be to someone's career. And besides, almost all the money for parapsychology comes from donors, not institutional funding. That's really depressing. And yet, somehow, these scientists manage to shrug off the never-ending insults, the depressing state of their profession, the lack of funding, the misrepresentations and the hostile attitudes, and get up every morning to pursue their passion. You have to really love what you do to put up with all that crap. I admire them for that.

The *Daily Kos* was not exactly an inviting atmosphere, but I had included my email address, which turned out to be useful. Psychic people began emailing me and a whole world opened up. They needed someone who understood them. These were people who were not professional psychics but needed someone to speak for them in a public arena over the noise of insults, misinformation, and general nastiness that psychic people encounter in our culture. Although I am also a sensitive person myself, I have developed a thick skin over the years.

In 2009, I started my own blog, The Weiler Psi, so that I could keep the skeptics out and give psychic people a place to comment free of that negativity. I didn't get a lot of views at first—only 109 for the first month—but things picked up quickly from there and, in October of that year, I got almost 2,000 views. At the end of 2012, I was exceeding 6,000 views a month.

When the TED controversy started, I was already an established blogger who covered parapsychology skepticism and was therefore well suited to covering the coming drama. I became one of the central voices in opposition and this was reflected in the enormous jump in my readership during the controversy. I reached about 20,000 views a month. (This was pretty good for a blog at the time.)

I started blogging on the controversy about two days after it began, and my initial post greatly increased its visibility. Later, I was responsible for breaking the story about the takedown of TEDxWestHollywood, which was the biggest news of the entire month-and-a-half long controversy.

That I was an important part of the goings on reflects the growing importance of blogs, comments, and forum threads at the time. For non-mainstream topics of many stripes, blogs had become the most important source of information. News, analysis, and commentary was posted about specialty topics where the readers generally share a common interest and knowledge. Bloggers had become an important part of niche information-sharing in our society. (They're still around, but other formats are overtaking them.)

Almost everything in this controversy happened either on blogs, comment threads, or TED forums. Hundreds of people from all over the world converged online to contribute to this controversy, which put a lot of very interesting people in the same virtual room. From Nobel Prize winning physicist Brian Josephson, to scientist/writer/philosopher Bernardo Kastrup, to the TED staff and TEDx organizers, to TED curator Chris Anderson; everyone had their say in what was mostly polite, intellectual discussion, thanks to TED's having very good forum software for managing discussions.

Blogs like mine linked to the TED discussions, which, in turn, posted notification of those links. People could jump back and forth to view commentaries. If they liked something they could quote it somewhere, linking back to the blog that it came from. The whole system was set up for the kind of massive information sharing that is possible only on the Internet. I didn't even need to conduct interviews because, during the controversy, no one had an unpublished thought.

As a writer, I've always liked to read article comments and comment on articles myself. I also hang out on a parapsychology forum and comment there as well. Hanging around these various public discussions has allowed me to see a gradual change in the type of conversation surrounding parapsychology over the years.

There is almost always a polarized debate. People seem to be very certain about which side they're on and it doesn't seem to change quickly or easily. This means that on any given public comment thread, there are skeptics and proponents of parapsychology. Some threads have lots of skeptics who pretty much drown out everyone else, and other threads are the opposite, with skeptics being overwhelmed. It has a lot to do with the nature of the article. Negative articles about psychics draw a lot of skeptical comments and very few proponent ones. Neutral or positive articles about parapsychology have far fewer skeptics and far more proponents.

Over the past few years it seems as though the nature of the debate is changing, though. The number of skeptics on the Web has stayed about the same, but they seem to be encountering far more resistance. It's no longer safe for skeptics to trot out Randi's Million Dollar Challenge as this is virtually guaranteed to be countered with researched objections that the challenge isn't legitimate. That particular argument doesn't come up as often as it used to.

By and large, the average skeptical comment on Internet articles is a declaration of what the poster presumes to be fact. As most people who read comments on the Internet are aware, this is a rather common approach on most topics, but especially controversial ones. A lot of that kind of pontificating happened at TED as you'll see. Rarely does one see a balanced weighing of scientific evidence by commenters on any topic. Part of it is just human nature and part of it is a reflection of the ongoing paradigm change.

All of this experience researching the science and being involved in trading comments with skeptics turned out to be useful for understanding the TED controversy. I didn't do a lot of commenting myself because it's all very much the same after a while, but I was able easily to assess the kind of commenting that was taking place. I had something to compare it with.

I knew how the scientific arguments were going to play out because I knew both sides of the discussion. Most accusations against Sheldrake would be more or less impossible to prove. The TED staff was obviously unaware of how untenable their position was, otherwise they might never have gotten into the huge mess that they ended up with.

CHAPTER FOUR

CONTROVERSY THE OLD FASHIONED WAY: SLANDER AND INSULTS

O n March 7, 2013, the controversy began in earnest. The same day Emily McManus responded to the blog post by Jerry Coyne, TED took down a TEDx video by Rupert Sheldrake, claiming it presented pseudoscience. The fact that there was such a short amount of time between the skeptical complaints and the actions taken by TED demonstrates how little thinking went into the process at that point.

I came to the TED site solely for the controversy. I do not normally hang out there as most of the videos are of no interest to me and I don't have the time to check up on every forum out there. But I do hang out on the Parapsychology and Alternative Medicine Forum on Mind-Energy. net[14] and someone else brought up the controversy on one of the threads. After seeing this I hopped over to TED to have a look. This is what editor Emily McManus had posted:

Rupert Sheldrake's TEDx talk: Detailing the issues

There's been a lot of heat today about Rupert Sheldrake's TEDx Talk. And in the spirit of radical openness, I'd like to bring the community into our process.

While TED does not vet speakers at independent TEDx events, a TEDx talk can be removed from the TEDx archive if the ideas contained in it are wrong to the point of being unscientific, and that includes misrepresenting the scientific process itself. Sheldrake is on that line, to some commenters around Twitter and the web. His talk describes a vision of science made up of hard, unexamined constants. It's a philosophical talk that raises general questions about how we view science, and what role we expect it to play.

When my team and I debate whether to take action on a TEDx talk, we think deeply about the implications of our decision—and aim to provide the TEDx host with as clear-cut and unbiased a view as possible.

You are invited, if you like, to weigh in today and tomorrow with your thoughts on this talk. We'll be gathering the commentary into a couple of categories for discussion:

1. Philosophy. Is the basis of his argument sound—does science really operate the way Sheldrake suggests it does? Are his conclusions drawn from factual premises?

2. Factual error. (As an example, Sheldrake says that governments do not fund research into complementary medicine. Here are the US figures on NIH investment in complementary and alternative medicine 2009-2010: [$294.5 million for 2009 and $311 million for 2010.]

As a note: Please know that whether or not you have time or energy to contribute here, the talk is also under review by the TED team. We're not requiring your volunteer labor—but we truly welcome your input. And we're grateful to those who've written about this talk in other forums, including but not limited to Jerry Coyne, PZ Myers, Kylie Sturgess and some thoughtful Redditors.[15]

It seemed rather weak to say that they were receiving a lot of "heat" when it was only three bloggers. All of these people were participants in the skeptic community. It's a little like getting an opinion on evolution from three creationists. In any event, these questions should have been put to Sheldrake personally, as he was the person most qualified to answer them or, perhaps in lieu of that, some other sources favorable to Sheldrake should have been sought out that might be able to address these concerns from a different angle. To rely only on opinions from people who were ideologically opposed to Sheldrake's work was asking for trouble. (Although the TED staff probably didn't realize this.) Nevertheless, they showed good form at this point by opening the topic up for discussion.

They set up a comment section so that the TED community could discuss it. Right away, TED started getting blowback from commenters such as Troy Tice who strongly felt that this action was unwarranted.

> I am disgusted by this attempt at censorship. It reminds me of a similar attempt in 2006 to quash a panel on parapsychology at the meeting of the British Association for the Advancement of Science. When asked by Sheldrake if he had read any of the literature of parapsychology Professor Peter Atkins – one of the scientists who tried to keep Sheldrake, Peter Fenwick and Deborah Delanoy from speaking – replied, "No, and I would be very suspicious of it." I don't pretend to know whether or not Professor Coyne has ever looked at the evidence deriving from, say, the ganzfeld experiments, but, to borrow Atkins's phrasing, I would be very suspicious of it since a few posts down he confidently declares there to be "no evidence" for anomalous cognition.

Other commenters such as Bill Hoffman defended TED's actions:

> This talk is nonsense and filled with factual and logical errors. These are numerous and have been delineated in detail in this comment log (e.g., Dark Star) and elsewhere on the net (Jerry Coyne). This talk should never have made it through the vetting process for TEDx. Since it did, however, I would label it as having been judged not to meet TED standards because it contains factual and logical errors.

The "factual and logical errors" that this person is referring to were not delineated in detail as he supposes, but merely opinion. The confusion of fact and opinion was a mistake that a lot of skeptical commenters made. They weren't paying enough attention to the fact that Sheldrake's speech, *The Science Delusion*, which is also the title of his latest book, was about what he considers to be ten dogmas of modern science. His main theme was that science was operating under a set of unquestioned assumptions:

1. That nature is mechanical.
2. That matter is unconscious.
3. The laws of nature are fixed.
4. The total amount of matter and energy are always the same.
5. That nature is purposeless.
6. Biological inheritance is material.
7. That memories are stored as material traces.
8. The mind is in the brain.
9. Telepathy and other psychic phenomena are illusory.
10. Mechanistic medicine is the only kind that really works.

Sheldrake proposed to turn these assumptions into questions: Is nature mechanical? Is matter unconscious? Etc. Sheldrake was questioning the underlying philosophy that dominates Western scientific thinking that is generally known as materialism and he offered a few examples that suggested that there was sufficient evidence to question those assumptions. The speech was a typical length for TED speeches in that it was slightly under twenty minutes long. In fact, speakers are required to keep their speeches within that time frame. This poses a problem for scientific topics as there simply isn't time within the speech to fully lay out a scientific argument. It is therefore not fair or justified to expect a talk on a controversial subject of such short duration to fully explore the scientific issues involved.

What made the criticism particularly problematic was that the central theme of this speech was philosophical, not scientific. The speech could only be considered to have factual errors if the speaker was making scientific claims that were factually incorrect. Philosophizing and raising questions do not fall in that category.

The rushed process and the general lack of thoughtful criticism seemed to be a very clear sign that this was going to be yet another chapter in the hundred-year controversy, but the TED team was also promising to pay attention to the arguments that were being put forth. This was perhaps part of what took the controversy well beyond any previous boundaries. For those who understood the nature of the controversy, this was special. Someone in charge was actually going to be open minded.

For Rupert Sheldrake, this was business as usual. He is a plant biologist and a biochemist, who researched the role of auxin, a plant hormone, in the cellular differentiation of a plant's vascular system. With his colleague, Philip Rubery, he worked out the cellular mechanism of polar auxin transport, on which much subsequent research on plant polarity has been based. A former Research Fellow of the Royal Society, he studied natural sciences at Cambridge University, where he was a Scholar of Clare College, took a double first class honors degree, and was awarded the University Botany Prize. He then studied philosophy and history of science at Harvard University, where he was a Frank Knox Fellow, before returning to Cambridge, where he took a Ph.D. in biochemistry. He was a Fellow of Clare College, Cambridge, where he was Director of Studies in biochemistry and cell biology. Sheldrake, in other words, is notable even without his involvement in consciousness studies.

But it is his work in parapsychology that has caught everyone's attention. He is, perhaps, best known for extending the idea of morphic fields, which was first popularized in the story of the hundredth-monkey, and for his experiments with dogs that seemed to know when their owners were coming home.

In his first book, *A New Science of Life: The Hypothesis of Formative Causation,* published in 1981, Sheldrake introduced the idea that phenomena – particularly biological ones – become more probable the more often they occur, and therefore biological growth and behavior get formed into patterns laid down by previous similar events. That is to say, all living things are shaped not only by ordinary evolutionary forces, but also by a collective memory specific to that group. As a result, newly acquired behaviors can be inherited by future generations who tap into the specific memory field of their species to learn this behavior rather than acquiring it through ordinary physical means.

In 1981, the editor of the scientific journal, *Nature,* wrote about *A New Science of Life*

> "This infuriating tract... is the best candidate for burning there has been for many years."

> "Sheldrake's argument is an exercise in pseudo-science. Many readers will be left with the impression that Sheldrake has succeeded in finding a place for magic within scientific discussion – and this, indeed, may have been a part of the objective of writing such a book."

For scientists who work in the field of parapsychology, this virtually amounts to a badge of honor. It seems that the more important the theory or experiment, the more likely that it will draw vitriolic criticism.

Sheldrake's newest book, titled *"The Science Delusion"* in the UK and *"Science Set Free"* in the US, challenges the strong materialist mindset of contemporary mainstream science. Rupert makes the point that this underlying philosophy is flawed and needs to be re-thought for science to move forward.

Back at TED, the thread was supposed to last just one day, but got extended to two, during which there were a whopping 523 comments. It ended March 9, the day I posted about it. But the action had already begun.

The Dirty Little Secret

On its forum, TED was discovering, possibly for the first time, the kind of parapsychology discussion that always takes place. If they were hoping for well-reasoned, well-supported skeptical arguments putting the smackdown on Sheldrake and his supporters they were sorely disappointed. That never happens.

Sheldrake has a large audience. It is not possible to study parapsychology even casually without running across his name. Even though he was in India at the time the controversy erupted, unable to defend himself personally, a lot of intelligent, thoughtful people knew his work and were more than up to the task of arguing on his behalf. Many people who didn't know his work and knew nothing about parapsychology supported his talk on grounds that they could make up their own minds. The usual patterns emerged in the skeptical commenting, which came across as being very authoritative:

> "It's not about the authority or reasoning of the person, but about the authority of the evidence and the validity of the reasoning. The evidence is overwhelmingly against Sheldrake, and the reasoning he uses is seriously flawed."

> "However, Sheldrake's views are those of a quack. Inviting quacks and then tearing them down still gives a venue to the quacks. What's the point, if it is well-known quackery? Better to have two really valid talks than one quack and one counterpoint."

> The answer is because it is clear now that these things are not science. They did not hold up. How many millions of human centuries of

thought and effort need to be wasted on such fancies before we can say "enough"?"

It's important to be skeptical of such complete certainty. It's just opinion. The problem with statements like those above is that they are just bland generalizations. What is flawed about his research? Why are his views those of a quack? Why are these things not science? It's important to answer these questions before passing judgment.

The same terrible condemnation of all things Sheldrake just got repeated over and over again in response to most pro-Sheldrake comments. Often by the same skeptic.

The comment above is the kind of thing that people say when they don't know very much about a topic but have a strong opinion. In parapsychology discussions this sort of problem occurs all the time.

When such discussions continue, people who know more about the topic will usually present evidence that contradicts such statements, but the skeptical commenter will rarely concede and there will be a back and forth argument.

The comments I quoted above sound convincing, but I know from my own studies that they were not factual. It is not necessary to believe me, though, because, while the editors at TED read all of the skeptical comments, *they didn't feel that any of them had enough merit to be adopted by TED.*

Here's an example of why these discussions never end. In this case a skeptic was presented with scientific evidence that refuted his earlier points. Here's how he responded:

... However, his published papers that are supposed to be the evidential basis for his TED speech are in largely disreputable journals whose adherents fail to live up to the standards of scientific enquiry. *The Journal of the Society for Psychical Research* is not a credible scientific organization or journal. It's *(sic)* very title presumes that which it believes to be true. It is akin to Answers in Genesis claiming "peer review" because the papers of its proponents are published in the "Creation Research Society Journal" – a publication they have set up themselves and police themselves.

The reason for Sheldrake standing accused of having no evidence is because he fails to meet even the basic "sniff test" of credibility that would remotely attract the attention of a credible journal. Claiming that he has that evidence because it is published in a rag that already accepts its conclusions on no evidence isn't acceptable scientific evidence."

Again, the comment is being presented as self-evident fact when in reality these statements have been made up on the spot just for the sake of attempting to win the argument. Rather than being convincing, it demonstrates both a complete ignorance of the subject and total cognitive dissonance. This was unfortunately typical of many skeptical comments on this thread. All evidence was dismissed with a wave of the hand. The skeptical arguments weren't based on a careful consideration of the facts, but on ignorance of those facts. In this case it was glaringly obvious that the skeptic has no idea what the evidence actually was, but that he would use any means to argue against it. That, in a nutshell, is your typical psi wars argument and they happen all the time on different forums.

To understand what was happening at TED requires an understanding of this situation. The moderators at TED were looking for reasons to shut down the Sheldrake video, but *the exact opposite* was happening. If TED was hoping that the skeptics who had rallied to their cause would provide them with sufficient cause to take down the video on scientific grounds, then they were surely disappointed.

The skeptics all throughout the thread assumed the mantle of being in favor of science but used no real science to defend their positions.

A couple of pro-Sheldrake statements summed up the moral side of the argument. Sandy commented:

"Censorship is just wrong. I don't need to be "protected" from unconventional ideas. I can use my own critical thinking skills to consider the evidence and make up my own mind. There are lots of people in the world I disagree with, but I would still fight for them to have the freedom to express their own opinions.

Has TED really sunk so low to even entertain the prospect of censorship? Does it think so little of those of us watching these talks that we need big brother to approve everything we see on the internet? I'm a grown-up. I'd like the opportunity to make up my own mind in regard to what I agree or disagree with. Giving up such a right would be akin to joining a cult."

And, in a very well thought-out post, Steve commented:

"Let us be clear what Sheldrake's talk was and was not about. It was not about morphic resonance or psychic functioning; it was not about dogs who know their owners were coming home; it was not about the sense of being stared at; it was not about whether the speed of light has actually changed; nor was it even a collection of amusing anecdotes about Terence McKenna (although such things did come up and Sheldrake could, no doubt, have talked at length about any or all of them). What his talk was actually about was certain philosophical views which many hold, and which many think are connected with science in a way that Sheldrake, and many academic philosophers of the top rank, do not. That is, his talk was about certain metaphysical views which have become associated with science and which, according to Sheldrake, and many others in academia, are actually metaphysical views which are not only unconnected with science but are actively constraining science (the drive to deny/do away with, rather than explain, consciousness, for example). That the philosophical views Sheldrake was criticizing are loudly espoused by many (with little or no formal academic training in philosophy), and that such criticism gets those people hot under the collar, is no reason to censor such critical views. Indeed, the shrill tone of the uninformed and often off-topic criticisms by those in favour of censorship shows exactly why Sheldrake's ideas are very much ideas worth spreading."

And, author, scientist and artificial intelligence researcher Ben Goertzel specifically addressed the points TED made in taking down the Sheldrake video:

***

1. Philosophy. Is the basis of his argument sound—does science really operate the way Sheldrake suggests it does? Are his conclusions drawn from factual premises?
***

This seems an ill-founded question. To ask that *philosophy* draw conclusions from factual premises, seems to presuppose that the way to judge ANY philosophy is according to some "objective" standard regarding what is factual !!
But the very question of what constitutes "factual" evidence, is part of the scope of philosophy...

Is TED really committed to a narrowly-construed, "naive reductionist" philosophy of science and the universe? If so, why?
***

2. Factual error. (As an example, Sheldrake says that governments do not fund research into complementary medicine. Here are the US figures on NIH investment in complementary and alternative medicine 2009-2010:
***

I didn't notice any real factual errors in his talk.... Yeah, he engaged in some minor rhetorical exaggerations, but he is not the first TEDx (or TED) speaker to do that !!!

You are right that governments fund research into alternative medicine—but it's pretty minimal compared to what's spent on drug therapies. His statement, as you cite it, is a minor rhetorical exaggeration, it's not as though he contradicted some recognized fact of science...

From the way you have formulated these two questions, it almost appears you are grasping at straws, in search of some reason to ban Sheldrake's video. Certainly, if you were going to hold EVERY TED or TEDx talk to strict standards of

— no rhetorical exaggerations

— no statements not clearly drawn from premises accepted as factual by 95% of scientists

then a heck of a lot of videos would have to be taken down!!!

So why do you want to hold Sheldrake to a standard other than the common one?

Because PZ Myers and some other extremist zealots want you to?

Not a good reason!!"

I've seen a lot of these discussions in my time on the web. I've learned a lot over the years watching skeptics attack over similar things. But this was the first time I'd seen so many well-informed people come out of the woodwork to support the other side. Whether it's because Sheldrake has high profile supporters or because the discussions on TED have well-informed people, I don't know. It was eye opening for me, in any case. Most of the time, these discussions are overrun with such intense skeptical negativity that most people quickly give up trying to discuss anything. Once people realize that skeptics are not going to engage in a real discussion, most lose interest. All you get are variations of the party line. At no point will the skeptic ever give credence to anyone else's point of view.

And that's the gist of most parapsychology discussions online. The skeptics attack anything positive with an authoritative sneer. Push them just a little bit and it becomes clear that they don't know what they're talking about. Push them some more and it becomes apparent that it doesn't matter to them. They'll keep insisting they're right no matter how much evidence you present to the contrary.

But, at TED, people were arguing with the assumption that their opinion might be meaningful, and they trusted the crew at TED to take them seriously. In fact, this was something encouraged at TED. Emily McManus, the host of that comment thread wrote:

> (...) And to say an early THANK YOU—this has been a truly fascinating conversation to be part of. I've read every word and so have some of my coworkers. We won't be able to make a decision that pleases every single flavor of opinion on this thread, but: You have been heard.

I think that it was this promise of reasonable objectivity that drew in the pro Sheldrake crowd. The people at TED were, after all, intellectuals and could perhaps be counted on for impartiality. Surely if they saw how poor the skeptical arguments were and how this contrasted with the pro-Sheldrake arguments, they would change their minds about removing Sheldrake's video. At the time, this was also the view that I held. I had no reason to doubt TED's sincerity.

And so the intellectuals braved the nonsense of the skeptics to get their voices heard. The first shots in yet another battle of the parapsychology culture war had been fired.

This brings me to my next chapter. It's necessary to include some of the science of parapsychology in this book, because it's largely unknown. You would never know the truth just by looking at articles on the web or reading Wikipedia. It's this evidence that TED would ultimately have to contest in order to truly make their pseudoscience claim.

CHAPTER FIVE

YUP, IT'S A REAL SCIENCE

Most people have very little contact with scientific research into psychic ability outside of the occasional item they might see in a magazine or newspaper about a new study. Very few people, many scientists included, know that credible research even exists. Yet, to understand what TED was getting itself into, it's important to look at what scientific research into psychic ability is out there.

The scientific study of paranormal ability is called parapsychology, and the premiere organization involved in this research is the Parapsychological Association. They publish a peer reviewed scientific journal, The *Journal of Parapsychology*, and they belong to the American Association for the Advancement of Science. The AAAS serves some 261 affiliated societies and academies of science, serving 10 million individuals. This number effectively makes parapsychology *accepted* by the mainstream as real science. The scientific experiments in parapsychology follow protocols that studies in other scientific fields do. Scientists plan a project, carry out the experiment, and the results are submitted to a peer reviewed journal. If deemed satisfactory, they are published in those scientific journals. That's as good as it gets.

Contrary to popular belief, the use of professional psychics or other gifted individuals in experiments is very rare; nearly all experiments test people without any extraordinary professed psychic ability. This virtually eliminates possible fraud from test subjects because, not making money from their ability, they have nothing to gain from cheating. Using people with ordinary ability is also helpful in designing experiments that have a better chance of being replicated. Parapsychology, like many other fields of research, is a statistical science in which results are measured in odds against chance. It is typical to combine many studies into a meta-analysis in order to discover trends that cannot be determined from individual studies.

There is no smoking gun in parapsychology; no single study by itself is convincing and no results are so obvious that they cannot be questioned. It is only with the accumulation of evidence over time that a clearer picture emerges.

If an experiment is controversial (and psi experiments ALWAYS are), the experiment needs to be replicated; it can take years before enough evidence is accumulated. The advantage of this is that the same experiment will be done by a wide variety of people in different locations at different times, which tends to remove experimenter error or bias as a probable explanation of the results. It is replicated experiments that constitute the best scientific evidence of psychic ability.

The intense skepticism that parapsychology faces is a curse, but it is also a blessing. There are peer reviewed papers which examine all of these experiments, which, in turn, allows us to see the best criticism that exists for these studies. If the studies hold up to this criticism, then we can safely assume that criticism from less well-informed people is unimportant. All the skeptical blog posts, TV appearances, podcasts and news articles don't count for anything if the scientific criticism doesn't hold up. These studies, and the scientific criticism that accompanies them are the headwaters from which all else flows.

There are four experiment groups that meet the replication requirement to a significant degree.

The Ganzfeld Studies

No other class of psi experiments has generated the controversy that this one has. The Ganzfeld studies in their present form have been around since the 1970s and the Autoganzfeld Study is a computerized version of the same thing.

The Ganzfeld (a German word meaning "total field") experiment is a technique for scientifically determining the presence of telepathy. It uses even, non-patterned sensory stimulation to produce an effect that is similar to sensory deprivation. By reducing external stimuli and distractions, the experiment increases the likelihood that the receiver will be aware of information coming telepathically from a sender.

This telepathy experiment is straightforward. Person A is shown a photo which he/she then sends telepathically to Person B, who must pick the correct one out of four photos. This establishes pure chance at 25%. By running the experiment many times, you can determine whether the results exceed chance. This experiment routinely yields results of around 33% correct guesses, and sometimes it is much higher. What made these experiments especially noteworthy is that Ray Hyman, a well-known skeptic, meticulously picked over them. After the results of the 1985 meta-analysis Ray Hyman wrote:

> Honorton's experiments have produced intriguing results. If independent laboratories can produce similar results with the same relationships and with the same attention to rigorous methodology, then parapsychology may indeed have finally captured its elusive quarry.[16]

(Although to this day he remains unconvinced.) These studies were performed at U. of Amsterdam, Netherlands; U. of Edinburgh, Scotland; Institute for Parapsychology, N.C; and U. of Gothenburg, Sweden. This material is covered in depth in Dean Radin's book: *The Conscious Universe*, and is summarized this way:

> The overall hit rate of 33.2 percent is unlikely with odds against chance beyond a million billion to one.

The abstract from a 2010 paper by Patrizio E. Tressoldi, Lance Storm and Dean Radin, titled *Extrasensory Perception and Quantum Models of Cognition*, concludes:

> Today, using modern experimental methods and meta-analytical techniques, a persuasive case can be made that, neuroscience assumptions notwithstanding, ESP does exist. We justify this conclusion through discussion of one class of homogeneous experiments reported in 108 publications and conducted from 1974 through 2008 by laboratories around the world. Subsets of these data have been subjected to six meta-analyses, and each shows significantly positive effects. The overall results now provide unambiguous evidence for an independently repeatable ESP effect.

The people responsible for these papers are some of the leading parapsychology experts in the world, and, based on extensive widely replicated experimental evidence, they have concluded that telepathy is real. It meets all the requirements of good science and the degree to which it has been proved is far beyond ordinary thresholds.

Ganzfeld Skepticism

This conclusion is reinforced by the nature of skeptical criticism of the Ganzfeld experiments. A perfect example of this is skeptic Prof. Richard Wiseman and Julie Milton's meta-analysis of the autoganzfeld data where they purportedly showed that there was really no effect. In reality, author Chris Carter pointed out the following:

> It later turned out that Milton and Wiseman had botched their statistical analysis of the ganzfeld experiments, by failing to consider sample size. Dean Radin simply added up the total number of hits and trials conducted in those thirty studies results with odds against chance of about 20 to 1.

> Not only that, but Milton and Wiseman did not include a large and highly successful study by Kathy Dalton due to an arbitrary cut-off date, even though it was published almost two years before Milton and Wiseman's paper; (...)[17]

Skeptics have been citing this meta-analysis for years after its flaws were exposed. As recently as 2010 in Stanley Krippner's book *Debating Psychic Experience* Prof. Chris French used this failed meta-analysis to argue against the validity of the Ganzfeld experiments. (If you have to intentionally conceal or disregard key facts to make your argument hold up, you have already lost.)

This is just one example of the extensive criticism of the Ganzfeld experiments by skeptics over the years, but nearly all of that criticism, like French's, is full of basic factual errors.

One has to look to scientific papers to find criticism that even acknowledges the basic facts of this experiment, such as a 2013 *Psychological Bulletin* paper by Rouder, Morey and Province.[18] They have no expertise in parapsychology, but felt justified in commenting on that field of science anyway. Unsurprisingly, they got it wrong. Their paper attempted to refute the Ganzfeld results not by demonstrating flaws in the experimental design or the statistics, but instead by using nonstandard ways of interpreting the data[19] and by changing statistical parameters, often to ridiculous extremes.[20]

To put this more simply, valid, relevant criticism would go something like this:

"You've made mistakes here, here and here. They have undermined your experiment and skewed your results."

What the skeptical criticism is actually saying is this:

"We made changes to the statistics and decided to omit some studies based on our own interpretation of what constitutes valid data. Our version shows that these experiments failed."

The most important point here is that the skeptics aren't finding flaws in the study design or statistics that the researchers used: they're changing the rules of the game to keep positive results out. All of the important flaws were discovered and corrected decades ago. The fact that the skeptics have to create their own methods to attack the research is basically a form of surrender.

While an alternate method of evaluating the data might seem reasonable at first glance, it would allow anyone to come up with any result they wished. If you can re-interpret data any which way, then there is no way ever to come to a conclusion about any test results.

Besides the fact that this is not good science, the other problem is that simply providing an alternative way of evaluating the data isn't persuasive on its own. It has also to be shown to be significantly *better* than the existing method. That hasn't been done.

It's easy to see why something as groundbreaking as demonstrating that telepathy is real would find little acceptance. Few people have the time or the interest to sort out controversies like this. A reporter or mildly interested scientist would only notice that the matter didn't appear to be settled.

The Staring Studies

This is the work of Rupert Sheldrake. It is especially irksome to skeptics because it is quite popular and easy to understand. Unlike the ganzfeld experiments, it does not require an exotic set up or very much in the way of equipment.

This experiment tests people's ability to tell whether they're being stared at from behind. What makes this experiment convincing is that the starer and the person beng stared at are not necessarily in the same room. Instead, the person doing the staring can be in a different room or doing the staring via a TV monitor.

This experiment is so simple that it can be done by high school students. [21] As with the other studies mentioned, this one has been replicated many times by many different organizations.[22] Studies have been conducted at Cornell University, Stanford University, U. of Edinburgh, U. of Adelaide, and by Rupert Sheldrake.[23]

Between 1998 and 2002, a total of 30,803 trials had been conducted with 1,558 subjects. This yielded a total of 16,849 times when people correctly identified that they had been stared at. This meant that people were right 54.7% of the time which gave a P value of 1×10^{-20}

The P value represents inverse odds against chance where 0.01 is considered good enough to count, and the smaller the number the more successful the experiment was. The total shown in the lower right corner is a very low number and is considered to be very good evidence of psychic ability. It is easier to understand as odds against chance, which is 10^{20} to 1.

Staring Studies Skepticism

The quality of skeptic criticism of the staring studies is no better than what was delivered for the Ganzfeld. There exists a small handful of peer reviewed papers that criticize Sheldrake's work.[24][25] Sheldrake elaborates on Colwell, Schröder, and Sladen on his website:[26]

> ... In their principal experiment, they used methods based on my own procedures, and followed my own randomized sequences of trials. They obtained strikingly significant (p<0.001) positive results that closely resembled my own findings (Sheldrake 1998, 1999). However, they argued that their participants' positive scores did not support the idea that people really can feel stares; instead, they were an artifact that arose from "the detection and response to structure" present in my randomized sequences.

> ... Marks and Colwell claimed that their pattern-detection hypothesis invalidated the positive results of staring experiments carried out by myself and others. If these experiments had involved pseudo-random sequences and feedback, as required by their

hypothesis, their criticism might have been relevant. But this is not how the tests were done, as they would have seen for themselves if they had read my published papers on the subject. First, in more than 5,000 of my own trials, the randomization was indeed "structureless", and was carried out by each starer before each trial by tossing a coin (Sheldrake 1999, Tables 1 and 2). The same was true of more than 3,000 trials in German and American schools (Sheldrake 1998). Thus the highly significant positive results in these experiments cannot be "an artifact of pseudo randomization". Second, when I developed the counterbalanced sequences that Marks and Colwell describe as pseudo-random, I changed the experimental design so that feedback was no longer given to the subjects. Since the pattern-detection hypothesis depends on feedback, it cannot account for the fact that in more than 10,000 trials without feedback there were still highly significant positive results (Sheldrake 1999, Tables 3 and 4).

In other words, Colwell, Schröder and Sladen were criticizing a problem that didn't exist in studies they hadn't thoroughly read. I wish to emphasize here that this is peer reviewed research, the highest quality criticism of the staring studies that exists. And it was bad.

The *Journal of Consciousness* had a special issue in 2005 that specifically addressed criticism of the staring studies and invited several skeptics to weigh in. For the sake of brevity, I'm only addressing specific criticism of the research itself and its methodology.

Anthony Atkins brought up several issues: 1. We can't detect the signal. (This is true, but irrelevant.) 2. Children might be biasing the study by saying "yes" more often to get positive feedback. (An examination of the statistics did not confirm this to be the case.) 3. The studies varied slightly from one to the next and this made putting them together for a meta-analysis somewhat unreliable. (It is true that the studies varied, but it's extremely unlikely that this would be the cause of consistent positive results over many different studies.) 4. Belief or reasoning bias. This was a somewhat confusing criticism because he starts with an unpublished study showing schizotypal personality types scoring higher, and then goes on to conflate them with schizophrenics, who have a mental disorder. (A schizotypal is a normal functioning person with very high sensitivity. They are not at all similar to schizophrenics.)

Ian Baker agrees that the results are promising, but that only studies done through videos should count because only their controls were good enough.

Jean Burns argued for the possibility of alternation bias, where test subjects can guess the pattern of trials and sometimes anticipate what comes next. (This is only possible in studies where subjects were given immediate feedback. Since those studies did not produce results that were different from studies where no feedback was given, this was determined to be a non-issue.)

That covered the majority of the specific criticisms, which weren't all that strong. It was all of the well-this-might-have-been-better-if . . . variety. Of all the skeptics who weighed in, no one was able decisively to refute the evidence; it was more like chipping around the edges. They didn't even agree on what the problems might be.

It's notable that the scientists who were most familiar with parapsychological research, Braud, Radin and Schlitz, all felt that the research adequately demonstrated the staring effect.

As it was Sheldrake's TED video that was being removed and he was being accused of pseudoscience, this examination of the scientific evidence is illuminating because, when it comes down to the hard facts, this is the literature that you turn to. What it demonstrates is that while it's easy for skeptics to *say* that Sheldrake is a pseudoscientist, there is no way that you could reach that conclusion by looking at either the evidence or its scientific criticism.

The RNG Studies

RNG stands for random number generator. This study is a model of simplicity. The test subject tries to mentally influence a random number generator. Then the researcher simply crunches the numbers to find out whether the numbers are completely random or not. To be sure that the numbers they start with are completely random (this is harder than it seems), they use scientific grade random event generators. (It uses data from radioactive decay, which is truly random.) The study can be done quickly and easily with no chance of tampering by the test subject. And it's fairly easy for the subjects to have an effect, although a very small one.

The nature of this testing procedure allows for many trials to be done. As explained by Dean Radin:

> From a wide range of sources, we found 152 references dating from 1959 to 1987. These reports described a total of 832 studies conducted

by sixty-eight different investigators, including 597 experimental studies and 235 control studies. Of the 597 experimental studies, 258 were reported in a long-term investigation generated by the Princeton University PEAR laboratory, which also reported 127 control studies.

The overall experimental results produced odds against chance beyond a trillion to one. [27]

RNG Studies Skepticism

In a 2006 paper from skeptics, Bösch, Steinkamp and Boller argued that the positive results as outlined in 13 meta-analyses, spanning almost 20 years, were the result of publication bias.[28] In other words, they suspected that so many studies were conducted but not published that this skewed the overall results. This is called a "file drawer problem." While this was backed up with reasonable sounding statistical evidence, theories and charts, it overlooked a basic human logistical problem as explained by Dean Radin et al. in their rebuttal:

> In any case, imagine that we had used precognition and estimated that the file drawer consisted of "only 2,681" non-significant, unpublished, irretrievable studies. Such a figure would have required every investigator who had ever reported an RNG experiment to also conduct but not report an additional thirty studies. Is that plausible? Not counting the PEAR Lab, which has no file-drawer problem due to a long-established laboratory policy, the most prolific investigator has been Helmut Schmidt. On average, Schmidt published about three studies per year for thirty years, many times the average rate of the other researchers. To achieve the estimated file drawer of 2,681 studies, each of the other ninety investigators would have had to match Schmidt's prodigious output for a full ten years, and for not a single one of those studies to be reported or retrievable, even in surveys among colleagues who have known each other for decades. This is a highly implausible scenario ...[29]

Skeptic M. H. Schub, in his 2006 paper, took the kitchen sink approach, commenting not only on a perceived file drawer problem, but on many other problems as well, including quality assessment, statistical significance, applicability of random effects modeling, optional stopping, repeatability, nonsense hit rates, reduced variance in control studies, ad hoc models and changing z scores.[30] It's worth noting that except for the file drawer problem, the paper by Bösch, Steinkamp and Boller did not mention any of these issues. All of the issues raised by Schub have very convincing rebuttals, as outlined in the cited paper by Dean Radin et al., but even the casual reader can see, by simply stepping back, that this criticism was over the top. How likely is it that one lone reviewer managed to find these problems and that all the researchers, peer reviewers and even other skeptics missed so many serious issues over the course of so many years?

Like the criticism of the Ganzfeld and the staring studies, what I have presented represents the highest quality criticism that's been made of this research.

The Presentiment Studies

Author's note: The replications for these studies came after the TED controversy was long over, but I've included them because they meet the criteria for best evidence.

In 2011, psychologist Daryl Bem, a professor, researcher and writer of textbooks published his study *"Feeling the Future: Experimental Evidence for Anomalous Retroactive Influences on Cognition and Affect"* in the Journal of Personality and Social Psychology.

Grab your popcorn because this is quite a story. Bem is a professor emeritus at Cornell University and well known in the field of psychology, having published many, many papers and introduced a couple of theories of human behavior. He's not your average nobody in other words. His contribution to parapsychology has been his ability to publish in respected journals. This newest experiment was no exception and, of course, it was immediately attacked.

In defending his work from skeptic James Alcock's criticism, Bem wrote: (Alcock's criticisms were not peer reviewed and are therefore not included.)

> I believe that Alcock has also put his finger on what is so particularly newsworthy about his critique: the striking contrast between his harsh assessment of my work and the collective assessment of the two editors and four reviewers who vetted it for the Journal. *JPSP* in one of the

most rigorously refereed journals in the entire field of psychology, with a rejection rate of 82% in 2009. Moreover, authors' names and other identifying information are removed from a manuscript before it is sent to reviewers so that their evaluations will be based purely on its merits and not be influenced by knowledge of an author's reputation or the prestige of his or her institutional affiliation.

The contrast between the assessments of Alcock and the Journal's editors and reviewers is also particularly newsworthy because it is not simply a reprise of the familiar disagreement between skeptics and proponents of psi (ESP). Like Alcock, several of the reviewers expressed various degrees of skepticism about the reality of psi, while still urging its acceptance. Unlike Alcock, however, they are all active researchers who regularly contribute to the mainstream experimental literature in psychology and cognitive science. Their task was to evaluate the logic and clarity of the article's exposition, the soundness of its experimental methods, and the validity of its statistical analyses. They did not have to agree with my conclusions regarding psi to make those assessments. As Joachim Krueger, an experimental psychologist at Brown University, put it so charmingly: "My personal view is that this is ridiculous and can't be true. Going after the methodology and the experimental design is the first line of attack. But frankly, I didn't see anything. Everything seemed to be in good order (quoted by Peter Aldhous in the *NewScientist* 16:29, November 11, 2010)."[31]

The study was simply flipping a couple of pieces from a well-known and oft used psychology study so that instead of testing a response after stimuli, the study tested the response *before* the stimuli. The results couldn't be dismissed on the grounds of study design, a favorite target of skeptics, which didn't leave much to harp on. Not that they didn't try.

"Feeling the Future" skepticism

In a 2011 paper, Wagenmaker, et. al.[32] used Bayesian statistics to show that there was actually no effect in the study. However this particular brand of statistics requires that you set a number for prior probability of the effect being tested. Wagenmaker set this number at 99,999,999,999,999,999,999 to 1 in favor of Ho. Basically, this is a statistical number that is guaranteed to remove pretty much any effect from a study. It's straight up ridiculous. But he also had to set the effect size, known as H1. For psi studies, this should be in the area of 0.18 based on previous work. Wagenmaker had this number ranging from 0.8 to 10. What he was basically saying was that psi absolutely can't exist, but if it did we'd see X-Men everywhere. It was fairly obvious that this was statistics butchery. It wasn't a very effective skeptical argument.

Here we had what was arguably the most bulletproof psi study ever published in one of the most prestigious journals. It was a big deal at the time. The question on everyone's mind was this: can it be replicated? Enter Richard Wiseman.

This is the same person that botched a meta-analysis of the Ganzfeld studies, claiming no effect when his own analysis showed that there was one and replicated Sheldrake's study on dogs who know when their owner is coming home, but changed parameters and claimed that it failed. It doesn't take a genius to see where this was headed.

In 2012 Wiseman, French and Ritchie published three failed replications of Bem's work.[33] The skeptics of the scientific community published article after article on those failed replications, using them as examples of why replication is so important in science. There was just a teeny tiny problem that skeptics overlooked in their haste throw Bem's study under the bus. Bem explains this in an interview on Skeptico:

> Without accusing him of actually being dishonest, he has now published the three studies that he and French and Ritchie tried to get published in several journals that rejected it. I replied with a comment on that. If there's anything dishonest there, it's when you publish an article, even if it's of your own three experiments—they did three experiments that failed trying to replicate one of my experiments—you always have a literature review section where you talk about all the previous research and known research on the topic before you present your own data.

> What Wiseman never tells people is, in Ritchie, Wiseman and French is that his online registry where he asked everyone to register, first of all he provided a deadline date. I don't know of any serious researcher working on their own stuff who is going to drop everything and immediately do a replication... anyway, he and Ritchie and French published these three studies. Well, they knew that there were three other studies that had been submitted and completed and two of the three showed statistically significant results replicating my results.

But you don't know that from reading his article. That borders on dishonesty.[34]

Wiseman conveniently leaving out important data? Who woulda thunk it? In actuality, Bem's experiment was well on its way to having a number of successful replications. In 2016 Bem published a meta-analysis of 90 studies.[35]

So what was the reaction of the skeptical community to a replicated psi experiment that met the most rigorous scientific standards? Did they concede the possibility that psi exists? Or did they conclude, instead, that if this experiment succeeded, then the entire field of psychology must have something wrong with it?

If you guessed the latter, congratulations. You understand how this game is played. An article for Slate had this hilarious headline: "Daryl Bem Proved ESP is Real which means science is broken"[36] This is just my opinion, but I think that throwing out an entire field of science to make one positive result go away is just a little bit on the extreme side.

Summary

The Ganzfeld, the staring studies and the RNG studies are all mature, replicated experiments that provide convincing evidence for psychic ability. (The presentiment replications came after the TED controversy was long over but it was still a significant experiment at that time.) In presenting the best skeptical arguments criticizing the best parapsychological research, I have demonstrated that the criticism isn't decisive or even very convincing. There are, of course many other criticisms that have been made but there is no point in addressing all of them. If the skeptical scientists publishing peer reviewed papers cannot seriously challenge the credibility of the studies, then lesser criticisms can safely be disregarded.

And that includes skepticism from magazines, newspapers, blogs, videos, podcasts and any other source. Including TED. There is simply no foundation of skeptical scientific criticism of parapsychology upon which to base the various derogatory statements that are made about this science.

The TED staff, and their science board, were never going to find the definitive proof they were looking for. Parapsychology is not a pseudoscience, Rupert Sheldrake is not a pseudoscientist and his ideas are not wacky nonsense. They were not protecting the public from dodgy ideas: quite the opposite. Since they had no scientific basis for what they were doing, they were, arguably, engaging in promoting pseudoscientific beliefs themselves.

The entire house of cards, upon which mainstream non acceptance of psychic ability is based, hinges on total belief in the skeptical point of view and an utter disregard for any other point of view. Once the skepticism itself is challenged, it all falls down. The TED staff effectively insulated themselves from questioning their own skepticism by relying solely on skeptical sources and left themselves with no avenue to change course.

Psychic ability has been proven to exist by any sane scientific standard. Only by never questioning the skepticism and dismissing everyone who thinks differently as "woomeisters" can anyone avoid that rather obvious fact. Parapsychology is controversial only because of the rather extreme cognitive dissonance it creates in some people, not because of any deficiency in the science itself.

CHAPTER SIX

EVERY GOOD CONTROVERSY NEEDS A RABBLEROUSER

Rupert's Story at the Time

Rupert was far away from this brewing controversy. Here's his
recollection of that time, which he emailed to me:

> When the TED controversy got going, I was travelling in India with
> my wife with only intermittent email contact. The first I heard of it
> was when I was staying in a small town called Maheshwar, on the
> Narmada River in Madhya Pradesh. I got several emails from people
> saying they supported me against the suggestions that my talk should
> be taken down. I didn't know what they were talking about and it was
> a few days before I realised the scale of this controversy. I was out of
> email contact for another couple of days before I realised the talks
> actually had been taken down and the TED Science Board had made
> a statement trying to justifying their decision.

Meanwhile, I created my initial blog post on March 9. The title comes from the informal name that has been given to the kind of antagonistic polarized arguments that erupt any time there is a discussion about the merits of parapsychological research.

The Psi Wars Come To TED

TED is a nonprofit devoted to Ideas Worth Spreading. It started out (in 1984) as a conference bringing together people from three worlds: Technology, Entertainment, Design. Since then its scope has become ever broader. This is an organization on a collision course with consciousness research and it was only a matter of time before the war spilled over into their territory.

In this case, the brouhaha started when apparently skeptics by the names of Jerry Coyne and PZ Myers tried to have a video by parapsychologist Rupert Sheldrake removed from TED talks because they felt he was unscientific. (Here is the video.) To the Immense credit of TED staff, they opened up the controversy to the public. Even more to their credit, the staff person who did this, Emily McManus, is an atheist who set aside her personal beliefs to open up the discussion. A comment section was set up for this topic and the floodgates opened. (You can find it here.)

The open discussion that took place is the kind of situation that skeptics cannot win if knowledgeable people show up to the discussion. It's kind of like asking "who won WWII?" Most people (in the West) will argue that it was chiefly the U.S. and Britain. However, if someone with the real facts shows up, the discussion changes dramatically. The credit for winning actually goes to the Soviet Union. Once you examine the evidence it's not really up for discussion. The Eastern Front stretched for over a thousand miles and it was where about 85% of WWII was fought. This isn't emphasized in high school history books, so most people don't know about it. The psi discussion is a lot like that. Skeptical arguments against psi don't hold up against knowledgeable disagreement. For that reason, skeptics usually avoid just this sort of battle. They get into positions of authority and work behind the scenes to fulfill their agenda. This strategy has worked magnificently on Wikipedia where their compulsive persistence has served their agenda well.

I've been on many comment threads about psi on various on line websites and tangled often with skeptics, but what happened on the TED comment thread was something new. A tipping point has been reached and it was really clear in the thread. It's the first time I've ever seen the skeptics overwhelmed on a public forum. Maybe the JREF crowd just didn't get the word. That skeptical organization usually shows up for these things. (It's easy to spot. Someone will favorably mention the million dollar challenge and that comment will instantly get 15 likes.)

Even without them, there were quite a few skeptics. Mostly well-mannered too. TED seems to attract a better crowd. A few people from the Parapsychology and alternative medicine weighed in on the debate, which brings to mind a sort of showdown between the Montagues and the Capulets.

I did not read through the whole 478 comments because, frankly, the discussion is always the same with minor variations. The skeptics claim that there is no proof, etc., but provide no compelling evidence and the pro psi crowd counters with a barrage of links and counter arguments. The skeptics attempt to define evidence according to radically narrow definitions and the pro psi crowd calls them on it. Back and forth, back and forth. What was interesting to me was how many well-informed posters were pro psi and how willing they were to work together to get their side of the debate heard. They even made a very strong effort to "like" comments from their side, which is new as well. That is usually a skeptical tactic. Somewhere, somehow, these people have learned how to counter the skeptics and they did it very effectively.

This supports my hunch that the Internet is changing how science is done by making the skeptical gatekeeping much more difficult. Information about consciousness research has spread far and wide and its supporters are growing ever more vocal. Among those supporters is a growing group of people who are persistent and engaged enough to do battle with the skeptical paradigm. Their numbers are apparently growing, from what I've seen, while the number of skeptics has stayed pretty much even. It looks like the tipping point has been reached. Skeptics are not winning.

Hopefully the staff at TED took notice because a wrong move on their part will create all sorts of havoc.

From a political standpoint, I think that the discussion made it crystal clear that many of the people on the pro Sheldrake side would regard it as censorship if Sheldrake's video was removed. If the staff chose to remove the video they certainly would be making the excuse that the video was not scientific in nature, but this would not be considered credible by the pro psi crowd which has already made it clear that that, in their opinion, Sheldrake is on solid scientific ground. The only really sensible thing to do is to leave the video up and let people decide for themselves. This has become the most conservative, low risk solution.

While the skeptical point of view is the mainstream position in science, the TED talks are for and supported by an informed public unconstrained by academic politics and belief systems. As the hosts of TED are learning, this public finds consciousness research fascinating. Whether they like it or not, TED must serve this audience or risk being viewed as hypocritical gatekeepers of the status quo.[37]

[If you have the print version of this book all blog posts and relevant links can be found at weilerpsiblog.wordpress.com]

The blog post was mildly popular, but I sensed that it had wider implications. It was just a hunch at the time. I sent senior psi researcher Dean Radin a link in case he hadn't seen it already, and no, he hadn't. He thanked me for bringing it to his attention and in a new blogpost, put up a link to my blog under the heading, "psi wars." He had a cool logo to go with it. At the time, this wasn't any big deal; it was just one more Internet argument with many of the usual suspects or their doppelgangers. I had underestimated the impact that the TED brand would have on the discussion.

Within the psychic/parapsychology community, this story began to pick up steam. From Dean Radin's blog it made its way to *The Daily Grail*, and was picked up by several other blogs. What was happening with Sheldrake was piquing the interest of many people. Perhaps it was the fact that this was right out in the open where people could follow what was going on and people felt that it was worth their time to give an opinion. Mostly this type of censorship happens behind closed doors, not in public where people can question it and certainly not where they can comment on it. It's changed in the last ten years, as we've all gotten used to life on the Internet. Communication is different now and more open. There are some new, more democratic rules of information-sharing that have taken hold. The Internet recognizes expertise, but, below the level of mass media, there are no gatekeepers. If you have something worthwhile to contribute, regardless of your academic credentials, people, sometimes the experts themselves, will recognize you and acknowledge your contributions. In the world of blogging, the Internet is the ultimate meritocracy.

Bloggers like me serve a niche function that didn't exist before the Internet. We act like newspaper editors and journalists rolled up into one, reporting and offering commentary on specialized topics that require a certain amount of background knowledge. Some mainstream publications, such as *The Huffington Post*, acknowledge this to a certain extent by hosting an army of bloggers, but they don't tend to use them as a resource for writing articles. Bloggers generally aren't regarded as knowledgeable enough to qualify as legitimate sources unless they have PhDs or have demonstrated their credentials elsewhere. But that is slowly changing.

On any specialized topic you will almost certainly find bloggers who are experts in that field and people who follow the topic who are near experts. The parapsychology community has many of the latter. It is one of the most popular of the "fringe" topics, and, with a great deal of excellent literature on the subject and more coming out every day, it is possible to educate oneself without pouring over obscure research material.

As someone who follows parapsychology discussions, I had seen enough of them to know that this one was shaping up a bit differently. No one in the mainstream press would notice something like this, and, even as the controversy heated up and developed into a larger story, the mainstream press still did not understand what was going on.

Over at TED, the initial discussion had ended after two days of intense intellectual sparring, and everyone was waiting to see what TED would do next.

As it was not immediately obvious which way the winds were blowing, I was quite curious. The situation was unique and called for a unique response. Did this organization have the guts to back down and allow the Sheldrake video to stay up? Or were they going to cave to skeptical pressure? While most of the time these questions are fairly predictable within the world of parapsychology, what they did next surprised nearly everyone.

CHAPTER SEVEN

MEET THE IDEOLOGUES, ER, SKEPTICS

keptics have a high-status position in our minds and in our media. We, and the media, tend to assume that critics know what they're talking about and typically aren't pressed to justify their position. That is left solely to the original claimant. The belief is that the claimant must satisfy the demands of the skeptics to have credibility.

This has the effect of granting 100% credibility to skeptics and 0% credibility to anyone else, particularly when the original claimant has a controversial non mainstream position. That may sound good, but, in practice, the original claimant has no avenue to success. As it is impossible to argue from a position of zero credibility, it is an absolutely unwinnable situation.

To understand why, you have to understand what skepticism really is.

The assumption that skeptics have to be convinced is based on the belief that they can be convinced. Skeptics are perceived to be tough, but also reasonable and fair. Anyone who has tangled with skeptics, however, knows this to be nothing more than a pleasant fiction.

I have a lot of not-very-pleasant things to say about skeptics, so right off the bat I need to put in this disclaimer. Skeptics are people and people are complicated. Not all skeptics fit the mold I describe and some only fit it partly, some in seemingly contradictory ways, and others don't fit it at all. Some skepticism is moderate, reasonable and helpful. Like many people who have studied parapsychology, debating skeptics has helped to sharpen my skills and I pay more attention to the details than I would have otherwise. The conflict that skepticism creates can be very healthy.

I also want to make another point crystal clear: although the vast majority of parapsychology skeptics are atheists, the vast majority of atheists are not skeptics. It's a point that's easy to miss, especially when it comes to high profile atheists such as Richard Dawkins, author of *The God Delusion*, which has been described as:

> ... often little more than an aggregation of convenient factoids, suitably overstated to achieve maximum impact, and loosely arranged to suggest that they constitute an argument. This makes dealing with its "arguments" a little problematical, in that the work frequently substitutes aggressive, bullying rhetoric for serious evidence-based argument.[38]

In fact, this sort of skepticism is better portrayed as a fundamentalist offshoot of atheism that makes the moderate atheists look bad. In a 2013 University of Tennessee, Chattanooga, study of atheism, he would fall into the category of "Anti-Theist."

> If any subset of our non-belief sample fit the "angry, argumentative, dogmatic" stereotype, it is the Anti-Theists. This group scored the highest amongst our other typologies on empirical psychometric measures of anger, autonomy, disagreeableness, narcissism, and dogmatism while scoring lowest on measures of positive relations with others.[39]

They comprise only 14.8% of all atheists. (For comparison, about 13% of Christians worldwide are fundamentalists, but in the U.S. that number is about 28%.) The vast majority of atheists, in other words, are open minded reasonable people. Some of them, such as parapsychologist Ed May, consider psychic ability to be a fact. Just so there is absolutely no doubt: *Atheism Does Not Equal Skepticism*.

Now that we have that out of the way, skepticism about the paranormal comes in all flavors, ranging from the nuanced and thoughtful to the bigoted and hateful. I've met skeptics from everywhere in this spectrum; I have a friend from my college days who fits the description of a closed-minded skeptic perfectly. I like him despite this, because, as with other skeptics, there is more to him than just how he responds to the paranormal. (Interesting update: he completely changed his mind after a life threatening accident that left him partially paraplegic. His premonition of danger was very strong that day and he never forgot that.)

Dyed in the wool, a priori skepticism towards the paranormal is the exception, not the norm. About 75% of the population of the U.S. believes there is truth to some form of the paranormal. According to a 2005 report from Gallup; "The poll shows no statistically significant differences among people by age, gender, education, race, and region of the country."[40] At least half of the population has had what they would characterize as a psychic experience.[41] Of those that remain, most people have doubts that can be overcome by evidence. They are cautious about ideas that seem foreign to them, but they make judgments based on their experiences and the existing data.

The people that I'm talking about in this book, though, **are not that kind of skeptic**. They are not really skeptics, by definition, so much as they are believers of a different sort. How they behave can better be described as **pathological disbelief**. Where most people who are skeptical are simply unaware of the research and have reached their conclusions only because they don't personally have a feel for psychic ability and/or have encountered mostly skeptical opinions (or perhaps a psychic they thought was fake), a certain percentage of skeptics are intractably skeptical to the point where they are better described as ideologues. They are not carefully examining facts but are espousing a particular belief system.

It's important to understand that skepticism itself is reactionary. It creates nothing original because it is only a reaction. It is, at its core, doubt and nothing more. It leads nowhere and inhibits interesting avenues of inquiry by shutting them off before they get started. This can be very useful in refining our thinking and removing useless avenues of inquiry and exploration, but that's about it.

When I first started researching and blogging about parapsychology, I learned more about this in my comment section. I would present evidence that showed positive experimental results and skeptics would either ignore or dismiss it preemptively. This happened over and over again, so that eventually I realized that this was a pattern. I wasn't encountering careful, informed objections to evidence, but rather knee-jerk emotional reactions from people who were ignorant and rude. We've all met the blowhards who can never be wrong; the professor that gave you a C because of the subject matter in your essay even though it was written and well thought out; the boss who doesn't listen when warned of coming problems but blames everyone else when they occur; that person in your social organization who acts as if they're the only one with the answers. It's those people. Just as some religious people go off the deep end and become bigots, so some science-minded people go off the deep end and become intolerant of scientific ideas that are outside of the mainstream or their worldview. What they are doing is defending a particular kind of limited, materialistic view of science.

Just as fundamentalists of pretty much any religion regard everyone else with disdain for not adhering to The Truth, there are science fundamentalists as well who act much the same way. These people are also just as prone to ridiculous levels of hypocrisy as their fundamentalist religious counterparts.

Psychology of the Skeptic

The other day, my wife and I had a friend over, whose boyfriend is a skeptic. He's a mellow sort and doesn't get involved with skeptic organizations or any of the more hardcore stuff, but he does listen to Skeptoid podcasts. He's male, white, well educated, intelligent, under the age of 35 and had a strong religious upbringing, which he rejected. He's now an atheist and he fits the skeptical profile exactly. While proponents of parapsychology, psychics and believers are an extremely diverse group, this is not true of skeptics who have crossed the line into ideologue territory. Their profile is very narrow.

One of the characteristics that appears again and again in research into self-identified skeptics is that they had a strongly religious upbringing which is usually described in various ways, the gist of which is that it was "crammed down their throats."

L. David Leiter, who was originally a skeptic and part of a skeptic organization but later disavowed that brand of skepticism while keeping his membership, studied the skepticism, which he encountered for a number of years. He discovered that many of those involved in skeptical organizations had a falling out with a previous religion that was forced upon them by family. Their rebellion sent them into the arms of what they felt to be non-faith-based philosophical thinking. However, they were overzealous:

Instead of becoming scientifically minded, they become adherents of scientism, the belief system in which science and only science has all the answers to everything. This regrettable condition acts to preclude their unbiased consideration of phenomena on the cutting edge of science, which is not how a true scientist should behave.[42]

On the Myer Brigg's personality test, self-identified skeptics are most likely sensing, thinking (ST) types. That is to say that when making decisions they focus on information from their five senses as opposed to interpreting or adding meaning to what they experience, and they look at logic and consistency as opposed to feelings and hunches. They tend to be decisive (J) as opposed to staying open to new ideas. (P)[43]

STJ types also tend to rise to positions of authority. The ultimate skeptic is an extroverted (E) STJ type. ESTJ types are, at their best practical, realistic, matter-of-fact people. They are decisive and quickly move to implement decisions as well as organize projects and people to get things done. They focus on getting results in the most efficient way possible while taking care of routine details. They generally have a clear set of logical standards which they systematically follow and want others to also. They can also be forceful in implementing their plans.[44] Let me emphasize, however, that having an ST personality trait does not mean that the person will be a skeptic, only that skeptics are most likely to be ST personality types.

Sensing, thinking (ST) personalities tend not to rely on intuition and feelings, therefore shutting out those characteristics that are most conducive to the psi experience. This helps to explain why so many ST type personalities can be found among skeptics.

The parallel between ideologically driven skepticism and fundamentalist religion has also been noted. Ideologue skeptics and religious fundamentalists share such traits as right-wing authoritarianism and traditionalism and a marked tendency to be authority-seekers. They also share a distrust of mystical or paranormal experiences. The ideologue skeptics regard them as delusional and the religious fundamentalists as dangerous. While the latter attribute unquestioned authority to their version of the bible, the former do the same with mainstream science.[45]

PZ Myers, one of the original skeptics who criticized Sheldrake's speech, put up a blog post in early May of 2013 actually criticizing the way skeptics deal with science:

> I was also annoyed by the skeptic movement's appropriation of the
> term "scientific" all over the place...except that it's a "science" that
> doesn't make use of accumulated prior knowledge, that abandons
> the concept of the null hypothesis, and that so narrowly defines what
> it will accept as evidence that it actively excludes huge domains of
> knowledge. It's toothless science that fetishizes "consumer protection"
> over understanding.[46]

Professor Myers is a good example of how even skeptics who are
obviously ideologues can vary in their adherence to that set of beliefs.
As I said before, they are people and are therefore complicated.

Ideologues in general, are just an ordinary offshoot of an ordinary
personality type. My general feeling about this is that evolution
gave rise to personality types who initially worked together in the
tribe size of hunter gatherers. This typically was between 150 to 200
people, who more or less lived together their entire lives. This lifelong
familiarity provided the necessary cohesiveness that allowed NF and
ST personalities to work together despite their radically different
perspectives. This is important for understanding psi skepticism
because the greatest weakness of this offshoot of the ST personality
type is not understanding the importance of meaning and therefore not
understanding the value that NF personality types bring to the table.
The ideologue skeptic personality types are capable of cooperatively
producing a great deal of work, but need other personality types to
help steer them towards work that is meaningful.

That's certainly what I've observed in organized skepticism. Left to
their own devices, they will typically produce work that is prodigious,
organized and logically consistent, but not very important.

A great example of this is a website called "Quackwatch"[47] created
and managed by Stephen Barrett who is dead set against chiropractic
care. It's a clean, well-organized website with a tremendous number
of clickable links all directing the viewer to different Quackwatch web
pages, very few of which provide much in the way of useful information.
They are more designed to sway a person's viewpoint than guide them to
anything useful. A section titled "Health Freedoms" is a good example.
The first two paragraphs read:

> If quacks can't win by playing according to the rules, they try to change
> them by switching from the scientific to the political arena. In science,
> a medical claim is treated as false until proven beyond a reasonable

doubt. But in politics, a medical claim may be accepted until proven false or harmful. This is why proponents of laetrile, chiropractic, orthomolecular psychiatry, chelation therapy and the like, take their case to legislators rather than scientific groups.

Quacks use the concept of "health freedom" to divert attention away from themselves and toward victims of disease with whom we are naturally sympathetic. "These poor folks should have the freedom to choose whatever treatments they want," cry the quacks—with crocodile tears. They want us to overlook two things. First, no one wants to be cheated, especially in matters of life and health. Victims of disease do not demand quack treatments because they want to exercise their "rights," but because they have been deceived into thinking that they offer hope. Second, the laws against worthless nostrums are not directed against the victims of disease but at the promoters who attempt to exploit them.[48]

The rest of that article continues in the same vein. It contains lots of content with very little meaning.

The NF's (intuitive, feeling) personality is far more likely to understand what is important, but will lack the interest and motivation to create on the same scale. There is no one personality type that covers it all. Humans are social creatures and personalities are a reflection of an evolutionary tribal system designed to maximize the variety of thinking types while minimizing the consequence of their individual weaknesses. In a huge global society, however, this system breaks down. ST types tend to do better and rise faster within corporate, academic and government food chains, without significant influence from NF types to temper their worst tendencies. In a small tribe, a leader gains status because of trust; in modern society leaders gain status because of rules. This puts far more skeptics in positions of authority than one would find in a hunter/gatherer society, and it allows their worst over-controlling impulses free rein.

There is, of course variety within the ST personalities ranging from moderate to fundamentalist. Many, if not most people with ST personality types are not irrationally skeptical of psychic capacities. As I stated earlier, in this book I am focused only on the subgroup that consists of the skeptical ideologues.

On a neurological level, using the popular (but inaccurate[49]) left brain/right brain description, ideologue skeptics and other fundamentalists are "left" brained. That is to say, they have strong tendencies toward linear, logical thinking while doing poorly at creativity, intuition, insight and holistic thinking in general.

Most people are familiar with the dysfunction that comes with being too "right" brained. Being "flighty, a dreamer, impractical, illogical and irrational come to mind. What are less well known are the traits that come with being too "left" brained. These include denialism, rigid thinking, arrogance, narcissism and a lack of awareness of hypocrisy or irony. An overly narrow focus as well as narcissism and inflated self-worth are examples of over reliance on the "left" brain. Denialism and extreme gullibility have been documented in some people who have had right-side strokes (and are thereby forced to over use their left brain. This includes for example, denial that they have had a stroke by coming up with endless, mostly irrational reasons for why they can't move their left arm.[50] These stroke victims are also likely to believe whatever they read. There are some similarities to ideologue skeptics. "In overly logical and analytical individuals, fMRI scans have shown the left brain actually inhibits the right brain—via the corpus callosum nerve fibers—from offering its contribution to the entire cognitive process. "[51]

The part of our brain that is creative, intuitive and holistic is where our minds go to get an overall perspective of what our senses are telling us. While an openness to experience and possibility is frequently mistaken for gullibility, gullibility is actually far more likely to occur when a person's focus is too narrow. Holistic, creative and intuitive thinking ability is what allows us to get out of a rut by mentally flying above it to have a look at where we are going. Ideologue skeptics and other fundamentalists lack this ability, so they tend to stay in their ruts, unquestioningly believing things which support their beliefs, while denying any things that don't. This translates into an intolerance for ambiguity and nuance, which are important to psi functioning.[52]

An ideologue skeptic is first and foremost a reactionary. Like other fundamentalists they firmly believe they are doing good by attempting to rid the world of ideas that they consider harmful to other people. They see themselves as defending the truth, but, in fact, they are just intolerant. The intolerance towards psi is part of a general attitude of intolerance that reaches into other parts of their lives.

For example, one of the things skeptics are infamous for is their attitude towards women. Very recently a dam burst on this topic within the skeptical community. And it was all kinds of ugly.

Charges of Rape, Sexual Assault and General Misogyny

The women of the skeptic movement are not happy, and they have been becoming steadily more vocal about how badly they have been treated. The misogyny is fairly widespread and includes inappropriate touching, insulting and/or vulgar remarks as well as hate speech. There is even a charge of rape.

This issue is incredibly divisive among skeptics, who seem to be either very much on the side of the women or very emphatically dismissive of their complaints. In addition to exposing an undercurrent of irrational anger and sexism it also demonstrates that not every male skeptic acts or feels this way. Some of the skeptics, who could be described as ideologues, have gone out of their way—and in some cases risked their reputations—in defense of these women. It's a good demonstration of what I stated at the beginning of this chapter: skeptics are people and people are complicated.

In early March, skeptical blogger Michael Nugent put together a list of fifty misogynistic comments that skeptics made, as part of a discussion with another skeptical blogger. He stated:

> I'm using examples that were published on The Slymepit website. I could add examples from Elevatorgate, YouTube and elsewhere, but I think there is enough here to be representative of the "nasty pushback" we are discussing.
>
> 1. If I was a girl I would kick [named person] in the cunt.
>
> 2. [named person] comes off as the most disgusting human being I have ever encountered. What a fucking self-pitying arrogant twat/bitch/cunt/asshole. Oh, was that sexist? Boo fucking hoo; stop complaining and grow a pair. Oh, was that sexist again? Fuck you.
>
> 3. But for her victim ploy [named person] needs to believe that there are people who want her to be raped, and all her little smelly-skepchick-snatch-sniffers are more than happy to magic them into being in their own tiny shiny minds.[53]

This brouhaha started back in October of 2012, when Rebecca Watson, who goes by the moniker Skepchick, published an article in Slate detailing her discomfort when attending skeptic events:

... women started telling me stories about sexism at skeptic events, experiences that made them uncomfortable enough to never return. ... I was occasionally grabbed and groped without consent at events. ...

... And Jen McCreight stopped blogging and accepting speaking engagements altogether. "I wake up every morning to abusive comments, tweets, and emails about how I'm a slut, prude, ugly, fat, feminazi, retard, bitch, and cunt (just to name a few)," she wrote. "I just can't take it anymore."[54]...

That same year, Damion Reinhardt (male, by the way) updated a list of alleged skeptic sexists with links to the source of the allegations. There were well known skeptics whom women accused of making sexist remarks: Richard Dawkins, Sam Harris, Christopher Hitchens, Daniel Dennett, D.J. Grothe, Ron Lindsay, Steven Pinker and Michael Shermer[55] as well as 25 others.

This issue returned to the background for a while, only to resurface in August of 2013. On August 6, Karen Stollznow published an article in *Scientific American* detailing her alleged sexual harassment (which turned out to be false) from an unnamed skeptic[56], who was later identified as Ben Radford, deputy publisher of the *Skeptical Inquirer*.[57]

(Stollznow, it turned out, was an ex-girlfriend of Radford and he sued Stollznow for defamation and won, so her charges appear to be baseless.[58] He informed me of this in 2015 and as it was going to be a while before I updated my book, I published this information on my blog on the same page that I advertised my book in the hopes that people would see it. It's a reminder that things can be more complicated than they appear.)

That accusation apparently was enough for other women to come forward. Carry Poppy accused D.J. Grothe, president of the James Randi Educational Foundation, of "constant duplicity, dishonesty, and manipulation" and of misogyny.[59] And an anonymous woman PZ Myers knows and trusts came forward with an "awful secret" that he published on his blog, alleging she had been raped by prominent skeptic, Michael Shermer.[60] (This was an anonymous, possibly baseless allegation, and he has not been formally accused of, or charged with a crime.) As if that wasn't enough, Bill Nye (the science guy) was named as a sexual harasser on a tumblr post.[61]

It's quite likely that not all of these allegations have merit, (as was demonstrated in Radford's case) but, taken as a whole, they don't paint a pretty picture. This is exactly what Rebecca Watson has been complaining about for years. It's a demonstration of a very hardened sexist attitude which comes from a general attitude of intolerance. (Just as an aside, this sort of behavior is virtually non-existent in New Age circles. It does occur, but not enough to get this type of response. Leaders who stray from the path are typically sleeping with their students, not engaging in misogyny.)

As an aside, you can also use misogyny as a guide for comparing the culture of ideologue skeptics with the boy's club culture in the hard sciences. There are many scientists who spend their entire adult lives immersed in logical, linear thought processes, so we should see a corresponding amount of misogyny in the sciences. And, in fact it is there. Misogyny is alive and well in the hard sciences as was discovered by professor Ben Barres, who has transgendered from female. (He was formerly Barbara Barres.) He gets far more respect for his work now that he is a male.[62]

As a female in a male dominated scientific field, Barres experienced countless instances of biased behavior towards her, solely based on her gender, which she/he was later able to compare with completely different behavior toward him as a man.

Misogyny is an aspect of personality that involves a lack of empathy and a predisposition towards intolerance and unconscious biases. It can be argued, therefore, that this overload of linear, logical thinking is at least partly to blame for mainstream intolerance towards subjects like parapsychology.

So what does it mean that there is so much misogyny in the skeptical movement? It means that as a group, skeptics have a behavior problem; something that has not gone unnoticed by the skeptics themselves. Ethan Clowe, a skeptic who has recently withdrawn from the movement, remarked on the pervasive mean-spirited behavior he witnessed. He detailed a few things he'd been told about:

Volunteers being called up early in the morning and yelled at.

Explosive arguments over mundane topics that result in vows of "I will not work with this person until they are kicked out!"

Skeptical activists trying to organize boycotts of other skeptical organizations because the said group has a policy etc. that someone doesn't agree with.[63]

Myron, a skeptic and scientist with the New York State Department of Health, had this to say:

> ... Well, the invective is worse and much more common and people in the non-skeptic realm are starting to notice. Someone out there right now might be asking themselves, "Why be a skeptic? They're a bunch of argumentative, know-it-all, navel-gazing assholes!"[64]

Widespread behavior of this kind is an indication that, as a group, these ideologue skeptics have a flawed ability to think clearly. As a group they lack empathy and an internal ability to conceptualize the various repercussions of behaving badly. That, in turn, is an indication of a lack of ability to think holistically, which is vital to rational thinking.

Critical Thinking vs. Rational Thinking

Ideologue skeptics pride themselves on critical thinking. It goes something like this: The best way to think is in a logical, unemotional fashion. Never jump to conclusions, and never let emotions overwhelm your ability for sound inferential reasoning. Draw conclusions only when there is enough evidence to support them and don't go beyond the limits of logical probability. Logical problem solving and critical analysis are central to this idea.

Characters such as Spock, Sherlock Holmes and Henry Higgins come to mind. They are admired for their powerful intellect and reasoning abilities. The problem with this approach, however, is that is entirely reactionary. Not surprisingly, so is the skeptical movement. It defines itself almost entirely by what it is against. Psychics, UFOs, homeopathy, bigfoot, ghosts, hauntings, crop circles, etc. The flaw in this type of thinking is that it is unable to make intuitive leaps to new alternative paradigms and reach conclusions in nonlinear fashion. It doesn't do anything *new*. Skeptical thinking starts with the premise that these things can't exist and goes from there to the only logical conclusion that can be reached: that they must not exist.

It is logical, but not rational; reactive and not innovative. The subjects listed above require a holistic approach to understanding because they involve ambiguity. The sum of the evidence, not its parts, makes the argument for their existence compelling, but, to do that, one must first imagine that they can be real.

Rational thinking requires imagination, creativity, insight and intuition as well as logical, linear thought.[65] To be rational we must be able to move beyond mechanical, analytic arguments and into the realm of *what if.* Only then can we be said to be thinking rationally.

Pseudoskepticism

Ideologue skeptics, who deny the existence of psychic ability, do so almost entirely with pseudoskeptical arguments. Most skepticism that you're likely to see surrounding parapsychology is actually pseudoskepticism in disguise. It can be a bit difficult to recognize without a good understanding of the subject in question, but, with practice, it gets easier to spot because it's generally accompanied by an arrogant insulting attitude and sweeping statements.

Marcello Truzzi attributed these eight traits to pseudo skepticism:

1. Denying, when only doubt has been established
2. Double standards in the application of criticism
3. The tendency to discredit rather than investigate
4. Presenting insufficient evidence or proof
5. Assuming criticism requires no burden of proof
6. Making unsubstantiated counter-claims
7. Counter-claims based on plausibility rather than empirical evidence
8. Suggesting that unconvincing evidence provides grounds for completely dismissing a claim

While I regard most of what I discuss in this book as pseudoskepticism, I will refer to it as skepticism and the people who engage in it as skeptics. That's how they refer to themselves and it minimizes confusion in the book for me do so as well.

If you're aware of the evidence for parapsychology and if you go through the skeptical comments at TED, you can find evidence of all of these traits to varying degrees.

Most people are much more levelheaded and reasonable. Yet, on the Internet, you can find a large number of overly zealous skeptics posting comments continually. I've found them typically in editorial positions on the Internet, where they have the opportunity to shut out topics that they find disagreeable and shape information according to their beliefs without having to engage in any real discussions about the merits of their own viewpoints.

In real life, this person is possibly your boss. They prefer management positions and actively seek them out and the authority that comes with it. They are the people who overestimate their own successes and underestimate yours; they will come into a situation that they are unfamiliar with, but quickly form an opinion and treat everyone else as though they're doing it wrong. On the Internet is where they do the most damage because their single-minded nature typically allows them to win in situations where being obsessive is a winning strategy (think Wikipedia editing).

The ideologue skeptics also have organizations that promote their reactionary, materialistic values. They have that in common with other ideologues in that they gravitate towards groups that see the world in black and white terms. They have much in common with other ideologues such as those in the Tea Party, which attacks liberal values and programs; fundamentalist Christian organizations, which attack women's rights; white supremacy groups, which attack minorities and terrorist organizations, which attack Western societies to name a few. As you may have guessed, one thing they all have in common is that they do a lot of attacking.

These are the people whom the media trusts and grants the final word over pretty much any controversial subject you care to name. Their opinions are always sought and never questioned. If that ever changed, parapsychology would cease to be a controversial subject.

The problem with this approach is that it grants 100% credibility to skeptics and 0% credibility to anyone else. In any disagreement the skeptics are always assumed to be right. This is unambiguously 100% bias because it allows no avenue for opinions to change. If you advocate for a controversial subject, your automatic zero credibility gives you no chance to persuade anyone of anything.

There is also a variation of this sort of group that specifically attacks parapsychology and frontier sciences. Two of these organizations have achieved international prominence: JREF, the James Randi Educational Foundation and CSI: The Committee for Skeptical Inquiry, formerly known as the Committee for scientific Investigations of Claims of the Paranormal (CSICOP). Both organizations have strong ties to atheism. We'll take a look at them and other skeptical groups and websites in another chapter.

CHAPTER EIGHT

TED THROWS DOWN WITH
SHELDRAKE AND HANCOCK

The TED staff seemed to be panicking. The types of comments that appeared in the original Sheldrake discussion could have, and should have, steered TED towards a more conciliatory approach. The fact that the original TED complaints were so easily disputed should have been a clue that something was wrong. There was no reason to hurry. They could have taken a month to sort things out quietly and it wouldn't have mattered. Perhaps the unexpected heat of the controversy unnerved the TED staff a bit. There is no way to know except by TED's actions, which were certainly not well thought out.

TED has a science board, which advises them on scientific issues, and it was upon their recommendation that the Sheldrake video be removed.

On March 14, 2013, having already taken down Sheldrake's video, they included a new list of complaints for Sheldrake:

> According to our science board, Rupert Sheldrake bases his argument on several major factual errors, which undermine the arguments of talk. For example, he suggests that scientists reject the notion that animals have consciousness, despite the fact that it's generally accepted that animals have some form of consciousness, and there's much research and literature exploring the idea.

He also argues that scientists have ignored variations in the measurements of natural constants, using as his primary example the dogmatic assumption that a constant must be constant and uses the speed of light as example. But, in truth, there has been a great deal of inquiry into the nature of scientific constants, including published, peer reviewed research investigating whether certain constants – including the speed of light – might actually vary over time or distance. Scientists are constantly questioning these assumptions. For example, just this year *Scientific American* published a feature on the state of research into exactly this question. ("Are physical constants really constant? Do the inner workings of nature change over time?") Physicist Sean Carroll wrote a careful rebuttal of this point.

In addition, Sheldrake claims to have "evidence" of morphic resonance in crystal formation and rat behavior. The research has never appeared in a peer reviewed journal, despite attempts by other scientists eager to replicate the work.

On the surface, this appeared to be a very damaging indictment of Sheldrake's speech, but I preferred to wait for Sheldrake's response before passing any judgment. Too often, these sorts of skeptical accusations are totally overblown.

In addition to Sheldrake's talk, Graham Hancock's talk from the same conference in London was also removed. This was curious as he is first and foremost an archeological journalist. While his books on archeology are highly controversial and have been labeled pseudo-archeology by skeptics, they were not the subject of his talk. He is not a scientist and certainly not a parapsychologist. He was giving a personal account of his travails with marijuana and how psychedelic journeys with an exotic plant mix known as Ayahuasca had helped him kick a marijuana habit which had taken over his life. This is what TED said about Hancock:

Graham Hancock's talk, again, shares a compelling and unorthodox worldview, but one that strays well beyond the realm of reasonable science. While attempting to critique the scientific worldview, he misrepresents what scientists actually think. He suggests, for example, that no scientists are working on the problem of consciousness.

In addition, Hancock makes statements about psychotropic drugs that seem both nonscientific and reckless. He states as fact that psychotropic drug use is essential for an "emergence into consciousness," and that one can use psychotropic plants to connect directly with an ancient mother culture. He seems to offer a one-note explanation for how culture arises (drugs), it's no surprise his work has often been characterized as pseudo-archeology.

TED respects and supports the exploration of unorthodox ideas, but the many misleading statements in both Sheldrake's and Hancock's talks, whether made deliberately or in error, have led our scientific advisors to conclude that our name and platform should not be associated with these talks.

Graham Hancock is the bestselling author of *The Sign and the Seal*, about his search for the lost Arc of the Covenant made famous in the movie *Raiders of the Lost Arc*; *Fingerprints of the Gods*, about his search for lost civilizations; and *Heaven's Mirror,* where he continues that search. His books have sold over five million copies and have been translated into 27 languages, so he's a big deal.

But he's not the sort of person that would normally be dragged into the parapsychology fight. His specialty is not normally on the skeptical radar and they aren't usually very concerned about that domain. It's not normally what they make a fuss about. What the heck did Hancock have to say that got them so riled up?

He said: "Materialism has nothing to say about consciousness." He also went on to point out that our industrialized society has a war on consciousness that criminalizes drugs that expand consciousness.

Singling out these two videos for a slap on the hand gives some insight into what sort of information TED was trying to keep off its site. Given their new guidelines for TEDx productions and their selectivity in attacking only speeches that questioned the philosophy of materialism, TED was tipping its hand as to its own philosophical position.

This philosophy, materialism, is popular in the mainstream media because it's popular in the sciences. It's the safe, conservative choice normally that prevents controversy. Or rather it was. The fact that a controversy was growing surrounding TED's actions was an indication that this was changing.

Before I get to the replies that both Sheldrake and Hancock made to these accusations let's take a step back and look at what was happening, because TED was clearly on the path to disaster.

It's time to put on our public relations hat and examine the choices that TED Curator, Chris Anderson, and the TED staff had:

1. Take down Sheldrake's video
2. Take down both Sheldrake's and Hancock's videos
3. Give into public pressure and put both videos back up on the main page.

Of the three choices the third would have ended the controversy with no consequence to TED. If you don't want that sort of stuff in programs under your name you can always handle that in the future. Now is the time to cut your losses and let your viewers have their way. Nothing is gained by turning this into a fight because there is no way to win; you're surely going to alienate people. The skeptics wouldn't have liked it, but they were going to stay loyal to TED no matter how things played out. But for those on the other side of the debate, this meant that TED wasn't "cool" anymore. The TED brand would be increasingly viewed as conservative and reactionary, or even worse, boring (That is what ended up happening).

This issue had all the signs of a serious disaster that could be damaging to TED's reputation. Those signs were:

1. The issue centered around the role of consciousness in physics. This is not settled in science. Quite the contrary, there is a great deal of evidence, which suggests that the mainstream materialist view is wrong.
2. When you start policing the content of the speeches, you have to demonstrate that this is done in an even-handed way across the board or risk being exposed as a hypocrite. TED would have had to eliminate a lot more speeches if they held everyone to the same standard.
3. TED's tag line is "Ideas Worth Spreading." That implies that they will take a chance on ideas that might not be mainstream and conservative.
4. Rupert Sheldrake and Graham Hancock are not nobodies. They have large followings that include some highly intellectual and well-respected people. Attacking them is going to draw a large crowd and plenty of negative publicity.

In other words, all signs pointed to a public relation nightmare. Other public entities, such as Wikipedia, or media companies such as the *Huffington Post*, should take note. Anyone who takes the skeptical side of this debate will be making a lot of enemies.

I don't see TED as some evil organization. Far from it. They do a lot of good. TED got its reputation by putting out high quality material. TED curator Chris Anderson makes this point in the Hancock comment thread:

> This is an important point that few understand. The role of curation. The only reason TED talks ever acquired a reputation for being worth watching is because we fought like crazy to ensure that only good stuff appeared on the site. People may say just let anything go. Then I invite them to open a website for serious content that does that, and watch what happens.

> The decision to open up to TEDx events and create a YouTube channel for them was a huge risk for this very reason. We believe overall TEDx brings in far more of the great than the problematic. But it is absolutely not an option for us to just wash our hands of any and all curatorial decisions on that channel. It's just really hard work to do that without upsetting people – as this episode so powerfully illustrates.

Anderson's reasons for curating TED videos is sound; it just wasn't applied with very much thought in this case.

There was also the matter of the science board that was anonymous. The reason for this, according to Anderson:

> The science board [is composed of] five volunteers from a variety of scientific disciplines, and [provides] a lot of wisdom on dealing with complex scientific issues of public interest. They give us informal advice when asked, and we make our own decisions taking that advice into account.

> If this was a public board a) they would probably all have to give up their day jobs to participate given all the incoming comments, suggestions and criticisms they'd have to deal with and b) the quality of their advice could be compromised as they would, in part, have to play to the public. This is why there is a long tradition of private advisers and referees in numerous organizations.

The reason that Anderson gives for keeping the board anonymous is somewhat of a red herring. The science board members do not have to respond to comments or even read them. Also, public disclosure generally forces people to be *more* fair minded, not the opposite. Closed doors usually just make room for dirty politicking.

Obvious secrecy looks bad from a public relations perspective as it's hard to earn the trust of those who disagree with you when you're deliberately hiding important information from them.

On March 18, both speakers addressed the criticisms that had been leveled against them and dropped their respective bombs on the skeptical arguments. At that point, the whole controversy began its long trip down the rabbit hole.

CHAPTER NINE

WHEN SKEPTICS ATTACK: SKEPTICAL ORGANIZATIONS AND WEBSITES

I f you really want to get to the heart of skepticism, the best way to do that is to look at the organizations that skeptics create and see how they operate. The behavior of these organizations is the behavior of the individuals, writ large. There are two national organizations worth considering: the James Randi Educational Foundation (JREF) and the Committee for Skeptical Inquiry (CSI). I'll look at one website that is representative of much of the skeptical web landscape.

I'll spend most of my effort on JREF because this required a lot of original research on my part.

(JREF more or less disbanded in 2016 and ceased being a public nonprofit organization. The million-dollar challenge has likewise been discontinued.) It is still seen by some as proof that psychics don't exist.

The James Randi Educational Foundation (JREF)

[The challenge ended in September of 2015, effectively ending the main reason for the foundation's existence. It continues as a grant making organization.]

JREF is a skeptical organization supposedly devoted to promoting critical thinking regarding claims of the paranormal. In reality it is an advocacy organization, known in politics as a pressure group. They lobby media and science organizations to dissuade them from taking parapsychology and psychics seriously. Like other pressure groups, they occasionally perform high profile publicity stunts to attract attention.

In fact, they are a magnet for controversy and scandal. The president of JREF, D.J. Grothe, has recently been accused of "misogyny and disrespect for women coworkers," and, "constant duplicity, dishonesty, and manipulation" by a female employee.[66] James Randi's significant other, Deyvi Pena, was convicted of identity theft. A disgruntled million dollar challenge applicant put out a $100,000 reward to anyone who could prove that the challenge was legitimate, and there is a long list of complaints by people who have either applied for the challenge or taken it; the challenge itself is the subject of unending criticism:

"Psychic offered a million dollars to prove his abilities." How many times have you seen that headline? James Randi, a magician, offers a million dollars to any person who can prove they possess psychic abilities. This is done through the James Randi Educational Foundation (JREF for short), and is referred to as the million dollar challenge (MDC for short).

Every few months, a story pops up in a prominent magazine about a prominent psychic who has been challenged to prove their abilities by taking the MDC. Celebrity psychics such as the late Sylvia Browne, James Van Praagh and John Edward have all been goaded at various times to apply for the challenge. All have declined.

Because the MDC is perceived in the media as a legitimate way to test psychic ability, declining to take the challenge is promoted as proof that the psychics are actually charlatans. Over the years, many people have applied for the challenge, a very tiny percentage has been tested, and no one has passed even the preliminary part. Some skeptics point to this as proof that psychic ability does not exist.

Mr. Randi is a very popular skeptic and the million dollar challenge is easy to understand and seems to provide a clear and easy way to establish the truth about psychic ability. Because the MDC is rather popular in mainstream periodical literature, it merits serious investigation.

A Review of the Literature

Parapsychological literature sheds little light on the workings of this challenge. There are no scientific papers reviewing the MDC and it is mentioned only briefly in some books about parapsychology. The most influential book in parapsychology, *The Conscious Universe*, by Dean Radin, spends only a sentence on Randi:

> They [Geller or Randi] are actually so *irrelevant* to the scientific evaluation of psi that not a single experiment involving either person is included among the thousand studies reviewed in meta-analyses.[67]

In the two most influential books that specifically address parapsychology skepticism, the JREF million dollar challenge gets only the briefest mention.

Chris Carter, in his book *Parapsychology and the Skeptics,* devotes a mere four and half pages to Randi without examining the challenge except to say this:

> The problem with this test is that Randi himself acts as policeman, judge and jury. Given his countless disparaging and insulting remarks concerning parapsychology, and his financial stake in the debunking movement, he can hardly be considered to be an unbiased observer.[68]

Robert McLuhan, despite the title of his book, *Randi's Prize*, has even less to say about the challenge, devoting only a few paragraphs to it:

> Randi himself laments that none of the stars in the psychic firmament – John Edward or Uri Geller for instance – has entered for it, (...) Another view, of course, is that, unlike the naïve individuals who actually do apply for the prize, they have more sense than to put themselves in the hands of a crusading sceptic who considers them to be the scum of the earth. (...)
>
> To offer an analogy: the difference between parapsychology and Randi's prize is the difference between a fleet of boats heading out to sea equipped with radar and large nets, and one man sitting beside a muddy stream waiting for fish to jump in his net.[69]

What is apparent is that scientists and scholars of parapsychology feel that the challenge is so insignificant as to not merit any significant consideration. Some serious examinations of the challenge do exist on blog posts on the Internet. Greg Taylor at *The Daily Grail*, published a very thorough article that examined it:

> First, and perhaps the most important, is the effect size required to win the challenge. While the JREF says that 'all tests are designed with the participation and approval of the applicant', this does not mean that the tests are fair **scientific** tests. The JREF need to protect a very large amount of money from possible 'long-range shots', and as such they ask for extremely significant results before paying out—much higher than are generally accepted in scientific research (and if you don't agree to terms, your application is rejected).[70]

Both the blog post by *The Daily Grail*, and another by Michael Prescott[71], questioned the rules for the challenge, pointing out logical errors and draconian terms in the application. For example, rules #4 and #8 allow JREF to use information as it sees fit and the applicant surrenders all rights to legal action. In other words, if the organization decided to lie and cheat the applicant cannot sue for damages.

Over the years, I have published a couple of articles on the Million Dollar Challenge on my blog,[72] which have made their way into various on line discussions about the merits of the challenge.

My main interest has been in the workings of the challenge. According to Wikipedia:

> In the October 1981 issue of *Fate*, Rawlins quoted him [James Randi] as saying "I always have an out".[19] Randi has stated that Rawlins did not give the entire quotation.[20] Randi actually said *"Concerning the challenge, I always have an 'out': I'm right!"*[21][22]. Randi states that the phrase "I always have an out" refers to the fact that he does not allow test subjects to cheat.[23]

Examining James Randi's Character

As the organization bears his name, this invites questioning about James Randi's character. Does Randi have an out? Is there some method he uses to make sure applicants never win? All of the criticisms of the challenge that I've read don't address this. They point out, correctly, that the challenge is unrealistically hard and that Randi, who is considered to be far from impartial, totally controls it.

The skeptical point of view is that Randi needs to control the challenge in order to prevent alleged psychics from cheating, and that he is qualified based on his considerable experience in magic to expose frauds. James Randi is a very accomplished magician and this does qualify him to expose people who are posing as psychics but are actually using magic tricks to dupe people. However, Randi has no scientific education, self-taught or otherwise. His critics contend that total control over the challenge allows Randi to cheat, or to create unrealistic rules that no one could satisfy in order to win.

In order to deal with the efficacy of Randi's challenge, we have to examine the character of James Randi. If he has a genuine interest in the truth, we can rely on his good judgment. So we look first at what his critics have to say.

While psi proponents acknowledge his considerable magic skills and that he has exposed a few frauds posing as psychics, he is widely regarded as deeply biased and more interested in publicity than the truth. Biologist Rupert Sheldrake, a target of Randi's criticisms, uses this widely circulated story to illustrate that point:

> The January 2000 issue of *Dog World* magazine included an article on a possible sixth sense in dogs, which discussed some of my research. In this article Randi was quoted as saying that in relation to canine ESP, "We at the JREF [James Randi Educational Foundation] have tested these claims. They fail." No details were given of these tests.

> I emailed James Randi to ask for details of this JREF research. He did not reply. He ignored a second request for information too.

> I then asked members of the JREF Scientific Advisory Board to help me find out more about this claim. They did indeed help by advising Randi to reply. In an email sent on February 6, 2000 he told me that the tests he referred to were not done at the JREF but took place "years ago" and were "informal". They involved two dogs belonging to a friend of his that he observed over a two-week period. All records had been lost. He wrote: "I overstated my case for doubting the reality of dog ESP based on the small amount of data I obtained. It was rash and improper of me to do so."[73]

Randi also claimed that in a tape of a dog experiment that Sheldrake had performed, the dog was responding to every passing car. He was later forced to admit that he had never seen the tape.

It is safe to say that no parapsychologist or paranormal investigator would ever work alongside Randi. In one telling instance, he was banned by the family and the investigators from entering a house where poltergeist activity was supposedly occurring.[74] Any testimony to Randi's integrity and honesty will not be found in the opinions of his opponents. Psi proponent Victor Zammit goes so far as to write:

> In fact his conduct shows him to be a conman, a mind-manipulator and someone *who himself admits* – and this is a matter of public record – to being highly skilled in deception, trickery and conning.[75]

In Will Storr's *The Heretics* he gets a stunning confession from Randi:

> Is James Randi a liar? I begin gently, by telling him that my research has painted a picture of a clever man who is often right, but who has a certain element to his personality, which leads him to overstate.

> 'Oh, I agree,' he says.
> 'And sometimes lie. Get carried away.'
> 'Oh, I agree. No question of that. I don't know whether the lies are conscious lies all the time,' he says. 'But there can be untruths.'[76]

We next turn to skeptics' perceptions of Randi. Does the skeptical community hold him in high esteem? Some do. In 1986, Randi was awarded a MacArthur Foundation Genius award for his work on exposing frauds.

Some skeptics are less generous. Former parapsychologist and CSI fellow Susan Blackmore reviewed Randi's book, *The Supernatural A-Z*, and commented that the book "has too many errors to be recommended."

Ray Hyman, a longtime skeptic and leading CSI fellow who has contributed more to the field of parapsychology than any other skeptic, noted:

> Scientists don't settle issues with a single test, so even if someone does win a big cash prize in a demonstration, this isn't going to convince anyone. Proof in science happens through replication, not through single experiments.[77]

Hyman and Blackmore are scientists who are among a very tiny handful of skeptics who have actual expertise in parapsychology and have made contributions to the field. While they do not criticize Randi directly, they lightly regard his scholarship and grasp of science.

Randi has been caught red-handed plagiarizing from skeptics *on his own forum*. He took comments from a forum user known as "Hawkeye" and changed the wording. When confronted, Randi responded with this comment:

> Chris: I admit, I shamelessly took your comments and dropped them in as part of SWIFT, simply because they exactly reflected my observations. I could have changed the wording, but getting SWIFT together each week – amid all the other duties that keep me here at least 60 hours a week – calls for some corner-cutting every now and then. Mea culpa...[78]

"Tkingdoll" noted:

> I see two real problems with Randi plagiarizing or otherwise cheating for any reason at all. The first is that the nature of his life's work demands that he act with 100% honesty and integrity, *because that's the standard he's demanding from those he exposes.* Why else would Randi pursue cheats unless he thinks cheating is bad? So why then is it OK to give the excuse "oops, you caught me in a blatant cheat, I was busy that week"?
>
> Or are we saying that cheating is OK as long as you admit it when you get caught? I hope we're not saying that.[79]

The most serious damage to Randi's integrity came from a long-term case of identity theft. Randi, who is gay, has a significant other, actually named Deyvi Pena, who went by the name José Luis Alvarez *for twenty years* before being caught in 2012. Somehow, Randi mistook Deyvi Pena, a young man from Venezuela on a student visa to study at the Art Institute of Fort Lauderdale, for a teacher from the Bronx.[80] Either Randi was duped by an obvious con right under his nose for many years or he knowingly conspired with Pena to hide the truth.

So, in regard to whether James Randi has impeccable character, the answer is clearly no, he does not. He appears to be willing to abandon honesty and integrity when it suits him. He does not seem to have enough personal credibility to be taken at his word and his detractors appear to have legitimate reasons for not trusting him. The million-dollar challenge is somewhat suspect on this issue alone, although he's not in charge of it anymore. For that reason it is necessary to look at how the challenge is run.

Examining the Challenge

How exactly does the challenge work? What is the procedure for taking an applicant from start to finish? This information is not readily available, and I have seen no formal explanation from JREF explaining this process in detail.

On the surface, the million-dollar challenge seems legitimate. It seems as though skeptics work on a protocol with psychics until a final procedure is hammered out. But Randi's people working on the protocol are not vetted in any meaningful way. There is no requirement that they understand scientific protocol or be able to conduct a scientific test. In the challenge forums I visited, no one, for example, seemed to take the experimenter effect seriously. There seemed to be an attitude that psychic ability was something that should function on demand, and testers did not have the specialized knowledge in parapsychology which would be necessary to design proper experiments.

The most glaring problems with the million-dollar challenge come from rules that can change on JREF's whim.

Scientific testing of psychic ability is statistical. That is to say, an effect is considered real when it is shown to *not* be due to randomness (or problems in the protocol). You do this by calculating the odds that something might occur due to chance. In the results you get from repeated tries, the higher the odds are against chance, the more likely it is that psychic ability is in play.

I'm explaining this because this crucial information is missing. You won't find it on the application or the FAQ for the million-dollar challenge. It should say somewhere that the preliminary test must overcome odds against chance of approximately 1,000 to 1, but it doesn't. And rumor has it that to win the challenge the applicant must overcome odds of one million to one. This kind of information is crucial to understanding how hard the challenge is.

An analogy would be to have a jumping contest to discover whether jumping was possible, but to not state anywhere how high a person had to jump in order to win.

Investigating through the forums

When I initially investigated the challenge, this is what I found: Applicants for the challenge were given their own thread on a sub forum specifically for the challenge, which is the only way for an outsider to track an applicant's progress. The forum appeared to be run by volunteers, and it was done very much on the cheap. Much of the information passed through the forum, some of it went through the mail and some of it was emailed. It was clear from reading the forum posts that the challenge process was a disorganized mess. The applicants dealt primarily with the volunteers, except when dealing with the staff, who apparently didn't always notify the volunteers about what they were doing. (The volunteers sometimes found out what had transpired from the applicants.) Randi or his staff could swoop in at any moment and change whatever they wished without notifying anyone or giving any justification for what he did. The volunteers seemed to be left to fend for themselves and had no authority to move an applicant forward in the process no matter how much work they'd done with that individual.[81] One of the signs this was badly run was that very few applicants ever got to the testing stage.

And the application process is dreadfully slow. A process that takes a year to two years is not unheard of. In the course of the Ziborov attempt, Startz (a forum name for a JREF MDC volunteer) made this comment:

> In fairness to Pavel, he has presented statistically sound protocols. JREF has been rather unresponsive as to what objections they have so that Pavel can revise them in accord with JREF's wishes.

> Let me be more pointed than, as a fan of JREF, I wish were necessary. JREF has asked for communications to be done by email. When I have done as JREF has asked, JREF has not had the courtesy to return emails. If JREF were one of my PhD students, rather than an organization with a long, successful track record, I would say this in a less pleasant way.

> Remie has sensibly pointed out that negotiations are better done by email than through this public forum. Following this wise advice, I have (on Pavel's behalf) sent in protocols by email (while posting informational copies to the forum). JREF's responses have been through the forum. There is no reason this could not have been settled in a week of back-and-forth email messages. Nearly all the delay time has been on JREF's end, not Pavel's.[82]

By forcing all the applicants to make a specific claim and set up a protocol, JREF is making the process difficult for people who have no experience in doing such things. Psychics are not scientists.

There is almost no transparency in the process and no attempt is made to satisfy outside objective observers that the testing is fair. There is no log of people who have been tested either. A complete report on the individual testing that would explain in detail what occurred *does not exist.*[83]

The forum is now long gone and the links to it no longer work.

PR Stunt or Serious Inquiry?

The easy way to tell a PR stunt from a serious inquiry is the way in which information is handled. A PR stunt requires important information to be controlled, and a serious inquiry requires all important information to be disclosed. The JREF million-dollar challenge is replete with information being controlled and makes no full disclosures. Here is an example:

The question of exactly how many people have been tested is *obviously* deliberately obfuscated. In the FAQ for the challenge one finds:

(3) To date, how many persons have been tested for the million-dollar prize offered by JREF?

That's not a simple question to answer. Many hundreds have made application, and most have had to be instructed to reapply sometimes several times because they did it incorrectly or incompletely. There are, at any given time, about 40 to 60 applicants being considered, but from experience we know that the vast majority will drop out even before any proper preliminary test can be designed. Of those who get to the preliminary stage, perhaps half will actually be tested, and some of those will quit before completion.

It *is* a simple question. Just add up the number of people who have been tested. (It appears that no more than a couple of people a year are actually tested, so I would put that number between 20 and 30.) Hiding this number is an obvious attempt to make the number look bigger than it actually is. This subterfuge is especially apparent on the Wikipedia entry for the MDC:

To date, over 1,000 applications have been filed but no one has passed a preliminary test, which is set up and agreed upon by both Randi and the applicant.[84]

These entries into Wikipedia are done under the auspices of an organization known as the Guerrilla Skeptics, whom I'll cover in a later chapter. They work closely with JREF, so it is no accident that applications have been confounded with actual testing. It is safe to say that the confusion of who has applied versus who has been tested is deliberate.

Investigating a Legitimate Applicant

Sometime in 2009 I started investigating an application for Pavel Ziborov that had just played out. At the time, the discussion forum for challenge applicants was open to public viewing, so I was able to follow what happened. I discovered foul play by Randi and wrote it up in my blog. Sometime after that, the applicant forum was closed to public viewing. What is there now is nothing more than a brief summary, which, in Pavel Ziborov's case, is inaccurate.

Pavel Ziborov's Attempt to be Tested

Around May of 2007[85]. Pavel Ziborov contacted JREF to apply for the challenge. After two years and almost 900 forum posts plus emails and letters, he and the volunteers had agreed on a straightforward protocol. Ziborov was to determine whether envelopes held a black or white piece of paper (50% chance) with 100 trials. It was agreed that he needed 67 correct answers to win which would have put the odds against chance at approximately 1,000 to 1. When this was submitted to Randi, it was changed to 20 trials with this explanation to Pavel:

> "Pavel,
> Thank you for your continued patience. Now that the TAM dust has cleared, we can again take a look at your protocol. As I said before, I asked other JREF staff to weigh in on whether or not they believed your proposed protocol was workable.
> Mr. Randi said:

Suggest that he merely identify for us which of two photos are in an envelope, 20 times. We cannot satisfy each and every whim, and it's too expensive.

I'd say, if he refuses, he's refused to be tested.

***

What do you think of simplifying the protocol to that level? Is that a possibility?

If not, I will do as Mr. Randi has suggested, and close your file.

Kindest regards,

Alison Smith
Research Assistant
James Randi Educational Foundation"[86]

This was straight up unethical. In addition to framing Pavel's possible refusal as chickening out:

1. Randi violated his own (unwritten) rule that applicants have eight hours to complete their challenge.

2. Pavel still had to comply with the 1,000 to 1 odds, so in order to achieve this with 20 trials he would have had to have a success rate of 80%, where he had claimed to be able to achieve 67%. He was being asked to succeed at something he never said he could do.

3. The take it or leave it demand violates the condition that "both parties have to agree to the protocol."

4. All of the JREF volunteers who had worked with Pavel were thrown under the bus as JREF blithely disregarded the protocol they had come up with.

The skeptic volunteers who worked on this application had worked with Pavel through several iterations of how to conduct tests where they had to teach him a bit of science. They did this because they believed in James Randi and JREF. The volunteers were *betrayed*.

In fact, many skeptics could not turn a blind eye to such an obvious miscarriage of justice. One of the people involved in the Pavel application wrote:

I realize that there is almost no interest in holding Randi and the MDC to the standards that they claim for themselves. I've always been in a ridiculed minority when I make these suggestions. It is clear that the Challenge is *not* about allowing people to demonstrate their claims, but rather about providing examples for our ridicule – partly for education, partly for group-bonding (my guesses). I am in the process of moving on from the idea of trying to persuade anyone to care to that of trying to get the JREF and Randi to be more upfront about this instead, in order to thwart criticism. I fully realize that this will be a futile effort as well.[87]

This comment was buried in a forum thread that only a handful of people will ever read. Rather than show their warts, JREF has provided a handy little synopsis of the outcome of the Ziborov application:

In accordance with the suggestions from other JREF staff, Pavel was given one last opportunity to simplify his protocol. He has declined, and his Challenge file has been closed. Pavel will have the opportunity to re-apply for the Challenge in one year, assuming he qualifies under the guidelines governing the Challenge at that time.[88]

This kind of dissembling is an indication that the JREF organization doesn't take their own challenge seriously. While they have acknowledged that it is a publicity stunt, it is this sort of organizational behavior that demonstrates something worse: outright dishonesty.

Other Challenge Applicants

I can't begin to list all the applicants who have complained about the challenge or investigate whether their protestations are valid. But here's one example of how irritated applicants have become over how they were treated. Homeopath John Benneth, who claims to have been stonewalled by Randi in his attempt to get tested, has issued a $100,000 challenge to anyone who can prove that the JREF million dollar challenge is legitimate.[89] No one has come forward to attempt to claim this prize.

Most of the complaints revolve around not getting tested at all despite numerous attempts. However, one complaint had to do with Randi's behavior during testing.

One contestant who actually got to the challenge and had some initial success was 11-year-old Natalya Lulova. In a trial where she was demonstrating that she could "see" without her eyes, Randi responded by claiming that the bridge of her nose was special, allowing her to see underneath her blindfold. He then did a massive taping job that, according to her guardian, left her in tears and unable to perform. [90] The website referenced in the footnote has pictures and a narrative of the event.

What about the Actual Test?

How about the actual tests that have been performed that have not demonstrated any psychic ability? Are these legitimate tests of psychic ability? If psychic ability exists, why has no one passed the test? In 1991, The TV show, *James Randi: Psychic Investigator*[91], employed many tricks to prevent actual demonstrations of psychic ability.

Astrophysicist Sam Nichols, who attended one of the shows, enumerated a long list of obvious deficiencies including this significant one:

> Never let the psychic get comfortable enough to feel settled; the guests were more or less dragged on stage with barely an introduction and then expected to exhibit psychic marvels.[92]

The idea behind the challenge is to expose frauds and delusional people who don't have the ability they claim to have. However, if you make the challenge impossible to fulfill, then you haven't proved anything, as noted by "Cuddles" on the Ziborov forum thread:

> It is therefore extremely important for the JREF to ensure that a test is fair to an applicant by ensuring that there is a high probability of success should they actually possess the claimed ability.[93]

> Short tests are more difficult than longer ones for psychological reasons. The pressure to succeed on any individual attempt is much higher and the applicant has no chance to relax. Patricia Putt had ten trials. [94] Pavel was allowed to have twenty. A 1979 test had three trials for four dowsers [95], and a test with so-called Baby Mind Reader Derek Ogilvie involved ten trials.[96]

The test is high profile, and a failure will be highly publicized. Psychic ability also declines in the presence of skeptics. This has been proved in scientific testing and is known as the experimenter effect.[97] In Randi's tests, the applicants are surrounded by people who hope that failure will occur.

Even if an applicant freely signs up for this sort of setup, as Patricia Putt did, a short, high pressure, high profile test run by skeptics is no legitimate way to test for psychic ability. That people fail, often in spectacular fashion (Putt did not get a single trial right), doesn't say anything about the abilities of the people who were tested except that they didn't succeed under these very adverse conditions.

In Putt's case, the problem had to do with the way she was tested. She normally speaks but was required to write out her psychic readings. She was being asked to succeed at something she had no training at and had not claimed that she could do.

The test protocol was presented to her as take-it-or-leave-it, just as with other applicants. She normally does under five readings a day and she was required to do ten. Portions of her readings were blacked out by Prof. Richard Wiseman who was conducting the test. Doing ten readings in one day is far more than most mediums do. She reported being mentally exhausted by the eighth reading. Other problems included having all young, female students as target subjects, making their experiences and personalities difficult to tell apart. Like other applicants, she did not have much control in the test design.

To sum this up, while the test had good controls against cheating, it was very poor at providing elements that were favorable to psychic functioning. An analogy would be putting a seed on a shelf to see if it will grow. The experiment is perfectly controlled but is guaranteed to fail.

All you can say is that the test demonstrated nothing. *Patricia Putt cannot be said to have failed the test because the design was completely inadequate to test anything.* That did not stop the press releases of course.[98]

To put this in perspective, the closest comparison to this test is probably the Afterlife Experiments[99] conducted by Gary Schwartz, which claimed to demonstrate statistically significant positive results from psychic mediums. The tests ran over several days and involved multiple mediums. Various versions of the same tests were run, and all the details and results were published. The experiments have been refined and replicated over the years and notable skeptical scientists have reviewed the literature and commented on it and it has become a part of parapsychological literature.

No reports of the psychic testing done for the million-dollar challenge has ever made it into parapsychological literature; zero, not one.

All that seems to happen is that when one of these tests is performed, the news travels around, a few newspapers pick it up, a few people blog about it and argue about it on the forums, and then it fades into history. *Because it's not important.*

There are obvious reasons for their insignificance:

1. Very few serious applicants for the challenge: With the age of the Internet upon us, potential applicants are much better informed than in years past. Even the most cursory Internet search will yield damning information about James Randi and the challenge. So only the most naïve people will pursue the prize.
2. No overall methodology: Every once in a while, someone braves the system and actually gets tested with an experiment that is unique, with very few trials and no replications. This renders the results useless as a measurement for anything.
3. Lack of data. To seriously discuss the relevance of any particular test requires that all details of that test be available for examination and critique.

The only thing you can say about the JREF million dollar challenge is that it is a publicity stunt, which does not do what it claims to do: legitimately test for psychic ability. Because of the poor way that testing is managed, the tests themselves are not indicators of anything, much less psychic ability. In its present form this challenge is, for all practical purposes, unwinnable.

It begs the question: if JREF is so sure about psychic ability not existing, why do they have to resort to this deceit?

CSI (formerly known as CSICOP)

This is another skeptical organization that is an advocacy group. Their tactics are different from JREF. Where JREF focuses on publicity stunts, CSI focuses on the media and creating confusion about parapsychology through invented controversy. CSI, formed in 1976 by members of the American Humanist Association (AHA), an atheist group, was originally intended as an organization that would test paranormal claims with scientific research. However, this went south right away when they tested the research claims of astrologer Michel Gauquelin and his wife Françoise. This is one of the campfire stories of parapsychology. It goes like this:

> The Gauquelin's had studied the birth data of more than 2,000 sports champions and found that a statistically significant number of them had been born with Mars 'rising' or 'transiting.' These findings had also been replicated by Belgian skeptics known as Comité Para. As this was just the sort of thing that CSICOP had been formed to investigate, it started its first, (and last), investigation. In order to debunk the so-called "Mars effect," they would have to show that the control sample had a higher percentage of champions than reported. However the control sample in their investigation turned out to have the same percentage as the Gauquelin's, meaning that they had just successfully replicated the Gauquelin study. This was not what they wanted and they attempted to cover up the results, which led to a split and defections from CSICOP, including Marcello Truzzi, the group's original co-chairman. The whole story of how the cover up happened found its way into a 31-page article by planetary motion specialist Dennis Rawlings, in *Fate* (October 1982)[100] with this editorial comment:

> They call themselves the Committee for the Scientific Investigation of Claims of the Paranormal. In fact, they are a group of would-be debunkers who bungled their major investigation, falsified the results, covered up their errors and gave the boot to a colleague who threatened to tell the truth.[101]

As late as 1997, over forty years after the Gauquelin study was first published, skeptics were still trying to debunk it through the usual method of continually recalculating data in an attempt to prove that the original statistics must have been wrong.[102]

I did a blog post on this organization, which I provide in full:

A Critical Look at CSI, (formerly CSICOP), a Pseudo-Scientific Skeptic Organization

Most psychic people have never heard of this organization. The original name was: Committee for Scientific Investigations for Claims of the Paranormal. (CSICOP) It's since been shortened to CSI. It should be noted that it is not a scientific organization, nor does it normally do investigations. It also has a popular magazine, The Skeptical Inquirer,which is not a scientific, peer reviewed journal.

What it does very, very well is *pretend* to be scientific. It is basically an atheist marketing organization dedicated to the systematic debunking of all psychic research through pseudo-science, talking points, ridicule and lobbying. In particular, it lobbies real scientific organizations, using its list of professors, researchers and other PhD fellows to discourage any active interest in any parapsychological studies. It maintains the pretense of objectivity, but in reality, it is anything but. Parapsychologist George Hansen writes:

> In examining the scientific status of CSICOP, sociologists Pinch and Collins (1984) described the Committee as a "scientific-vigilante" organization (p. 539). Commenting on an article in *SI*, medical professor Louis Lasagna (1984) wrote: "One can almost smell the fiery autos-da-fe of Torquemada and the Spanish Inquisition" (p. 12). Engineering professor Leonard Lewin (1979) noted that in *SI* articles "the rhetoric and appeal to emotion seemed rather out of place" (p. 9). Rockwell, Rockwell, and Rockwell (1978b) called CSICOP members "irrational rationalists" (see also Kurtz, 1978b; Rockwell, Rockwell, & Rockwell, 1978a). Sociologist Hans Sebald (1984) described contributors to *SI* as "combative propagandists" (p. 122). Adams (1987) compared CSICOP with the Cyclops; Robert Anton Wilson (1986) labeled CSICOP the "New Inquisition," and White (1979) called them "new disciples of scientism." McConnell (1987) wrote: "I cannot escape the conviction that those who control CSICOP are primarily bent upon the vilification of parapsychology and parapsychologists" (p. 191). Clearly, CSICOP has its share of detractors.

> CSI has a number of well defined characteristics:

> CSI membership is generally very well-educated, with many holding prominent positions within academia. Many are magicians and they are overwhelmingly male. Many members actively hold atheistic viewpoints and promote them.[103]

> CSI shares office space with the Council for Secular Humanism, an atheist organization, and Paul Kurz, one of the founders of CSI, has chaired both organizations. Thus, there is a strong link between CSI and active atheism.[104]

Something strange happens when these pseudo-skeptics get involved with science. I'm going to assume that the skeptics I've mentioned so far, and the ones I haven't mentioned yet, are smart people who do intelligent things in most areas of their lives. Most of them are PhD's and many hold university positions after all. Yet, when members of CSI actually attempt to involve themselves in parapsychological research, bad things happen and their research is highly questionable at best and downright embarrassing at worst.

CSI and its members have a history of bad research into the paranormal. It's not just that the research is sloppy, phrases such as "deliberately misleading" come up frequently. On those rare occasions when skeptics conduct research, they often omit positive research in the same area and focus exclusively on their results, which are almost always flawed in some important way. It appears to be a combination of willful ignorance of parapsychology methodology and statistics combined with a serious bias. The results aren't pretty. (I don't know if this is a complete list. It's what I could find.)

The Gauquelin Effect, 1975-78 (Astrology) by: Rawlings, Kurz, Abell, Zelen

Results: Ignored the only planetary motion specialist involved in the project, bad calculations by skeptics, eventual cover-up of the results and resignations by moderate skeptics from CSICOP. (exposed by Dennis Rawlings)[105]

Blackmore Parapsychology Studies, 1976-78 by Susan Blackmore

Results: Vastly overstated her experience, applied double standard to experiments, her studies were reported to be "carelessly designed, executed and reported."[106]

Critique of Sheldrake's paper: "Dogs that know when their owners are coming home, 1995 by Wiseman

Results: Got the same results as Sheldrake. Based statistical calculations on comments made by TV commentators. Set arbitrary criteria for judging that removed positive results, failed to adequately review Sheldrake's calculations or methods.[107]

Milton and Wiseman Autoganzfeld meta-analysis, 1999 by Milton, Wiseman

Results: Botched statistics and flawed methodology, omitted a relevant, positive study, included an irrelevant study.

When errors were corrected, the meta-analysis showed positive results.[108]

Skeptical Replication of Sheldrake Staring Study, 2001, by Marks, Colwell

Results: Allowed subjects to be distracted, dismissed answers from two acceptable subjects, introduced an unnecessary experimental restriction, dismissed or explained away positive results. Failed to acknowledge or refer to previous research.[109]

The Girl With the X-Ray Eyes, 2004, The Discovery Channel, by Wiseman, Hyman and Skolnick.

Results: Faulty experiment design, violations of the protocol, bad statistics by skeptics, general uproar from critics including Nobel Prize winner in physics, Brian Josephson.[110]

What you can see here is that first of all, there isn't very much research, and, second, there is a pattern of methodological and statistical failures. These are just the people associated with CSI. While they may be incompetent to judge the existence of psychic ability, they are at least performing the rituals of real science and they are to be commended for that I suppose; these skeptics have provided open access to their work, allowing their critics to check their math and their procedures and provide relevant criticism. This is, of course, faint praise, but considering the overall poor quality of most paranormal skepticism, it's as good as it gets.

[If you have the print version of this book all blog posts and relevant links can be found at weilerpsiblog.wordpress.com]

REF and CSI have a knack for getting the ear of the media when psychics are known to have failures. The late psychic Sylvia Browne was called out by the *Huffington Post* for a failed prediction she made ten years ago that kidnap victim Amanda Berry was dead. Amanda Later escaped from her captors, very much alive.

The *Huffington Post* interviewed me for the article, but what does one say? It was obviously wrong of Browne to act with such certainty, so that's pretty much the gist of what I said, and the reporter was pretty accurate in conveying my viewpoint. However, this was only a small portion of the article, and what I said was sandwiched inbetween a barrage of skeptical nonsense. Here are some tidbits:

> "The [Ariel Castro abduction] is a test case for all psychics," said Joe Nickell, editor of *Skeptical Inquirer* a magazine that encourages science-based analysis of paranormal and fringe-science claims. "Why didn't one psychic wake up in the middle of the night and know where they were?"

> "Nickell has also headed projects researching the success rate of psychics working on police investigations, and found no substantial evidence of their effectiveness."

> "One detective, a homicide commander, told me, 'You can be skeptical, but when you have a distraught family and a psychic has convinced them they have clues, it's hard to refuse,'" Nickell told Huff Post.

> "Problem is, according to Nickell, many of the so-called "clues" offered by the psychics are too vague to be of use. Once the police find out the answers through legitimate police work, the vague clues might seem to fit after the fact, a process he calls "retrofitting.""

> "Parapsychology researcher Ben Radford, a deputy editor at *Skeptical Inquirer*, said that anytime there is a high-profile, missing-person case, psychics and mediums come out of the woodwork."

> "We call them 'grief vampires,'" he told *Huff Post*. "But every single time, the psychics fail to find the person."

> "D.J. Grothe, one time president of the James Randi Educational Foundation (JREF), an organization that works to stop paranormal and pseudoscientific frauds and has long criticized Browne, said this latest psychic scandal is even more reprehensible than others."

"It's not just her lack of success that bothers me. It's that she deigns to give so-called psychic or spiritual advice to people when they're at their lowest and hurting most," he told Huff Post by email. "How reprehensible for this TV psychic to disrupt criminal investigations or cause a family to lose hope about their missing loved ones like that."[111]

And there you have it. Joe Nickell, editor of the *Skeptical Inquirer,* "parapsychology researcher" (no, he's not a scientist researching psi; he has not published any scientific papers in parapsychology); Ben Radford, a deputy editor at the Skeptical Inquirer; and D.J. Grothe, president of JREF all sounded off on a single failed psychic prediction by one psychic and used it to condemn all psychics with a mishmash of unrelated material. These people have the ear of mainstream media and play into its need for drama. CSI and JREF scored big that day.

This is kind of like getting a viewpoint on Christianity from one lapsed Catholic and one Presbyterian and then giving the bulk of the article to four fundamentalists.

Basically, the mass media allows a small group to act as though they represent the scientific point of view.

The Skeptic's Dictionary

The Skeptic's Dictionary is the work of retired professor Robert Todd Carroll. Created in 1994, it now includes hundreds of pages. It is actually an encyclopedia of sorts, not a dictionary. It is one example of a number of one-man-show skeptical resource sites that have a prodigious amount of information but are very lightly regarded by their critics. *The Skeptic's Dictionary* is probably the highest profile of these sites and like the others, it is criticized for being terribly biased and horribly inaccurate.

Skeptics have created a web of resources. CSI, JREF and *The Skeptic's Dictionary* all link to each other and use each other as source material for articles. Skeptics editing Wikipedia use the Skeptic's Dictionary as source material and this in turn gives the appearance of objective sourcing.

Google cannot tell the difference between good sense and nonsense. If a site is heavily cited, isn't commercial, and provides sources, it rises to the top of Google search. The skeptics work to push the Skeptic's Dictionary to the top of the search results, which skews searches toward a skeptical point of view.

Outside of Wikipedia, which I'll get to later, *The Skeptic's Dictionary* is pretty much ignored. Mainstream sources do not refer to it and it is universally regarded by psi proponents as biased trash.

It is amusingly easy to criticize. Tom McKinley Ball writes of a Skeptical Dictionary article[112] on Transcendental Meditation:

> However, readers seeking an honest assessment of the Transcendental Meditation may find *The Skeptic's Dictionary* appraisal frustratingly biased. The author cites no empirical evidence to support his criticisms of the TM program, uses inaccurate non-science sources as references and disregards the body of peer reviewed scientific literature that supports the program.[113]

Ball then goes on to refute the assertions point by point, which is too much information to include in this book. Jon Barron, writing for Baseline of Health Foundation on the Skeptical Dictionary article[114] about himself:

> When I read *the [Skeptic's Dictionary* page on Jon Barron], I found it uproariously funny, filled with misstatements, distortion of fact, and packed with innuendo and a number of juvenile comments— surprising, considering that the site's author is a retired teacher of "logic" and "critical thinking," albeit at a city college.[115]

Like Ball, Barron goes to great lengths to refute the erroneous statements.

In a web article about NLP (Neuro Linguistic Programming), author Andy Bradbury writes about his treatment at the hands of the Skeptic's Dictionary:

> [The] owner of the website – who appears to be the sole author of both the website and the book – has had more than a decade to get his facts right.

> In practice the material looks more like a rather mediocre encyclopedia than a dictionary, offering numerous articles of varying lengths rather than the correct spelling and brief definitions of individual words. But then again, "accuracy" is not a word I would associate with this particular material.[116]

Another critic is Rod Martin, Jr., of Project Atlantis who spent no time refuting the article point for point has this to say about his own project:

> The myth of Atlantis may ultimately prove to have been merely an exciting fiction, or it may one day stand as the biggest breakthrough in human history. Currently, we do not have enough proof either way. (...) Some who are skeptical of the past possible reality of Atlantis have grown arrogant, abusive and sloppy. It does not need to be that way. I hope there are some intelligent, civilized skeptics who are more interested in truth than ego.[117]

Martin brings up a good point. Insightful skeptical criticism is useful because it brings a fresh set of eyes to a problem and can uncover errors that people who are too close to a project can miss. Done correctly, skepticism helps people create better work. *The Skeptic's Dictionary* however, isn't that sort of skepticism.

Quackwatch, Chirobase, What's the Harm? Et al.

The skeptics have several websites that purport to provide objective information about a variety of "fringe" topics, but, in reality, they give heavily slanted opinions against non-mainstream–everything. Click on virtually any topic they list, and you'll find a one-sided, simplistic discussion. Like *The Skeptic's Dictionary*, these sites are each more or less the work of one person. They do excellent cross-referencing and have good search capability, but their actual content is very shallow.

These sites do not get much traffic thanks to their lack of depth and the obvious biases. They are mostly for preaching to the converted and for use as Wikipedia references to promote a skeptical point of view. What's the Harm[118] by Tim Farley is a particularly silly site. They list 368,379 people killed by alternative medicine. To get this number, they include an estimated 365,000 AIDS patients in Africa.[119] If you take out this one number, you are left with under 4,000 deaths over a large number of years which demonstrates that alternative medicine is actually incredibly safe.

The great absurdity of this site is that it gives these examples without providing any context. Everything in life carries a certain amount of risk. How harmful is this alternative medicine in relation to other things?

By way of comparison, approximately 200,000 people die each year from properly prescribed prescription medication and medical errors just in the U.S.[120][121] and approximately 1,275,000 people worldwide die each year in car accidents.[122]

CHAPTER TEN

SHELDRAKE AND HANCOCK
DELIVER THE SMACKDOWN

After the TED science board issued its criticism of the two videos, judging from the comments pouring in, it was clear that the criticism from TED's science advisory board probably wouldn't hold up to much scrutiny. Still, there was a sense of anticipation as everyone waited for the speaker's rebuttals, which were sure to follow quickly, and they did. They were every bit the crushing blow to TED's criticisms that they were expected to be. Rupert Sheldrake explained:

> I wrote a response while I was still in India and sent it to the TED administrators, asking them to post it on their site below the statement by the Science Board. Nothing happened. Meanwhile. I got back to England and received an email from Chris Anderson asking if we could speak on the phone. We had quite a long conversation, at least half an hour, as a result of which he then posted my response and deleted the Science Board statement. My first reaction when I heard of the controversy was to assume that this was something quite minor and I paid it very little attention. It was only when the talk was taken down and the statement by the Science Board posted online I realised that TED had been influenced by the views of Coyne and Myers and seemed to think that they spoke for the 'scientific community' rather

than simply for a small reactionary faction, the militant atheists. That's why I thought it was important to respond. I was incredulous rather than angry.

Response to the TED Scientific Board's Statement

Rupert Sheldrake
March 18, 2013

I would like to respond to TED's claims that my TEDx talk "crossed the line into pseudoscience", contains "serious factual errors" and makes "many misleading statements."

This discussion is taking place because the militant atheist bloggers Jerry Coyne and P.Z. Myers denounced me, and attacked TED for giving my talk a platform. I was invited to give my talk as part of a TEDx event in Whitechapel, London, called "Challenging Existing Paradigms." That's where the problem lies: my talk explicitly challenges the materialist belief system. It summarized some of the main themes of my recent book *Science Set Free* (in the UK called *The Science Delusion*). Unfortunately, the TED administrators have publically aligned themselves with the old paradigm of materialism, which has dominated science since the late nineteenth century.

TED says they removed my talk from their website on the advice of their Scientific Board, who also condemned Graham Hancock's talk. Hancock and I are now facing anonymous accusations made by a body on whose authority TED relies, on whose advice they act, and behind whom they shelter, but whose names they have not revealed.

TED's anonymous Scientific Board made three specific accusations:

Accusation 1:
"... he suggests that scientists reject the notion that animals have consciousness, despite the fact that it's generally accepted that animals have some form of consciousness, and there's much research and literature exploring the idea."

I characterized the materialist dogma as follows: "Matter is unconscious: the whole universe is made up of unconscious matter. There's no consciousness in stars in galaxies, in planets, in animals, in plants and there ought not to be any in us either, if this theory's true. So a lot of the philosophy of mind over the last 100 years has been trying to prove that we are not really conscious at all." Certainly some biologists, including myself, accept that animals are conscious. In August, 2012, a group of scientists came out with an endorsement of animal consciousness in "The Cambridge Declaration on Consciousness". As *Discovery News* reported, "While it might not sound like much for scientists to declare that many nonhuman animals possess conscious states, it's the open acknowledgement that's the big news here."

(Author's note: Original link cited in this reply no longer works.)

But materialist philosophers and scientists are still in the majority, and they argue that consciousness does nothing – it is either an illusion or an "epiphenomenon" of brain activity. It might as well not exist in animals – or even in humans. That is why in the philosophy of mind, the very existence of consciousness is often called "the hard problem". http://en.wikipedia.org/wiki/Hard_problem_of_consciousness

Accusation 2:
"He also argues that scientists have ignored variations in the measurements of natural constants, using as his primary example the dogmatic assumption that a constant must be constant and uses the speed of light as example … Physicist Sean Carroll wrote a careful rebuttal of this point."

TED's Scientific Board refers to a *Scientific American* article that makes my point very clearly: "Physicists routinely assume that quantities such as the speed of light are constant."

In my talk I said that the published values of the speed of light dropped by about 20 km/sec between 1928 and 1945. Carroll's "careful rebuttal" consisted of a table copied from Wikipedia showing the speed of light at different dates, with a gap between 1926 and 1950, omitting the very period I referred to. His other reference does indeed give two values for the speed of light in this period, in 1928 and 1932-35, and sure enough, they were 20 and 24km/sec lower than the previous value, and 14 and 18 km/sec lower than the value from 1947 onwards.

1926: 299,798
1928: 299,778
1932-5: 299,774
1947: 299,792

In my talk I suggest how a re-examination of existing data could resolve whether large continuing variations in the Universal Gravitational Constant, G, are merely errors, as usually assumed, or whether they show correlations between different labs that might have important scientific implications hitherto ignored. Jerry Coyne and TED's Scientific Board regard this as an exercise in pseudoscience. I think their attitude reveals a remarkable lack of curiosity.

Accusation 3:
"Sheldrake claims to have "evidence" of morphic resonance in crystal formation and rat behavior. The research has never appeared in a peer reviewed journal, despite attempts by other scientists eager to replicate the work."

I said, "There is in fact good evidence that new compounds get easier to crystallize all around the world." For example, turanose, a kind of sugar, was considered to be a liquid for decades, until it first crystallized in the 1920s. Thereafter it formed crystals everywhere. (Woodard and McCrone *Journal of Applied Crystallography* (1975). 8, 342). The American chemist C. P. Saylor, remarked it was as though "the seeds of crystallization, as dust, were carried upon the winds from end to end of the earth" (quoted by Woodard and McCrone).

The research on rat behavior I referred to was carried out at Harvard and the Universities of Melbourne and Edinburgh and was published in peer reviewed journals, including the *British Journal of Psychology and the Journal of Experimental Biology*. For a fuller account and detailed references see Chapter 11 of my book *Morphic Resonance* (in the US) / *A New Science of Life* (in the UK).

The TED Scientific Board refers to "attempts by other scientists eager to replicate the work" on morphic resonance. I would be happy to work with these eager scientists if the Scientific Board can reveal who they are.

This is a good opportunity to correct an oversimplification in my talk. In relation to the dogma that mechanistic medicine is the only kind that really works, I said, "that's why governments only fund mechanistic medicine and ignore complementary and alternative therapies." This is true of most governments, but the US is a notable exception. The US National Center for Complementary and Alternative Medicine receives about $130 million a year, about 0.4% of the National Institutes of Health (NIH) total annual budget of $31 billion.

Obviously I could not spell out all the details of my arguments in an 18-minute talk, but TED's claims that it contains "serious factual errors," "many misleading statements" and that it crosses the line into "pseudoscience" are defamatory and false.

And just like that the entire skeptical house of cards came crashing down. I've seen this so many times in parapsychology that I wasn't remotely surprised by it. On the surface the skeptical criticisms can seem very convincing, but as soon as they come up against an intelligent rebuttal they melt like a snowman in August. What set the TED debate apart from the normal state of affairs was that it was all out in the open where the skeptics had absolutely no way to hide from their mistakes or pretend that they weren't mistakes. Under these circumstances, TED could not afford to be making baseless accusations due to the threat of legal action. Their accusations had to be either valid or be removed. It's not very often that I've seen skeptics in a position where they were forced to be truthful and I was curious to see how they would handle it.

The situation was even more pronounced with Graham Hancock. While there might have been a slight bit of room for interpretation in regard to the accusations against Sheldrake's speech, Hancock exposed the accusations leveled against him as outright lies.

Response to the TED Scientific Board's Statement

Graham Hancock
March 18, 2013

(1) TED says of my "War on Consciousness" presentation: "...he misrepresents what scientists actually think. He suggests, for example, that no scientists are working on the problem of consciousness."

The only passage I can find in my presentation that has any relevance at all to this allegation is between 9 mins 50 seconds and 11 mins 12 seconds. But nowhere in that passage or anywhere else in my presentation do I make the suggestion you attribute to me in your allegation, namely that "no scientists are working on the problem of consciousness." Rather I address the mystery of life after death and state that "if we want to know about this mystery the last people we should ask are materialist, reductionist scientists. They have nothing to say on the matter at all." That statement cannot possibly be construed as my suggesting that "no scientists are working on the problem of consciousness," or of "misrepresenting" what materialist, reductionist scientists actually think. I am simply stating the fact, surely not controversial, that materialist, reductionist scientists have nothing to say on the matter of life after death because their paradigm does not allow them to believe in the possibility of life after death; they believe rather that nothing follows death. Here is the full transcript of what I say in my presentation between 9 mins 50 seconds and 11 mins 12 seconds: "What is death? Our materialist science reduces everything to matter. Materialist science in the West says that we are just meat, we're just our bodies, so when the brain is dead that's the end of consciousness. There is no life after death. There is no soul. We just rot and are gone. But actually any honest scientist should admit that consciousness is the greatest mystery of science and that we don't know exactly how it works. The brain's involved in it in some way, but we're not sure how. Could be that the brain generates consciousness the way a generator makes electricity. If you hold to that paradigm then of course you can't believe in life after death. When the generator's broken consciousness is gone. But it's equally possible that the relationship – and nothing in neuroscience rules it out – that the relationship is more like the relationship of the TV signal to the TV set and in that case when the TV set is broken of course the TV signal continues and this is the paradigm of all spiritual traditions – that we are immortal souls, temporarily incarnated in these physical forms to learn and to grow and to develop. And really if we want to know about this mystery the last people we should ask are materialist, reductionist scientists. They have nothing to say on the matter at all. Let's go rather to the ancient Egyptians who put their best minds to work for three thousand years on the problem of death and on the problem of how we should live our lives to prepare for what we will confront after death ..."

(2) TED says of my "War on Consciousness" presentation: "... Hancock makes statements about psychotropic drugs that seem both non-scientific and reckless."

I profoundly disagree. In my presentation I speak honestly and openly about my own damaging and destructive 24-year cannabis habit and about how experiences under the influence of Ayahuasca were the key to breaking this habit. I also say (3 min 46 seconds to 3 min 50 seconds) that "I don't think any of the psychedelics should be used for recreation."

(3) TED says of my presentation: "He states as fact that psychotropic drug use is essential for an "emergence into consciousness," and that one can use psychotropic plants to connect directly with an ancient mother culture."

Nowhere in my talk do I state as a fact that psychotropic drug use is "essential" for an "emergence into consciousness." Nowhere in my talk do I state that "one can use psychotropic plants to connect directly with an ancient mother culture."

(4) TED says of my "War on Consciousness" presentation: "He offers a one-note explanation for how culture arises (drugs), which just doesn't hold up."

I refute this. What I say (between 1 min 06 seconds and 1 min 54 seconds) is that some scientists in the last thirty years have raised an intriguing possibility—emphasis on POSSIBILITY—which is that the exploration of altered states of consciousness, in which psychedelic plants have been implicated, was fundamental to the emergence into fully symbolic consciousness witnessed by the great cave art.

(5) TED says of my "War on Consciousness" presentation: "... it's no surprise his work has often been characterized as pseudo-archeology."

Of what possible relevance is this remark? Many different people have characterised my work in many different ways but at issue here is not what people have said about my work over the years but the actual content of this specific TEDx presentation.

How could the TED science board be so far off the mark? Easy— they were giving their edicts on what *they thought* was in the presentations, not what was actually there. The original accusations were unconscionably sloppy. It is absolutely breathtaking that no one on the anonymous science board gave the slightest thought to performing basic fact checking before taking their accusations public.

As these intellectual bombs exploded and it was clear that the accusations were baseless at best and idiotic at worst, this should have been the end of it. TED should have apologized and put the videos back up after that embarrassment. Even Chris Anderson expressed some exasperation with the situation in responding to someone on Rupert's comment thread:

> I understand your frustration with the [Sheldrake] talk. We've read a lot of such comments. They're what initiated this whole process. But I'd prefer you to make the case in more temperate language. I personally didn't think the talk was 'crap'. I spoke with Rupert Sheldrake a few days ago and I think he genuinely respects scientific thinking. He just disagrees with a lot of it. Some of his questions in the talk I found genuinely interesting. And I do think there's a place on TED to challenge the orthodox. Maybe I'm expecting too much for this forum, but I was hoping scientists who don't buy his ideas could indicate WHY they find them so implausible.

It's surprising to see such a moderate comment coming from TED's curator, given what had occurred (and what was yet to occur.) But it illustrates the complexity of the people involved. The fact that some very poor decisions were made by TED doesn't mean that they were stupid or even wholly intolerant, only that they were caught up in something that they genuinely thought that they understood but didn't.

It's hard to understate just how big the TED science board failure was. They had utterly blown their opportunity to make their case. They should have carefully gone over the speeches, fact checked their claims and generally made sure that they weren't putting TED's reputation in jeopardy. TED decided to make a show of taking down first Sheldrake's and then Hancock's videos. It was a show of great confidence that they knew what they were doing, but, by making the whole affair public, they were now being forced to deal with something that was obviously very uncomfortable for them: they were flat out wrong.

But it wasn't over. They failed to acknowledge the weakness of their position, did not learn from their mistakes and, incredibly, took it even further.

CHAPTER ELEVEN

THE UNIVERSE JUST GOT WEIRDER: NONLOCAL CONSCIOUSNESS

Both Rupert Sheldrake's morphic resonance theory and Graham Hancock's "war on consciousness" rely on an interpretation of quantum physics known as nonlocal consciousness. It's not accepted by mainstream physics, but this isn't because of a lack of evidence, but rather a general unwillingness to look beyond the current theories.

In this chapter I want to demonstrate that there is a controversy in physics and neurology. This is a pretty important part of any discussion about whether materialism deserves to be questioned. If all evidence pointed to a universe that was mechanical in nature, then there wouldn't really be much to dispute. But this is not the case. If anything, quantum physics demonstrates that materialism is an oversimplified and outdated way of perceiving reality.

This controversy in physics has its roots in the 1927 Copenhagen Interpretation[123] of quantum physics, and lies at the very heart of the TED controversy. The Copenhagen interpretation says that a quantum particle in its wave state doesn't exist in one state or another, but in all of its possible states at once. Only with observation is a quantum particle forced to choose one probability, and that's the state that we observe. It can be forced into a different observable state each time, which explains why a quantum particle behaves erratically. The problem of what constituted "observation" was tabled on the grounds that it didn't matter because the basic mechanics of quantum physics were conforming to the mathematical models. Still, it was an attempt at the most basic question we can ask:

What is reality?

However, there are great mysteries in quantum physics that no one has solved and that are open to wildly different interpretations. It's a shame that we typically get only one point of view, because that doesn't even begin to cover the whole truth of the situation. Here's the reason why:

Many features of quantum physics defy our notions of a material reality. In particular, we have a feature of our reality called nonlocality. "Nonlocal" is a label used in quantum physics and it's been adopted by new age gurus and psi scientists because it's tremendously convenient shorthand for describing a complex concept.

To understand this term, it helps to first understand what we mean by "local". In physics this refers to an interaction between two forces that are in contact with one another. This is called a "local interaction." If you roll two billiard balls so that they hit each other, you have a local interaction. This is true whether it's billiard balls or molecules or electricity. Contact is required for one thing to affect another even if it's energy making contact with other energy. This is basic Newtonian physics, where, to go from point A to point B you have to travel the distance in between. (One ball has to roll towards the other.) All physics beyond the subatomic level operates this way (or at least it appears to).

At the subatomic level however, nonlocal interactions do occur. Nonlocal means that it requires no movement and no contact for two separate things to be affected by one another. Distance is not a factor. This nonlocal interaction is called entanglement. It's not magic or even controversial physics. It's a fact so basic you can find it in introductory books on quantum physics.

According to the best measurements available, this appears to be instantaneous. An effect that is instantaneous is operating outside of time because time and space/distance are inseparable. Time is measured by movement and movement requires space/distance. In a nonlocal interaction distance is treated as though it does not exist. So the term "nonlocal" essentially means "beyond space and time." It sounds very mystical, but it's totally a thing and an equation called Bell's theorem demonstrates that for quantum physics to work, the universe must be nonlocal. What that means is, if this is a correct interpretation of our universe, is that time and space are, practically speaking, an illusion. Something though, is making a universe that is beyond space and time appear to have both space and time. What is that thing? The only conclusion you can possibly come to is that consciousness is not only responsible for our perception of reality, but that it essentially creates that reality. (Our consciousness creates a 3D reality with space and time out of a reality in which neither exists.) You can see how this makes the whole "nonlocal" part of physics a pretty big deal and why mystics would latch onto it. The logic is inescapable, and you don't have to be a physicist to see that.

Disproving a nonlocal universe would mean disproving Bell's Theorem, which has so far withstood all challenges, so physics is left with a very large elephant in a very small room. There is no way other way to account for this.

But that's not all. In quantum physics there is the double slit experiment that demonstrates something called "the observer effect" (a.k.a. QMP, the Quantum Measurement Problem). This experiment demonstrates that an undisturbed subatomic particle behaves like a wave. It goes through the double slits in a crisscrossing pattern with spots where the waves cancel each other out on the wall behind the slits. However, if it is measured (i.e. "observed"), the particle behaves like something solid, leaving individual points on the wall.

That's pretty strange that the act of measuring a subatomic particle would transform its characteristics so radically, but it gets even weirder still. Other experimental set-ups have demonstrated that the transformation can occur *before* the particle is measured. This means that the particle isn't affected by the measurement, but by *the information that it is going to be measured* This is a problem in mainstream physics because information is a product of consciousness and consciousness is not supposed to directly affect our reality. Yet that is what it appears to do.

In order to test whether consciousness affects the double slit experiment, Dean Radin conducted this experiment with one important variation. Instead of using a physical measuring device he had test subjects attempt to consciously "observe" the particles to see if they would transform as if they had been measured. These experiments have been successful. He writes:

> Because it is central to interpretations of quantum mechanics, the physics literature abounds with philosophical and theoretical discussions about the QMP, [quantum measurement problem] including speculations about the role of consciousness. One might expect to find a correspondingly robust experimental literature testing these ideas, but it is not so, and the reason is not surprising: The notion that consciousness may be related to the formation of physical reality has come to be associated more with medieval magic and so-called New Age ideas than it is with sober science. As a result, it is safer for one's scientific career to avoid associating with such dubious topics and subsequently rare to find experiments examining these ideas in the physics literature. Indeed, the taboo is so robust that until recently it had extended to any test of the foundations of quantum theory. For more than 50 years such studies were considered unsuitable for serious investigators.[124]

The world of theoretical physics forks at this point into mainstream and non-mainstream. In mainstream theoretical physics, consciousness is treated as though it were an unimportant emergent property of the brain. But there is another way to interpret the evidence and not everyone ignores it. Physicists Bruce Rosenblum and Fred Kuttner outlined the problem in their popular book: *The Quantum Enigma*. They give a summary on their website:

Here are quantum theory's reality and connectedness problems in a nutshell:

> **Reality:** By your free choice you could demonstrate either of two *contradictory* physical realities. You can, for example, demonstrate an object to be someplace. But you could have chosen to demonstrate the opposite: that it was *not* in that place. Observation *created* the object's position. Quantum theory has *all* properties created by their observation.

> **Connectedness:** Quantum theory tells that any things that have ever interacted are forever connected, "entangled." For example, your friend's freely made decision of what to do in Moscow (or on Mars) can *instantaneously* (though randomly) influence what happens to you

in Manhattan. And this happens without *any* physical force involved. Einstein called such influences "spooky actions." They've now been demonstrated to exist.[125]

An important point here is that Rosenblum and Kuttner aren't going out on a limb; they are spelling out the obvious implications of non-controversial quantum physics research. They are not alone in seeing these implications either; those physicists include heavyweights: Albert Einstein, Werner Heisenberg, Niels Bohr, Pascual Jordan, Eugene Wigner, Bernard d'Espagnat, Richard Feynman, John Bell, and Martin Rees in addition to mathematician John Von Neumann.

The problems of nonlocality and consciousness have also been tackled theoretically. The most well-known theory dealing with non-locality is physicist David Bohm's Holographic Universe. He holds that the universe is one (or two) dimensional space and that our reality is actually a 3D projection of this. Every bit of the universe is actually the whole universe, and, if you divide it, you get two smaller wholes and not two halves. Consciousness is not an explicit feature of this theory although there is room for it as an explanation of why we perceive a holographic model of the universe instead of a two-dimensional version. Those interested in exploring this subject are recommended to read *The Holographic Universe: The Revolutionary Theory of Reality*, by Michael Talbot.

A better integration of the consciousness problem in physics was posited by Robert Lanza, MD., which he calls Biocentrism. Lanza is one of the world's most prominent scientists in the field of stem cell and regeneration biology. He was prompted into looking into the nature of life and death after the death of his sister. He has neatly put this into seven easy-to-understand principles:

The 7 Principles of Biocentrism

First Principle of Biocentrism: What we perceive as reality is a process that involves our consciousness.

Second Principle of Biocentrism: Our external and internal perceptions are inextricably intertwined. They are different sides of the same coin and cannot be divorced from one another.

Third Principle of Biocentrism: The behavior of subatomic particles—indeed all particles and objects—is inextricably linked to the presence of an observer. Without the presence of a conscious observer, they at best exist in an undetermined state of probability waves.

Fourth Principle of Biocentrism: Without consciousness, "matter" dwells in an undetermined state of probability. Any universe that could have preceded consciousness only existed in a probability state.

Fifth Principle of Biocentrism: The structure of the universe is explainable only through biocentrism. The universe is fine-tuned for life, which makes perfect sense as life creates the universe, not the other way around. The "universe" is simply the complete spatiotemporal logic of the self.

Sixth Principle of Biocentrism: Time does not have a real existence outside of animal-sense perception. It is the process by which we perceive changes in the universe.

Seventh Principle of Biocentrism: Space, like time, is not an object or a thing. Space is another form of our animal understanding and does not have an independent reality. We carry space and time around with us like turtles with shells. Thus, there is no absolute self-existing matrix in which physical events occur independent of life.[126]

While Lanza's material is outside the mainstream, he uses the same technique as Kuttner and Rosenblum in that his interpretation of the data requires only plain vanilla quantum physics—nothing controversial to support it.

That Lanza can do this speaks volumes as to why there is an intractable controversy: The existing data for quantum physics can support physics theories that are consciousness-centric just fine. This is a point that is utterly lost on skeptics, even those with a physics background. The typically informed, intelligent skeptical position is summarized neatly by physicist Nico van Kampen:

Quantum mechanics provides a complete and adequate description of the observed physical phenomena on the atomic scale. What else can one wish? ...The scandal is that there are still many articles, discussions, and textbooks, which advertise various interpretations and philosophical profundities ... Many physicists have not yet learned that they should adjust their ideas to the observed reality rather than the other way round.[127]

This is more or less a plea to completely ignore the consciousness problem entirely. It is a classic example of how an ST personality thinks: practical, straightforward, not interested in intangibles like philosophy. Because this is an expression of his values and attitudes, we have to treat it as such. He is not wrong to think this way, but he is also trivializing a very important area of inquiry. There is certainly merit in focusing on practical elements of particle physics, but there is much more to it.

There is certainly room for disagreement on this as demonstrated by Nobel Laureate Frank Wilczek:

> The relevant literature [on the meaning of quantum theory] is famously contentious and obscure. I believe it will remain so until someone constructs, within the formalism of quantum mechanics, an 'observer,' that is, a model entity whose states correspond to a recognizable caricature of conscious awareness.[128]

The world of physics is suffering from a split personality. On the outside, the world of theoretical physics presents a face to the world of having a basic working theory of the universe that can be solved by working on the same problems some more. But it achieves this illusion at the price of ignoring its greatest and most intractable controversy, the possibility that consciousness is a fundamental part of the universe.

Neuroscience

The problem of understanding what consciousness is in neuroscience is known as "The Hard Problem;" a term coined by Australian philosopher David Chalmers. The problem is this: How do you get from physical systems; i.e. the brain, which is composed of matter and energy, (which, according to mainstream physics, are the same thing), to *experience* (ideas, thoughts) which is neither matter nor energy? As an example, we know that a group of photons with a wavelength of between 620 and 740 nanometers can travel to the back of our eyes and hit the retina, which is a membrane containing photoreceptor nerve cells on the inside back wall of the eye. This is translated into electrical impulses that travel through the optic nerve to the brain where neural action is triggered. So far, so good. But this is where the trail ends for science. No one has the slightest idea how you get from what is essentially a chemical signal to seeing the color red. Something mysterious is translating a signal (something material) to information (something immaterial). Cognitive scientist and materialist skeptic Steve Pinker explains:

> The Hard Problem is explaining how subjective experience arises from neural computation. The problem is hard because no one knows what a solution might look like or even whether it is a genuine scientific problem in the first place. And not surprisingly, everyone agrees that the hard problem (if it is a problem) remains a mystery.[129]

To put this another way, when a person has a thought/experience/idea, it is facilitated by the brain, but the thought/experience/idea is not the brain function that it seems to come from. Energy and matter are the mediums used for information, but they not information itself. You can arrange the word "hello" out of hydrogen molecules or entire galaxies and the meaning remains the same. The pattern can only be interpreted by consciousness and loses all of its meaning without it. In order for matter and energy to create meaning and information, they would have to be conscious, because whatever form they take is meaningless without consciousness to interpret it. This very much applies to whatever chemical and electrical activity is occurring in our brains.

The current mainstream scientific thinking is that the problem is a mechanical one and that we will eventually solve it by better understanding of the processes of the brain. Scientists have certainly mapped out a great deal. By following the blood flow of the brain, scientists can determine whether we are looking at a face or a place or a bottle or a shoe. You can affect consciousness with a variety of chemicals, and you can you can have people relive memories almost as if they were there by stimulating parts of the brain. It's easy to understand why some neurologists believe consciousness ends at death and only exists in the brain, but it is not the whole story.

Mapping consciousness in the brain or observing how brain activity affects consciousness only tells you that there is a strong correlation between the brain and consciousness. It doesn't tell you anything about which causes which. You can argue, as Graham Hancock did, that consciousness is like the TV signal. If you damage or change the TV, this signal will be distorted and/or changed on the TV, but the signal itself is not part of the TV and does not require the TV in order to exist. The existing correlation for brain function and consciousness is not evidence that the brain causes consciousness.

There are other problems with the mechanical theory. One is that when people have their memories triggered via electrical impulse, they aren't suddenly transported back to that experience as though they were there; they understand that it is a memory that they are experiencing. Some part of the mind has taken a step back and is managing the experience. This is not what a theory of brain = mind would predict.

Another problem with the mechanical theory is that while brain damage generally results in a damaged mind, this is no sure thing. In fact, you can also have these two combinations:

Healthy brain and unhealthy mind (due to psychological trauma).

Unhealthy brain and healthy mind (people overcome brain damage or brain defects to lead healthy, normal lives).

A strictly materialistic view of the brain would require the mind to slavishly comply with whatever was happening to the brain. Yet it is well documented that psychological trauma, which originates entirely in the mind can have a lasting effect on the brain. Likewise, brain damage, even sometimes quite extensive, can be overcome by the mind, as famously demonstrated by neuroscientist Jill Bolte Taylor in her book *My Stroke of Insight*.

Near-Death Experiences

Near-death experiences, (NDEs), might be the smoking gun of consciousness research. Some of these happen while there is little to no brain activity, demonstrating that consciousness is doing something beyond what that brain is capable of. Lack of oxygen, hallucinations, and drugs do not duplicate full blown near-death experiences. No skeptical arguments have yet held up to serious scrutiny. A discussion of the skepticism can be found in Chris Carter's book, *Science and the Near Death Experience*.

Neuroscientists in general are not interested in NDE's. It is a very popular subject with the public but held in derision by skeptics. The gap between what the skeptics think the evidence is and what there actually is, is breathtaking. A perfect example can be found in a recent Skeptiko podcast hosted by Alex Tsakiris. His August 2013 interview with NYU psychology professor, Dr. Gary Marcus, author of *Kluge: The Haphazard Evolution of the Human Mind,* sheds light on the mindset of many mainstream neuroscientists:

> **Alex Tsakiris:** Have you read any word on it? [*Near-death experiences*] Have you read any of the leading guys out there?

> **Dr. Gary Marcus:** I've read a few words here or there but it doesn't make sense to me. It would be like you asking me have I read anything on astrology. I mean, I know about astrology but I don't see the causal mechanisms.

> ... whatever the answer is, it is biological. It is about how our brains work. I would maybe broaden that to say there could be things beyond neurons firing that we don't understand about the physiology of the brain, but ... whatever it is, it's a property of the brain...[130]

Dr. Marcus has stated that he has very little knowledge about NDE research, yet he also has very strong opinions about it. This is the sort of confusing milieu that "fringe" topics live in. How are these topics supposed to be treated fairly when the experts have strong opinions without really knowing anything about them?

It's not standard to question the knowledge of doctors, professors and other professionals who have strong opinions, yet this is what is required to determine whether they know what they're talking about. It's only when savvy interviewers like Alex Tsarkiris come along that we discover the true extent of this "expert" knowledge.

There are, in fact, scientists who have been studying NDE's for long time. Cardiologist Dr. Pim van Lommel; Dr. Sam Parnia, director of Resuscitation Research; and Professor of Psychiatry, Dr. Bruce Greyson have dealt extensively with skeptical objections.

The basic problem is that the research, which could revolutionize how we think about consciousness, is being ignored solely on the grounds that mainstream science doesn't think it's plausible.

All of Biology

It's actually impossible to keep consciousness out of the sciences, if for no other reason that it requires a conscious person to do science and all of science is information, which is a product of consciousness. But once you start looking at the markers of consciousness, they turn up all over the place and are completely unavoidable. All of biology involves the biological codes of DNA written into all living things. A code is a set of instructions and instructions are information.

Information, of course, is a product of consciousness. So here we are with another big question: how is it that all biological organisms are designed to include something that only consciousness can interpret?

Getting back to TED. All of their assumptions about the two speeches relied on a mainstream *interpretation* of physics, whether they realized it or not. Like most skeptics, they treated this interpretation as though it were the truth. It's not surprising that they did so; the worldview of mainstream theoretical physics has a huge influence on our society. It certainly affects our first impressions of "fringe" topics. If you start with the assumption that consciousness can't possibly be anything more than a product of brain chemistry, as the TED staff surely did, then of course you're not going to be open to ideas based on models of reality that contradict this. But there's a problem with this. By settling on a particular type of interpretation when many radically different but equally valid interpretations are available, mainstream science (and by extension TED) is making a *cultural* choice, not a scientific one.

A good anthropologist will immediately recognize what is happening because this is just part of what it is to be human. Scientists have formed their own culture and this culture has set up its own values, ideas, attitudes and beliefs. That culture has taken on a life of its own and like other cultures is highly resistant to change. Within any culture, certain core beliefs are never questioned and within that milieu they are taken for fact. But like any other culture, science has its heretics who question those core beliefs. And these heretics are generally sanctioned in some way. Due to the Internet, those heretics have a much stronger voice and their numbers are growing.

The controversy, in other words, is far bigger than just taking down a couple of speeches at TED. It goes far beyond charges of pseudoscience and ideologue skeptics. It is a full-blown intellectual culture war spanning decades and continents of which the TED controversy is merely one battle. It stretches deep into the psyche of western civilization and its schizophrenic approach to dealing with consciousness and science. Consciousness, and by extension spirituality, are slowly forcing themselves into the scientific discussion and pushing hard against the scientific culture of materialism. While no one can answer the question: "What is reality?" we do know one thing for sure: the skeptics don't have the answers, despite what they claim.

CHAPTER TWELVE

TED DOUBLES DOWN ON THE CRAZY

On March 18, after both Sheldrake and Hancock refuted TED's reasons for having their videos taken down and it was obvious that TED's charges were baseless. The TED leadership backed down and crossed out the objections of their science advisory board on the blog page where they first appeared. Now that the charges of pseudoscience had been completely dropped and all complaints dismissed, Sheldrake and Hancock should have been exonerated completely and their videos reinstated on the main page. In a completely baffling move however, the TED staff not only kept the two speeches off their main video web page, they decided to conduct a do over, but in an apparent move to avoid more criticism of their criticism, they didn't put forward any new objections. TED put up a blog post to explain their position:

> The obvious question is "how do you ensure the quality of these [self-organized TEDx] events"?
>
> Our approach is to empower organizers to achieve greatness, by providing detailed guidelines – and guidance – on what works and what doesn't. And we're constantly amazed at how good most of

these events are. But we also count on the community to help when things go wrong. Occasionally a TEDx event will include a speaker who causes controversy or upset. When that happens, someone in the community will flag the talk, and we have to decide how to respond.

One option would be to have an "anything goes" policy. We could just say that these events are the responsibility of the local organizer and wash our hands of it. The problem with that stance is that we would soon find the TEDx brand and platform being hijacked by those with dangerous or fringe ideas. And eventually credible speakers would not want to be associated with it. TED's mission is not "any old idea" but "ideas worth spreading." We've taken a deliberately broad interpretation of that phrase, but it still has to mean something.

The hardest line to draw is science versus pseudoscience. TED is committed to science. But we think of it as a process, not as a locked-in body of truth. The scientific method is a means of advancing understanding. Of asking for evidence. Of testing ideas to see which stack up and which should be abandoned. Over time that process has led to a rich understanding of the world, but one that is constantly being refined and upgraded. There's a sense in which all scientific truth is provisional, and open to revision if new facts arise. And that is why it's often hard to make a judgment on what is a valuable contribution to science, and what is misleading, or worthless.

Some speakers use the language of science to promote views that are simply incompatible with all reasonable understanding of the world. Giving them a platform is counterproductive. But there are also instances where scientific assumptions get turned upside down. How do we separate between these two? We have done two things as a tentative answer to this question:

We've issued a set of guidelines to TEDx organizers

[Here's the pertinent guideline for choosing speakers:

"Avoid pseudoscience. TED and TEDx are platforms for showcasing and explaining genuine advances in science, and it's important we retain the respect of the scientific community. Speakers should avoid the misuse of scientific language to make unsubstantiated claims."]

124

and we've appointed a board of scientific advisers. They are (deliberately) anonymous, for obvious reasons, but they are respected working scientists, and writers about science, from a range of fields, with no brief other than to help us make these judgments. If a talk gets flagged they will advise on whether we should act or not.

When Sheldrake and Hancock's talks were flagged, the majority of the board recommended we remove them from circulation, pointing out questionable suggestions and arguments in both talks. But there was a counter view that removing talks that had already been posted would lead to accusations of censorship. It's also the case that both speakers *explicitly* take on mainstream scientific opinion. This gives them a stronger reason to be listened to than those who simply use scientific sounding language to make nonsensical claims. So we decided we would not remove the talks from the web altogether, but simply transfer them to our own site where they could be framed in a way which included the critique of our board, but still allow for an open conversation about them.

What happened next was unfortunate. We wrote to the TEDx organizer indicating our intention and asking her to take the talks off YouTube so that we could repost. She informed the speakers of what was coming, but somehow the part about the talks staying online got lost in translation. Graham Hancock put out an immediate alert that he was about to be "censored", his army of passionate supporters deluged us with outraged messages, and we then felt compelled to accelerate our blog post and used language that in retrospect was clumsy. We suggested that we were flagging the talks because of "factual errors" but some of the specific examples we gave were less than convincing. Instead of the thoughtful conversation we had hoped for, we stirred up angry responses from the speakers and their supporters.

So much is wrong with this. Let's start with TED's main premise: *avoid pseudoscience.* All along TED has flown the science flag which means that they are obligated to play by the rules of science. They have entered into an agreement to abide by an objective and universal set of rules for evidence and requirements for proof. If their concept of "ideas worth spreading" is going by the rules of science, then they do not get to decide what those rules are. And in science you cannot simply claim that something is pseudoscience, you have to prove it, which they emphatically did not.

What they're doing in this blog post is all kinds of sleazy. They are implying that the speeches are pseudoscience, but not directly saying so. It is a tactic that is common in political campaigns and it's used as a PR gambit to slur someone without the legal problems associated with actual accusations. It is outrageous that TED was doing this to speakers that had been *invited* to speak at one of their independent conferences. It is just the sort of thing that gives ideologue skeptics a toe hold to accuse the speakers of pseudoscience by misreading the exact wording of the blog post. These accusations then spread through the skeptical community and get mistaken for truth.

In fact, this misinterpretation made it all the way into Rupert Sheldrake's Wikipedia biography, where it became fodder for the mainstream media. If it's in Wikipedia, anyone can reference it. (Hancock's Wikipedia page does not currently mention the controversy.)

Taking the talks down from the main page and sticking them in an obscure corner of the TED website with no links is a form of censorship: calling it something else is just hair splitting. Their timeline is off as well. Criticism was raining down on TED well before they even decided to take down Hancock's video. What Graham sought to do wasn't to generate outrage, but to merely see that his video was preserved on the web before TED banished it to a far corner of an obscure webpage with no way of searching for it short of knowing the link.

The reference to the "army of passionate supporters" was essentially a way of denigrating TED's critics as if they were groupies objecting for emotional reasons. But many, including myself, were objecting not as supporters of either speaker but on philosophical, scientific and/or moral grounds. TED also referred to the responses by the speakers as "angry." The responses were not angry but were a careful dismantling of the fictional complaints that were leveled against them. The whole tone of this paragraph suggests that the TED staff saw the opposition to their actions as rash and emotional despite all evidence to the contrary. They did not seem to be able to come to the realization that their lack of good arguments meant that they might be in the wrong.

Nothing was more galling, however, than the lame excuse that was given for putting up their poor criticisms of the speakers in the first place. In essence they were saying, "Hey, we were so eager to find things wrong with these speeches that we screwed it up. We can't concede that though, so give us some more time and we'll come up with things that are wrong with them."

Even leaving that dumbfounding statement aside, there is still the question of what the heck was going on? Taking down a video for scientific reasons is not supposed to be done on a whim; it is an attack on someone's reputation and it should be taken very seriously. At the very least the reasons for taking action should be completely spelled out and vetted *before any action* is taken. The letter continues:

We would like to try again.

We plan to repost both talks in individual posts on our blog tomorrow, Tuesday; note a couple of areas where scientists or the community have raised questions or concerns about the talks; and invite a reasoned discussion from the community. And there will be a simple rule regarding responses. Reason only. No insults, no intemperate language. From either side. Comments that violate this will be removed. The goal here is to have an open conversation about:

- the line between science and pseudoscience

- how far TED and TEDx should go in giving exposure to unorthodox ideas

We will use the reasoned comments in this conversation to help frame both our guidelines going forward, and our process for managing talks that are called into question.

Both Sheldrake and Hancock are compelling speakers, and some of the questions they raise are absolutely worth raising. For example, most thoughtful scientists and philosophers of science will agree it's true that science has not moved very far yet in solving the riddle of consciousness. But the specific answers to that riddle proposed by Sheldrake and Hancock are so radical and far-removed from mainstream scientific thinking that we think it's right for us to give these talks a clear health warning and to ask further questions of the speakers. TED and TEDx are brands that are trusted in schools and in homes. We don't want to hear from a parent whose kid went off to South America to drink Ayahuasca because TED said it was OK. But we do think a calmer, reasoned conversation around these talks would be interesting, if only to help us define how far you can push an idea before it is no longer "worth spreading."

TED claimed that the answers provided by Sheldrake and Hancock are "so radical and far-removed from mainstream scientific thinking that we think it's right for us to give these talks a clear health warning and to ask further questions of the speakers." As I've pointed out, "mainstream scientific thinking" is in the process of upheaval; the very reason that TED came down on these two speakers and why there were so many comments and such outrage is precisely because *we are in the middle of that upheaval.* TED never did provide any new criticisms by scientists and the skeptical arguments in the comment threads provided none either. How could they when their criticism was *cultural*, not scientific?

This is what it looks like when changes occur in science. The old guard doesn't go quietly into the night. They go down biting, kicking, screaming, hair pulling, back stabbing, choking and groin kicking. What they never, ever do is say these three words: You. Were. Right. In the end, the old guard simply gets overwhelmed, which is why it is such a slow process.

Greg Taylor at The Daily Grail had a good response to TED talking about a kid running off to South America to drink Ayahuasca:

> ZOMG won't somebody think of the children?! Seriously, if a kid can travel to South America and get their hands on some Ayahuasca, I'm pretty certain they're at a stage of life where they should be taking (and hopefully want to be taking) responsibility for their own actions, rather than blaming a TED talk. ...

The next day, March 19, TED created two different threads. One was for Hancock and the other was for Sheldrake, with neither thread giving any specific reasons for continuing to keep the two speeches off the main part of the TED site. That turned out to be a pointless inconvenience. The same people weighed in on both threads discussing much the same issues. It had the effect of simply generating more comments from crossovers. Vague charges of pseudoscience still hung over the speaker's heads.

The next day, Rupert Sheldrake wrote in his comment area:

> I appreciate the fact that TED published my response to the accusations leveled against me by their Scientific Board, and also crossed out the Board's statement on the "Open for discussion" blog.

There are no longer any specific points to answer. I am all in favour of debate, but it is not possible to make much progress through short responses to nebulous questions like "Is this an idea worth spreading, or misinformation?"

I would be happy to take part in a public debate with a scientist who disagrees with the issues I raise in my talk. This could take place online, or on Skype. My only condition is that it be conducted fairly, with equal time for both sides to present their arguments, and with an impartial moderator, agreed by both parties.

Therefore I ask Chris Anderson to invite a scientist from TED's Scientific Board or TED's Brain Trust to have a real debate with me about my talk, or if none will agree to take part, to do so himself.

Graham Hancock weighed in the next day, adding his own points and also volunteering to debate the TED science board.

I previously commented that I would not post further on this Blog page because it is so clearly designed to distract public attention from the disastrous way TED have handled their attempt to censor my "War on Consciousness" talk and Rupert Sheldrake's "Science Delusion" talk. That in my view is the important point, for it bears on the future of TED itself as a viable platform for "ideas worth spreading". I am heartened that so many of the 400-plus concerned people who have now posted here (and the 1000-plus who posted on the original Blog page) have refused to fall for TED's sleight of hand and continued to press the organization to rethink its policy.

Since TED have retracted and struck out all their justifications for the original deletion of my talk from the TEDx YouTube channel and since they have published my rebuttal, and done the same re Rupert Sheldrake's talk, I agree with Rupert on his new post.

There are no more specific points surrounding TED's misguided decision that he and I need to answer. Nor is it possible to make much progress through short responses to nebulous questions like "Is this an idea worth spreading, or misinformation?"

129

But I now make this one further post, simply to add my voice to Rupert's and to put on record that I, too, would be happy to take part in a public debate with a scientist who disagrees with the issues I raise in my talk. My only condition is that it be conducted fairly, with equal time for both sides to present their arguments, and with an impartial moderator, agreed by both parties.

Therefore I join Rupert in asking Chris Anderson to invite a scientist from TED's Scientific Board or TED's Brain Trust to have a real debate with me about my talk, or if none will agree to take part, to do so himself.

The speakers were in a strange situation where they knew neither the identity of their accusers nor what the charges were against them. Franz Kafka would have been proud. As they said, there was nothing to defend. They were being treated badly and for no demonstrable reason. The question that was on everyone's mind was whether TED would respond. Was there going to be A Great Debate? Because that would be awesome.

It became clear however, that TED was flying the Camp Skeptic banner, which was just another demonstration of what goes on with skeptics all the time. They complain bitterly about pseudoscience but won't say exactly why. They also won't debate because their lack of knowledge would be exposed. It was also relatively easy to see this pattern in the comment section, since most hard core skeptics use the same playbook: disparage the opponent with snide or otherwise unkind remarks, make sweeping generalizations about the speaker's work, back those up with irrelevant sources, and avoid all the hard questions that require actual knowledge of the subject in order to reply to them.

This is exactly what Chris Anderson did to Graham Hancock in the comment section on March 14' before TED crossed out its original critique of Hancock's talk:

Graham, greetings, and thanks for engaging here personally. We'll try to get you some more detailed comments early next week. I'm currently tied up at National Geographic in DC helping launch the TEDxDeExtinction event (which, by the way, is an indication that we have no problem with radical scientific ideas per se.)

I understand why you're upset at the talk being pulled off YouTube, but we're quite serious in saying we're not censoring you. The talk will live here as long it takes for this conversation to work itself out, and perhaps indefinitely. I must say, you're a compelling speaker and I personally enjoyed the talk quite a bit. I can understand why you and your books have attracted a huge following.

There it is again. He's portraying Hancock as being emotional, thereby implying that he's not thinking straight. It makes Anderson's compliment seem hollow.

> It would help your cause to let this whole discussion calm down a little. You seem to have whipped your supporters up into a bit of a frenzy. There's no conspiracy out to get you. We just have certain guidelines for our TEDx events that weren't fully implemented in this instance, and it's OK to have a public discussion about that.

And again with the portrayal of the opposition being "into a bit of a frenzy." Actually, this was the best-behaved set of discussions of this sort I'd ever seen. Whatever upset there was came from insulting comments like this one. And, in fact, the people who supported TED's decisions were the ones who were most likely to be rude, although most of the worst of those comments were deleted by TED staff.

Hancock, in the comments that Anderson was responding to, never mentioned a conspiracy against him. Yet he is portrayed by Anderson as somehow being paranoid.

There was actually a conspiracy that was out to get Graham Hancock, just as there was a conspiracy that was out to get Rupert Sheldrake. Skeptics teamed up to pressure TED to get rid of these talks. That's a conspiracy. Chris Anderson continues:

> So here's a suggestion. While I reach out and see if any of our advisors is able to go into more depth in answering your specific questions, perhaps you could help me understand why your work is widely characterized as pseudo-archeology, as in the current version of this Wikipedia page. http://en.wikipedia.org/wiki/Pseudoarchaeology
> Is that a distorted description of your views? Is mainstream archaeology simply misguided? Or is there some other explanation?

A Wikipedia page which allows literally just anybody to re-write science pages is a source of authority about Hancock? That was quite unfair, and I'll show why in a later chapter on Wikipedia. Wikipedia is the poster child of skeptics gone wild and some of the attacks on non-mainstream subjects are legendary.

This would be hilarious if it wasn't so pathetic. The curator of TED was relying on a reference source that schoolchildren are taught to avoid. Chris Anderson again:

> Do you agree that we should have *some* form of guidelines for our TEDx organizers as to what constitutes credible science, or do you think our approach should be [to] let anyone put anything they want out there and just let the public decide?

And here, instead of addressing Hancock's complaints, which were later shown to be valid, Anderson reels off a couple of rhetorical questions to promote his point of view but which *do not address Hancock's speech at all*. It's a straw man argument. He has compared Hancock's position to a fictional situation and then attacked the fictional situation. This kind of attitude and method of arguing was an indication that TED was deaf to criticisms.

At this point, it seemed as if the controversy might be peaking because it didn't appear that there was a lot more to do. The only question left was whether TED would arrange a debate. In fact, there turned out to be a great deal more to come. The TED controversy was just warming up.

CHAPTER THIRTEEN

WIKIPEDIA:
THE RESOURCE FROM HELL

I had originally intended simply to do some research on Wikipedia, a well-known stronghold of ideologue skepticism, create a chapter on it and move on. Yet events suddenly lurched forward, as they sometimes do, and I found myself in a far more involved role than I had initially intended.

I ended up getting some first-hand experience which morphed into several blog posts which in turn added yet another voice to a growing chorus of complaints about the awful state of Wikipedia and its editing process. But before I get into that story, I think a bit of background is necessary about Wikipedia's problems, which are both endless and probably insurmountable.

Wikipedia matters because of the sheer numbers of visitors it draws. The term Parapsychology has about 300,000 views a year. Rupert Sheldrake's biography Wikipedia page has about 180,000 views a year and Graham Hancock's page has roughly 120,000 views a year.

Google search results place Wikipedia at or near the top of nearly every category where it has a page, so this online encyclopedia is one of the first resources that anyone looking for objective information on the Internet sees. While it is acceptable for bland, non-technical, noncontroversial topics it is a complete disaster on pretty much any other subject and especially those that people have differing opinions about.

Wikipedia is the world's largest online encyclopedia. Yet this enormous resource was only founded in 2001:

> Initially, Wikipedia was created to complement Nupedia, an online encyclopedia project edited solely by experts, by providing additional draft articles and ideas for it. Wikipedia quickly overtook Nupedia, becoming a global project in multiple languages and inspiring a wide range of additional reference projects.

> As of June 2013, Wikipedia includes over 26 million freely usable articles in 285 languages, written by over 39 million registered users and numerous anonymous contributors worldwide. According to Alexa Internet, Wikipedia is the world's seventh-most-popular website, visited monthly by around 11% of all internet users. According to comScore, Wikipedia receives over 85 million monthly unique visitors from the United States alone.[131]

Google and Wikipedia have a symbiotic relationship. Wikipedia doesn't run any ads, which allows Google to create more ad revenue, which has led to complaints of preferential treatment.[132] How this works is somewhat roundabout. By putting websites with no commercial intent at the top of search results everywhere, Google is making sure that commercial websites show up farther down the search results, limiting the number of views that they get.

This ensures that the best way for businesses to improve their search results is by buying ad space on Google.[133] (This isn't necessarily bad. Most people prefer to get their information without a blizzard of auto play advertisements, pop up ads, moving survey requests and hidden ads.) In a 2012 study using 1,000 search terms, Wikipedia ranked in the top five in a whopping 96% of web searches. The study asked if this dominance was deserved:

> We all love Wikipedia, but should it really be so prominent and all conquering in Google? We know that Wikipedia is a vast site with millions of pages and thousands of editors offering unique vital content on multitudes of subject matters. But should Wikipedia be the de-facto resource for pretty much all subjects? Surely some pages are riding on the back of other quality pages or perhaps lazy references

to the site from businesses and bloggers across the internet. Google obviously loves Wikipedia and still ranks it despite there being next to zero content on some of the pages.[134]

Search optimization expert Lisa Barone points out that what this does is put non expert information at the top of search results.[135]

The search engines are supposed to reward authoritative, expert content. Wikipedia is not a subject matter expert on anything. It's an open-ended encyclopedia where anyone can contribute to make the article on a given topic "better" and "more accurate". The best and worst thing about Wikipedia has always been that anyone can edit any entry. That fact may make it a fun project idea, but it doesn't lend itself to promoting [good] quality information.

... There may be a high quantity of frequently updated information on the Wikipedia site, but the quality is equal to a middle school book report. Wikipedia is not the Encyclopedia Britannica.

... By ranking first for everything under the sun, it pushes down information that actually is authoritative and worthy of rankings, thereby "hiding" expert information.

In other words, Wikipedia is a very influential and important source of information and it is going to stay that way whether its information is accurate or not. It tends to provide increasingly poor information as topics become more technical and controversial.

The tragicomedy that is Wikipedia is perhaps best summed up on a talk page from April 2011 regarding their article, "Energy Catalyst," which is associated with the controversial technology known as LENR (low energy nuclear reaction), a.k.a. cold fusion. It was Brian Josephson and a senior staff writer from a distinguished technical magazine, *NY Teknik*, versus a couple of anonymous Wikipedia editors in an incredibly lopsided discussion. [136]

Professor Brian Josephson, a Nobel Prize winning physicist, was not only arguing physics with nincompoops, *but he couldn't get any changes past them.*[137] His expertise was ignored in favor of tedious, mendacious use of Wikipedia guidelines for editing, of which there are many. This discussion graphically demonstrates what is wrong with Wikipedia, where scholars are thwarted by an army of ignorant nobodies.

Few experts are willing to argue with people who have strong opinions, but don't know enough about the subjects they're editing. This sort of problem is common on Wikipedia. An article on Wikipediocracy noted:

> **Wikipedia disrespects and disregards scholars, experts, scientists, and others with special knowledge.** Wikipedia specifically disregards authors with special knowledge, expertise, or credentials. There is no way for a real scholar to distinguish himself or herself from a random anonymous editor merely claiming scholarly credentials, and thus no claim of credentials is typically believed. Even when credentials are accepted, Wikipedia affords no special regard for expert editors contributing in their fields. This has driven most expert editors away from editing Wikipedia in their fields. Similarly, Wikipedia implements no controls that distinguish mature and educated editors from immature and uneducated ones.[138]

It can be ludicrous. Economist David Henderson was not trusted to know his own birthday.[139] Economist John Lott had so much trouble getting his biography and ideas presented correctly that he turned it into a study. People who supported him and his position were accused of being sockpuppets. His experience and those of his associates was so bad that they offered this amusing tidbit:

> An entertaining thought: what would it look like if WP had a problem being cast in such poor light and we followed WP's own policies to resolve it? In that case we would readily publish material from all the WP detractors in the world, no matter what they happened to write, then cheerfully assure WP that we would correct any presentation here once *everyone* had reached consensus on what is said.[140]

Wikipedia is also infested with pure trolls and some of them have the time to do a significant amount of damage. In one case, a user named Qworty attempted to purge Wikipedia of all references to the occult and modern paganism, making some 13,000 edits.[141]

Since Wikipedia does not recognize expertise, it relies on secondary sourcing:

> A secondary source *usually* provides analysis, commentary, evaluation, context, and interpretation. It is this act of going beyond simple

description, and telling us the meaning behind the simple facts, that makes them valuable to Wikipedia.[142]

It seems like a good idea, but a secondary source *cannot be overruled even when directly contradicted by a primary source.* It's a horrible protocol that leads to critical errors. Take the case of Professor Timothy Messer-Kruse, an expert on the Haymaker riot and trial of 1886. If anyone knew what the best sources were, it was him. Yet he discovered that this was insufficient for Wikipedia. Messer-Kruse was relying on verbatim transcribed testimony that's online at the Library of Congress, which is the very best evidence available about what happened at the Haymaker trial, but because this was at odds with popular histories of the trial his change was refused. In an article for The *Chronicle of Higher Education,* he outlined an ordeal where he removed a line about there being "no evidence" and gave a full explanation of this on the Wikipedia talk page for that article.

But his primary source,—the actual transcripts—were not allowed and his edit was reverted back to the original. "You must provide reliable sources for your assertions to make changes along these lines to the article" was the explanation. This article had a gatekeeper who quoted Wikipedia's "undue weight" policy, which stated that minority views do not get the same weight as majority views. Messer-Kruse asked the obvious question:

> "Explain to me, then, how a 'minority' source with facts on its side would ever appear against a wrong 'majority' one?" I asked the Wiki-gatekeeper. He responded, "You're more than welcome to discuss reliable sources here, that's what the talk page is for. However, you might want to have a quick look at Wikipedia's civility policy."[143]

As Wikipedia regards books as reliable sources, Messer-Kruse waited to edit again until his book came out, hoping that this more scholarly source would help him put the facts straight.

> My improvement lasted five minutes before a Wiki-cop scolded me, "I hope you will familiarize yourself with some of Wikipedia's policies, such as verifiability and undue weight. If all historians save one say that the sky was green in 1888, our policies require that we write 'Most historians write that the sky was green, but one says the sky was blue.' ... As individual editors, we're not in the business of weighing claims, just reporting what reliable sources write."

Thus, the 1,530 entries in the published bibliography of titles that all got this one fact wrong would hold sway. By resorting to consensus opinion in matters of expertise (this is important for how psi is treated in Wikipedia), Wikipedia virtually guarantees that subjects which acquire new information will practically never be up to date.

Wikipedia's most pressing problem is that it doesn't acknowledge expertise and give it any preference, relying instead on consensus building between interested editors who are guided by a blizzard of rules. This allows kingdom building because people are not limited in their editing by their knowledge of a subject and as with most similar endeavors, human nature dictates that those who have the best command of the rules and do the most politicking will almost always prevail.

An awful lot of people from botanists to geologists are frustrated with the Wikipedia system in which mistakes are broadcast all over the world and cannot be corrected.

The editors are generally not good at science in general and tend not to be good researchers, instead relying on slapping things together [bold from original author]:

> **A lot of these articles are wrong, wrong in emphasis, wrong in basic facts, and most importantly wrong because there is no true distillation of the consensus view of the topic from the best sources. Why? Because the cutty-pasties don't really understand what they're writing about (how could they? In general, they haven't sat down and read it all before starting. They're just Magpies, a bottle cap here, a shiny piece of plastic there, ctrl v and I'm done).** And this entirely leaves aside the fact that **cutting and pasting is often from very old PD** [pure data] **sources that are no longer accurate (particularly in science-related articles, but not exclusively). The culture of tolerance for this stuff, and the false sense of accomplishment given to poor article writers with DYK** [Did You Know, -a regular Wikipedia contest in which a selected article is featured.] **baubles, leads to an ever expanding miasma of inaccurate articles, beyond the scope of the small handful of engaged editors to fix, if they were to try.** Sometimes, more is less. Bali (talk) 22:32, 28 October 2010 (UTC)"[144]

As one commenter on my site wrote:

However, since neither the editor writing the science article, nor the editor promoting it to be on the main page to get viewed 7000 times a day, have any background in biology outside of Wikipedia, the encyclopedia is slowly but surely rewriting evolutionary biology and taxonomy and dropping its poop onto the top of Google searches to replace science.

This highlights one of the most irritating problems about Wikipedia: it's used in search results on mobile devices, so that it's guaranteed to give more people more bad information than any other source in the history of mankind.

From the perspective of scientific articles, Wikipedia of course, does not fare particularly well as a resource. Studies of the accuracy of Wikipedia vary greatly in their conclusions because of how different aspects of articles are rated. In a rather well known *Nature* study of Wikipedia back in 2005, Wikipedia supposedly fared rather well compared to the *Encyclopaedia Britannica* but when the people at Britannica looked at the data they noted that Wikipedia had 30% more inaccuracies and that many of the so-called mistakes in the *Encyclopaedia Britannica* were actually mere differences in interpretation, which makes the differences between the two encyclopedias even more profound. Also, the *Nature* study did not account for readability, which can be a severe flaw of Wikipedia.[145]

According to a thesis paper by Spanish researcher Filipe Ortega[146], Wikipedia lost almost 50,000 editors in 2009. The core group of editors have picked up the slack. Who is this core? It is 87% male with an average age of 26.8 years. This hardly is the demographic to entrust with the world's knowledge. In the real world we would never tolerate people that young being entrusted with the accuracy of an important encyclopedia. Dean Radin writes of this in his blog:

> The most persistent editors on Wikipedia, by the way, largely seem to be 20-something students who are riding high on arrogance, because like all kids, they're suffering under the delusion that they know everything. (I recall this state of mind quite clearly from when I was 20-something.) For you young folks out there, believe me that grandiosity dissolves with life experience. The fact is that nothing is certain, *especially* what science pretends to know.[147]

Within such a consolidated system run by males under the age of thirty, it is the controversial sciences that are the most vulnerable to Wikipedia editing shenanigans. In 2003, Anthropogenic Global Warming Theory was subjected to near total control by a single editor who created or rewrote 5,428 unique Wikipedia articles, obtained Website Administrator status, and removed 500 articles and banned more than 2,000 Wikipedia editors. This continued until September of 2009 when his privileges were finally revoked.[148]

There are many topics, collectively referred to as frontier sciences, that get labeled fringe and/or pseudoscience by Wikipedia. Unsurprisingly, parapsychology is lumped into this group. This designation carries certain penalties as it allows for over the top sensationalizing of the controversy surrounding a subject. The articles are littered with useless trolling statements saying things like "critics say that this is pseudoscience." It does not matter how convincing the evidence is or even if it is acknowledged by experts in the field and there are peer reviewed studies and scientific journals associated with it. If someone can find a skeptical opinion piece in Scientific American, then that criticism is never going away.

Wikipedia is an ideal location for ideologues to set up camp and bend a corner of Internet to their will. I think it's important to understand why because it gets to the heart of what ails Wikipedia and will go a long way towards explaining why change will be so difficult.

Wikipedia is run by volunteers who have set up a system of rules that govern how articles are created for the encyclopedia. The ideologue skeptics are just one of many groups that have captured the process by getting themselves favorably positioned in the arbitration and rule making process. Once that is done there is really no way to stop them because they will resist any rule changes that negatively affect their power. The greatest crime of Wikipedia is that it does not recognize expertise, which puts knowledgeable people on the same footing as ideologues. There will of course, always be fewer subject experts than ideologues and the experts will not be inclined to fight their way through a system where expertise is necessary yet rendered irrelevant. Let me put this another way, just so it's clear: on Wikipedia, lies are given the same weight as truth. Wikipedia's rule system is designed in a way that can ignore a mountain of peer reviewed scientific research merely because a majority of editors doesn't want to include it.

Wikipedia not only has no failsafe that allows knowledge to override opinion, but even trying to do this would upset the ideologues who hold a sizable number of Wikipedia's editing, moderating and arbitrating positions. It's a problem that's not likely to get corrected in the foreseeable future. In the case of Sheldrake's page, he has gotten the fringe/pseudoscience stamp, which cannot be undone. The ideologues can "prove" this by referencing skeptical opinion pieces published by JREF, CSI, its fellows or even *The Skeptic's Dictionary*. There is no way out of this short of engaging in months long debates with exceedingly narrow-minded people.

The Parapsychological Association is a member of the American Association for the Advancement of Science, which should have put the whole pseudoscience matter to rest, but that would require reasonable Wikipedia editors and they are few and far between in matters of parapsychology or other "fringe" topics. It's all about whether someone can find a secondary source to support their opinion, no matter the bias.

The editors are anonymous and given wide latitude and discretion within a rule system that isn't immediately obvious to outside observers. The Wikipedia rules system rewards people who have no expertise, but do have a great deal of time to spend defending their ideological position on the subject of their choice. As I've demonstrated, a person who acquires the position of administrator can pretty much shut out anyone they don't like. Skeptics game Wikipedia quite openly to promote their viewpoints. There is even a list on Wikipedia of skeptical participants.[149] These are people who are intentionally warping Wikipedia articles pages to skew them away from a neutral point of view. This might be ok if all they did was limit themselves to providing relevant criticisms to various topics, but that's not what they do. They are there to push their belief system, which is why there has been so much discord on Rupert Sheldrake's biography page. Skeptics have a long list of subjects they hate, including, of all things, chiropractic care.[150] And you can find their opinions stamped on nearly all of them.

By quoting articles from CSI, JREF and the Skeptic's Dictionary they keep their sources all in the family. *The Skeptic's Dictionary* is cited in pages about pseudo history, applied kinesiology, psychokinesis, biorhythm, Deepak Chopra, astral projection, Pisces, and Werner Erhard.

The page on parapsychology[151] is an example of the kind of control skeptics exert. This is the third paragraph down (today):

> Critics state that methodological flaws can explain any apparent experimental successes[12] and the status of parapsychology as a science has been vigorously disputed.[13] Many scientists regard the discipline as pseudoscience, saying that parapsychologists continue

investigation despite not having demonstrated conclusive evidence of psychic abilities in more than a century of research.[14][15][16]

Not a single thing that the "critics" and "many scientists" say in this paragraph are factually correct. They are easily disprovable assertions that skeptics make over and over again without any evidence to substantiate them. Setting aside the fact that criticisms belong under "Criticisms," the citations for this are from longtime CSI member Ray Hyman, a skeptical book from 1982, an assertion by a popular psychology encyclopedia, a book from 1991 about skeptic's beliefs, and a skeptical psychology article from 1991. These statements come from opinionated, non-scientific sources, and it's a good example of manipulating the secondary source rule to make improper assertions.

Biased articles are used as source material to legitimize skeptical positions on other Wikipedia topics in a loop of skeptical thinking. As an added bonus for skeptics, getting their sources cited on Wikipedia raises the ranking on those sources in the search engines.

Articles on parapsychology used to be well-written back in the early years of Wikipedia, but they have taken on a biased, skeptical slant as the skeptics have exercised their control. Just recently, within a period of fifteen days, a single skeptic deleted 20 references to the pro-psi Skeptiko podcast. Reason given: pseudoscience.[152]

Greg Taylor, at the *Daily Grail* writes:

> I long ago gave up thoughts of trying to edit Wikipedia articles on TDG-related topics—reading through the history of some of those articles, it was quite obvious that there was a fairly large, and loud contingent of pseudo-skeptics in place there who would soon revert any open-minded content, no matter how well referenced and written the piece was. Certainly there's a place for keeping the 'riff-raff' out—you can't include every strange thing that people believe—and as an alternative encyclopedia you want to keep most of it to mainstream, accepted thought. However, Wikipedia edits by pseudo-skeptics often over-step that mark in order to bias articles towards mainstream opinion without fair representation of alternative views.[153]

Author and journalist Robert McLuhan presented this scenario:

> The danger of course is getting into a tiresome tit-for-tat, with teams of rival guerrillas coming out at night and trashing the opposition's most

recent efforts. In that case the victor would be whoever runs out of steam first. Actually I don't think it need come to that, and Wikipedia surely has ways of dealing with it. We don't need the last word; all we need to do is to put the carping in perspective, and ideally encourage readers to check out the subject for themselves in other sources, where they aren't going to be distracted by noisy sceptics.[154]

Editing the Sheldrake biography page

This was the environment that I knew I was getting into, but the research that I had done up to that point mostly pointed to incompetence and bad bureaucracy, which didn't really deal with what I was about to encounter.

My own involvement on Wikipedia as an editor began a few months after the TED controversy had ended. Rupert had mentioned in his June 2013 newsletter that there was a skeptical group on Wikipedia called the "Guerrilla Skeptics" whose mission was to edit Wikipedia to a skeptical point of view. Sometime between then and September the skeptics got to work on his page and edited it in a way that made him look bad. Judging by the timing it was a near certainty that the Guerrilla Skeptics were involved.

According the Guerrilla Skeptics they have about 90 editors, but they operate via secret Facebook pages and do not have an open list of members or their screen names so it is impossible to verify that number or know how many of them are active. Some of what they do is benign, like making sure that skeptics have good Wikipedia pages, but much of what they do is removing viewpoints they disagree with. In a training video[155] the organizer, Susan Gerbic, explicitly talks about targeting psychics, psychic programs and other people of the New Age variety. Her attitude is somewhat frightening: around 32:14 she says:

> "So they're getting their information from here, so, we can control this, this is so powerful you don't understand when you put one of these guerrilla skepticism edits up on Jenny McCarthy's page or Priceline, or Walmart or just some of these pages you're like glowing inside it's so powerful to feel like I've made such an impact. Hundreds of thousands of people can be reading my edit, homeopathy, we've changed that page drastically, the lead, the very very first couple of sentences of the page which most people it's the only thing they read we use the word "quackery" I mean it's so awesome" . . .

Wikipedia is an ideal place for that kind of chicanery because it does not distinguish between the quality of the sources. At about 1:04:40 Susan Gerbic makes this statement:

> I can't give my opinion on Wikipedia but I can through our spokespeople give an opinion of how I feel about a topic and so on so I'm writing through other people but I need that content first from the JREF or the CSI or from Ben Radford or from Ray Hyman whomever, I need the content first. And then I can [edit the page.]

Wikipedia's ignorance of expertise is a loophole that Skeptics happily jump through by creating and then citing skeptical sources. They typically cite notable skeptics or from articles in skeptical publications and if you go back to those sources you generally find poorly sourced, often inaccurate articles or in some cases, nothing more than opinion. Rarely do they venture far outside of their own skeptical camp to get their information. A good example of this can be found on a Guerrilla Skepticism blog post[156] by Susan Gerbic that outlines a strategy for attacking a Wikipedia article on Pet Psychics.[157] It includes references to experiments by Rupert Sheldrake, whom she names in her article. Her sources are: Richard Wiseman, a fellow of the Committee for Skeptical Inquiry, whose replication of the dog experiment was soundly refuted; Joe Nickell, writing for the *Skeptical Inquirer*; and Karen Stollznow writing for the . . . *Skeptical Inquirer*.

The list of notable skeptics and their organizations is so small that it fits on an ordinary sized Wikipedia page.[158] Of those listed, some skeptics are dead, most are not scientists, some are less notable than me and only four are scientists who have a legitimate claim to some expertise in parapsychology. Yet this tiny group of sources sways much of the editing of the frontier sciences, fringe topics, psychics and other similar articles. I knew that the skeptics editing the Sheldrake page would probably fanatically defend those sources, but there was nothing I could do about it. I stayed away from Wikipedia for two reasons: first, I was in the middle of writing this book and had very little time to spare, but the other reason was that I was aware of what it was going to be like to argue with ideologue skeptics. I've had a lot of experience over the years in dealing with them and, based upon my research, I had little doubt that I would encounter the worst sort on Wikipedia.

In an email to me Rupert mentioned that other people had come to his Wikipedia page to try to sort things out, so I began to follow what was happening. On Wikipedia, in the upper left-hand corner of every article is a tab for the article and just to the right of it, a tab for talk. The talk page is where all the editing for the page is (supposedly) discussed. It was there that I could more or less follow what was going on.

The discussions were exactly what I expected them to be: both sides talking past each other with the skeptical side relying mostly on specious arguments. Every discussion seemed to go on forever. It was exhausting just reading it.

Nevertheless, in mid-September, I finally dove in and contributed a little bit on the talk page because there was a conversation revolving around the TED controversy. I got an account under my own name and contributed what I could.

The first thing I noticed, and that everyone notices who tries to edit Wikipedia for the first time, is that it has a user interface from the age of the dinosaurs. It is very imposing because everything is in some funky version of html, where you can see all the code. It's very distracting and difficult to use. There is an updated version that is more like modern editors, but it's buried deep in menus and is hard to find and challenging even to figure out how to turn it on.

I had dealt with this kind of clunky interface before, so I was able to get up and going pretty quickly. The system is barely usable to hold a conversation, so that is almost all of what I did.

Soon, I was embroiled in an idiotic argument with a skeptic who was absolutely firmly convinced that a single sentence on one of TED's blog posts conveyed TED's entire position on the matter of Rupert Sheldrake's speech.[159] It was instantly maddening.

Rupert Sheldrake's biography on Wikipedia was a mess to the point of being slanderous. I volunteered what I already knew about Wikipedia from my research for this book to Rupert, with the warning that getting the page edited to a neutral point of view was going to be more trouble than it was worth. It was just another ideological battle forming on an obscure talk page[160] on one of millions of Wikipedia articles.

There is a strong skeptical group-think on Wikipedia that you can almost taste. The skeptics editing the Sheldrake page consistently treated me like a scientific ignoramus the entire time I participated. In their mind, only skeptical people could be trusted.

While I was still feeling my way around on Wikipedia I received a veiled threat on a page that Wikipedia automatically set up for my account.

Hi, I would recommend looking at WP:IMPERSONATE. The worst case of ignoring it is that a random administrator could temporarily block you, which wouldn't be so bad, just inconvenient until you get it unblocked. This is just FYI; it doesn't matter to me who anyone is. vzaak (talk) 06:42, 29 September 2013 (UTC) ...

... There's no downside in taking precautions when it comes to identity; "CSICOP, a known radical atheist pressure group" could be construed as an attempt to make the real Craig Weiler look bad. vzaak (talk) 10:47, 29 September 2013 (UTC)

... You can be blocked at any time, for no reason other than your account name. You could have been blocked ten seconds after you created your account. Making heated arguments simply draws more attention; it doesn't actually matter what the arguments are about. Murphy's Law says that a block would come at the worse possible time—say, in the middle of some argument—which might indeed look like a conspiracy. But it would only be Wikipedia's WP:IMPERSONATE policy aiming to protect people. vzaak (talk) 22:37, 29 September 2013 (UTC)

It was a kind of welcome from the Wikipedia mafia: *Nice name you got there. It would be a shame if anything happened to it.* A couple of days later I did my first blog post on my Wikipedia editing experience. It must have annoyed them, because a day later they started warming up the banhammer.[161]

Hi Barney. I'm a skeptic and have been following the Rupert Sheldrake stuff on the internet for some various months, I noticed the talkpage and noticed some woo-meisters are trying to add in various fringe theories. One of these users is Craig Weiler a known psi-believer. He's all over the internet stirring this controversy up and he has a lot of nasty comments against wikipedia. Please see here;

[6] and [7] as you can see he's asking other psi-believers to help him out add fringe stuff into Sheldrake's wiki. I believe this is going to end in trouble and suggest this user should be banned. Perhaps you could pass this onto an admin. Thanks. Dan Dan skeptic (talk) 06:14, 2 October 2013 (UTC)

While I was still busy trying to figure out Wikipedia, they were already trying to figure out a way to get rid of me. It was not an auspicious start. Dan_skeptic was right in that I was stirring up controversy. What I was witnessing confirmed my worst fears . . . and then some. There was not the faintest hint of people of different viewpoints working together, meaning that there was not much point in trying to work within the system. I used my blog instead.

I never really believed that it was going to be possible successfully to edit Rupert Sheldrake's biography enough to improve it. It was more productive to write about what was going on, which was analogous to giving the hornet's nest a good swift kick.

It did not take long before the banhammer machinery was put into motion. Another editor, who went by the name of Tumbleman, wrote this:

> What unfolded was surreal, stressful, and without question, cyber bullying. Within two days of discussing the article in talk, I was threatened with banning. Once I was able to overcome that first hurdle – I was then faced with 4 more attempts to remove me from the page. Finally the last one worked. I was banned, for life, from editing Wikipedia. The evidence for my banning was nothing more than a contentious discussion I had 8 years previously on a discussion forum that no longer exists. Additionally, my personal information and identity was outed by these editors, passed around (despite there being clear rules regarding this behavior) and a 'hit piece' was created about me personally on another site. Since then, other editors have been warned that would happened to me, could happen to them if they did not pull back.[162]

It was only a matter of time before they came after me. And sure enough, it did not take very long.

It was October 13ʼ. I got a notice on my home page and was directed to an administrator notice board.[163] A group of the ideologues had gotten together to try to get me banned. According to them I was violating Wikipedia policy by soliciting other people to come to the Sheldrake page. The evidence was unbelievably weak, so I imagine that they were looking for either a sympathetic admin or just sort of throwing whatever they could against the wall to see what would stick.

In any case, I managed to elude their attempt to kick me off of Wikipedia. Tumbleman was not so lucky.

There is actually a set of rules on Wikipedia for how to control an article. It's presented as a kind of joke but as Wikipediocracy puts it:

Editor's note: this essay appeared originally at Wikipedia, where it is accompanied by an elaborate disclaimer which assures the reader that the essay is intended to be humorous and that "**It is not, has never been, nor will ever be, a Wikipedia** policy or guideline. Rather, it illustrates standards or conduct that are generally **not** accepted by the Wikipedia community." Me, I'm not so sure.

1. Do your best to bait, prod, and aggravate somebody on the opposing side of an ideological war from yourself into acting uncivil out of frustration with you. If you have friends, get together with them to gang up on your opponents and get them angry and desperate.

2. When the opponent finally does something that can be construed as a violation of policy, get a friendly admin to block him/her.

3. When the blocked editor uses the means still available to him/her, such as his/her talk page and the e-mail feature, to complain about the unfairness of the block, get your admin friend to bind and gag the editor by removing talk page posting and e-mailing privileges for "trolling" and "harassment".

4. With the editor forcibly silenced and thus unable to speak in his/her defense, hold a lynch mob ban discussion on WP:AN/I, with your friends once again ganging up. This works best when the blocked user lacks friends to gang up on his/her behalf; if that happens, you'd really have drama, but if there aren't any, you'll just get an open-and-shut case where you and your friends say ~~"Burn the witch!"~~ "Ban him/her already!", and a handful of people who like to see a good lynching banning and hang out on that forum for that purpose weigh in too.

5. Now that an editor representing the POV you oppose is banned, make the banned editor into a bogeyman responsible for all that is wrong with Wikipedia, claiming that everything that editor believes in is Communism a "fringe belief" or a "harassment meme", and that no tactic is too extreme to counter this grave threat. They should block all IP addresses in Upper Slobbovia if that's where they think the banned editor is editing from!

6. If anybody else shows up with similar opinions on any subject to the banned editor, try to accuse him/her of being a comrade sockpuppet. If that won't stick, call him/her a meatpuppet and claim that he/she is proxying for the banned editor, and that everything they edit needs to be reverted on sight.

7. If they call this treatment unfair, blacklist ban them too.

8. The larger the body count from the serial banning of advocates of this particular POV gets, the easier it will be to summarily ban anybody new who shows up; just cite the "serial harassment" allegedly committed by people allegedly associated with the new editor.

9. Award barnstars to everyone who jumped on the dogpile![164]

Based on what I saw, the preceding list was almost exactly what I saw happening:

This led me to wonder if perhaps everything the ideologues were doing was designed solely to get people banned. They certainly were experts at gaming the system.

Just as Tumbleman was about to lodge a formal complaint against the skeptics, they struck first, getting a friendly administrator to ban him before he could act or even defend himself. They accused him of sockpuppetry, which is when users have more than one account editing on the same page. This had the added convenience of allowing them to summarily ban a different user, Oh_Boy_Chicken_Again. I knew who Tumbleman was in real life and also knew that he was not the creator of the other account. One was in Los Angeles, the other in Palm Springs.

The process by which Tumbleman was banned was eye opening for the efficiency of the operation. First, they complained and took him to the administrator notice board. Then they got him into arbitration and had an amazing display of cherry picked statements he'd made carefully arranged to make him appear to be disruptive. Then a single administrator ignored the majority of support that he had in arbitration and just banned him.

Just as soon as they got him banned, they then went around squashing any and all attempts to protest his obviously rigged removal. It was chilling.

Getting any changes through the skeptics was a lost cause. When there is a conflict between editors, these are supposed to be resolved through consensus. This is just the sort of wedge that skeptics need to enforce their point of view because they are more organized and interested in proselytizing their ideology than the people they are confronting. By having a larger number of editors on the page never agreeing to consensus and constantly pushing their own point of view, they were able to squash any attempts at cooperation.

The editing was so contentious that an administrator came to the page to try to sort things out, but proved to be useless at the job. This person was no better at effecting any sort of change than if he hadn't been there at all.

Along the way I endured the usual skeptical name calling: "woomeister" "conspiracy theorist," "alleged psychic" and others. The discussions had the feel of talking to High School freshmen who were full of themselves. As they were unable and unwilling to concede a single point or approach any conversation in an adult manner, it made no sense to engage them in discussions.

The constant drama of the Wikipedia editing provided me with five blog posts, each of which created a stir among the skeptics when they came out. I sensed quite a bit of frustration on their part and I drew a lot of skeptical criticism for not editing more. But I didn't see the point in that. The whole endeavor was ridiculously rigged in favor of the ideologues.

It really was a kind of war trying to edit that Wikipedia page. I never imagined that I would find myself staring at so many arbitration pages filled with accusations, but that's how the system rolls. The skeptics, who operated very much as a group, focused far more energy on attacking other editors than they did on working with them.

It did not take me long to wrap up the Wikipedia experience. It didn't take a genius to see that it was a lost cause. I put up one last post on this experiment:

Wikipedia: The Only Way to Win is Not to Play

This is my final post on trying to edit Wikipedia. There is no point to this charade anymore. After having taken a few days to reflect on what was happening, I've come to the same conclusion that many before me have reached as well: *It's not worth the effort.* Wikipedia is systemically broken to the point that trying to edit it is a complete waste of time. Wikipediocracy has compiled A Compendium of Wikipedia

Criticism. It's worth reading. Rupert Sheldrake's biography is no better than when I started and this is despite the efforts of numerous people.

Tumbleman was banned, Oh boy Chicken Again was banned, I was almost banned as was Lou Sander. That is four people who were trying to edit the article to a neutral point of view. Number of opposing editors banned or nearly banned? Zero.

Once you start looking for this type of problem on Wikipedia, the floodgates start to open.

> The Fairy-Tale Cult of Wikipedia, Wikipedia Woes – Pending Crisis as Editors Leave in Droves , The Acta Pauli blog and Wikipedia trolls Snared in the Web of a Wikipedia Liar, The Decline of Wikipedia, Why Wikipedia Can't Work, Tell a Lie Enough Times…, Yet More Problems With Wikipedia, Wikipedia Goes All-In on Transphobia, Wikipedia Bans 1,000 IP Addresses to Silence One Man, The Great Failure of Wikipedia and on and on and on. And remember that there is also an entire organization dedicated to outing all the terrible problems of this Encyclopedia. Wikipediocracy.

These articles, mostly culled from a quick search, go as far back as 2004, with many of the same problems recurring over the years. My articles are merely the latest in a long line of similar criticisms of Wikipedia.

Wikipedia's basic rule structure and philosophy of "anybody can edit" has produced a product that is so easy for ideologues to game that it is frankly useless to oppose them. Ordinary editing only occurs on those subjects where ideologues don't care and have left them alone. Everything else is just a time sink.

I am a fairly good scholar and writer myself. I have a bachelor's in Spanish, which is basically an English degree in another language. I've written over 200 articles for this blog, many of them researched, and learned a lot about sourcing along the way. I have a heavily researched book at the publisher and I am also very well read on parapsychology in general, I have a pretty substantial library of science books that I've read to become better informed.

So imagine how I might perceive this:

OK, so Craig.CSICOP promotes that extraordinary claims require
extraordinary evidence. That is not an unreasonable position. We
cannot take every claim people make at face value; for a start many
such claims are contradictory, so we need to ensure that claims are
passed through a filter to determine what's bullshit and what might
not be. Now, to make extraordinary claims without such evidence
is commonly done by humans. However, once someone's claims
have been assessed by the expert in this area, who point [sic] out
obvious fallacies, those persons who continue to promote such
unsubstantiated fantasies is [sic] all of these things: (1) immensely stupid
or deeply immoral (depending on whether the claimant is being an
idiot or trying to profit in some way despite knowing it's wrong) (2)
disrespectful of expert opinion (3) potentially harmful as regards the
public understanding of science, and (4) potentially harmful to people
with mental health issues. I'm sure you can appreciate that sometimes
things get a little heated when people who take their time to point out
that you are wrong and you respond with (1)(2)(3)(4) above. This btw,
is how Wikipedia works too. Barney the barney barney (talk) 16:16, 1
October 2013 (UTC)

I'm being lectured to by someone who is speaking on a range of
subjects that he is completely ignorant about, but fancies himself to
be an expert. I am supposed to argue my points with this person? And
convince him with facts? I actually made the attempt, but it turned out
exactly as expected. He comes into the discussion on Wikipedia as my
equal and he has other, equally ignorant people to back him up. Now
imagine me trying to reason with a whole group of them and you'll
be able to see the problem. Endless discussions that go nowhere and
that I end up losing because the ignorant people agree with each other.
Voilá, a Wikipedia consensus.

All around the web, people encounter truly bizarre situations on
Wikipedia, such as this attempt by a scholar to get a correction past *a
14 year old administrator.*

I've learned that *Anonymous Dissident,* who removed my links from
the French and German articles on the *Acts of Paul and Thecla,* is
approximately 14 years old. Wow, that's pretty cool Wikipedia! An
approximately 14 year old is able to eliminate a link to this site which is

being published by people with PhDs. Now I'm sure that Anonymous Dissident is very mature for the age of 12 approximately 14, but it does lower the status of Wikipedia considerably when scholars can't even add a little insignificant link to your so-called encyclopedia.

One of the commenters on that blog put the problem very clearly:

The sheer number of people who have had bad experiences is very great, even though it is difficult to find material about this using Google. But even so, there are any number who report being attacked by trolls, of finding their attempts to contribute—and Wikipedia is designed to entice participation, to make doing so addictive—met with violence, of dishonest "administrators", of no rational or sane way to resolve disagreements.

A stellar example of the kind of nonsense I have been putting up with is this attempt to get one single source removed. My argument was simple: There was an experiment involving Rupert Sheldrake and Steve Rose. Rose believed that the results did not support morphic resonance and Sheldrake did. The source being cited was Rose's argument. But Sheldrake also had a rebuttal to that. To cite only Rose and nothing else amounted to cherry picking so Rose's statement had to be taken in context to everything else. I argued that Rose's paper was therefore part and parcel of a primary source which is disallowed on Wikipedia.

What followed was a huge, bloated, mostly off topic discussion that did everything but actually address the point I was making. The skeptical position amounted to "no, we disagree" and that was about it. Why didn't they actually address the issue? Because they didn't have to. On Wikipedia you don't need to argue rationally or provide sufficient facts if other people have your back. There is no authority that differentiates between nonsense and informed discussion. Well, there is, actually, It's the RfC. But figuring out which sources are legitimate requires an expert on the topic, not a bunch of people flying blind. If you are not familiar with the nature of the whole parapsychology controversy then you're probably not going to make a good decision.

There is an administrator on the page, but neither the talk situation nor the article itself have improved *at all* since he's arrived. It's safe to say that he has utterly failed to make any difference.

I'm faced with a question: do I really care enough to battle into eternity with ideologues in the hopes of making a tiny change to a single article? I look to former Wikipedia editor, Abdul-Rahman Lomax, who had this to say about a similarly controversial article he'd been working on:

> [The Wikipedia Arbitration Committee] knows that Wikipedia has problems. What they do is to blame them on "disruptive editors," rather than on lack of functional structure, because it's easy to ban a disruptive editor, difficult to change structure. In fact, they know that it is *very* difficult to change structure, because at various points, the Arbitration Committee tried. They were shouted down, and they had *no spine.*

> ... And that's the real Wikipedia. A radically unreliable structure, massively inefficient—it can take weeks of work to get a simple change through, that should have been obvious from the beginning. . . . That, essentially and long-term, filters out sane editors. . . . The cabal has been able to maintain the Wikipedia article in an obviously poor and confused state because it's not worth going to RfC over hundreds of small changes.

Is it productive for me to try to edit? Definitely not. There is no point in entangling myself in the mess that is Rupert Sheldrake's biography page with the ideologues running the show. I've already been run around in circles a couple of times and I don't care for more of the same. This leaves the other option of trying to learn the system in order to use Wikipedia policy against the ideologues by trying to get them banned or at least soundly rebuked. Again, no. I'm not interested in doing that. It's not my idea of fun. It seems mean spirited and ugly to behave like they do.

The last option is to try to go up the ladder at Wikipedia and see if I can get structural changes in place for this obviously broken system. Here too, my answer is no. It would end up becoming my life's mission and given how deep the problem is and how long it's been going on, it's doubtful that I would accomplish anything anyway. Raging against The Machine is a fool's errand. Wikipedia is not an important part of my life and that's the way it's going to stay. I am not obsessive enough to want to take that on.

I am left with the knowledge that I am shut out of the topic where I have the most expertise. As a result, I am not left with any appealing options for participating on Wikipedia. So I will move on and Wikipedia will continue to deteriorate as a resource. The problem is too big for me to deal with it.

It's time to go outside of the box. "How do we fix Wikipedia?" is the wrong question. It can't be fixed. So whatever happens, it has to be something else.

> The solution is to remove [Wikipedia founder Jimmy] Wales from the equation, get rid of all the "administrators"/trolls/ children, and get rid of the system where the REAL system administrators remain unknown. Instead, introduce a fair, sane, and transparent system of governance, run by responsible people who do so under their own names in an accountable manner. I fear that only the government can do this. Little as I like the idea, I suspect that it needs to do so. Wikipedia is a howling success at gathering information, because of its contributors. It is a terrible failure in most other respects.

I don't have the answer, but there is at least one stopgap measure that's been suggested: I have heard several people mention that the Rupert Sheldrake Biography should be deleted from Wikipedia because it's impossible for him to be treated fairly. I find that hard to argue with. Not having any article on Wikipedia has to be better for Rupert (and perhaps many other notable people) than being slandered like this. And there it is: The only way to win is not to play. [165]

(For the print edition the original blog post and its links can be found at weilerpsiblog.wordpress.com)

All along the way my posts were getting noticed, mostly by people who were dealing with similar bullying issues on Wikipedia. The news site Reality Sandwich picked up a collection of my articles and created one of their own. But this last one somehow stood out. Deepak Chopra referenced it in an article he wrote for the *Huffington Post* and other major news sites.

If the powers that be at Wikipedia took notice of this kerfuffle, they gave no sign of it. That wasn't surprising. Criticism has been raining down on Wikipedia for years and they've managed to ignore it this entire time. This really wasn't all that different.

In some ways, Wikipedia is a microcosm of the overall zeitgeist regarding parapsychology and related topics. It mirrors the struggle occurring in the scientific world and demonstrates the futility of civil discussion. As I stated earlier, this scientific field has a fighting chance against the misinformation and outright lies that find their way onto Wikipedia articles about non mainstream science because it's the most mature of all non-mainstream sciences and it has a rather large public that knows this. It's relatively easy to convince unbiased people of the legitimacy of parapsychology because of the large volume of scientific studies and the fact that so many people have psychic experiences.

Eventually, the barrage of bad information, slanderous biographies and ideologue slanted articles will catch up with Wikipedia. Ideologues really excel at making enemies and because they "own" Wikipedia, the encyclopedia itself is making enemies. This will eventually be its downfall if it doesn't change.

Most people know not to rely on Wikipedia and check alternative sourcing if they really want to fact check something. Wikipedia does have a disclaimer that their information should not be trusted, but because of their placement on Google search, it's still quite possible that millions of people around the world are still relying on it. My guess is that either a better encyclopedia will somehow overtake Wikipedia by having a rule system that rewards expertise or that Wikipedia will finally change when they start running out of enough donations to operate. It's really that bad.

Update for 2020

Not much has changed in the intervening years at Wikipedia. If anything, the number of editors has shrunk and consolidated, with fewer new editors coming in, making ever more unlikely that sanity will be restored.

Women are still vastly under-represented on Wikipedia and still struggle to get articles written about prominent women. It's not uncommon for them to get marked for deletion soon after they're put up.[166]

Sometime shortly after the TED controversy, parapsychologist Stephan Schwartz threatened to sue Wikipedia for his slanderous biography and demanded its removal. He was successful and has no biography on Wikipedia to this day.

Stanley Krippner, who participated in the Maimonides dream studies gave me this personal account of his recent efforts to clean up his Wikipedia biography:

"It is notable that in the COMMENTS section, Wikipedia focuses only on my parapsychology work. They do not cite favorable book reviews on, for example, Post-Traumatic Stress Disorder: Biography of a Disease. They ignore my publications in humanistic psychology, hypnosis, and dreams. They simply focus on the dream telepathy work I did half a century ago. And they ignore the recent meta analysis that shows our work has been successfully replicated. On the website for Montague Ullman, they ignore his pioneering work in psychotherapy, community mental health, and dream education. They simply debunk his work in dream telepathy."

… "Wikipedia cites a book by a scoffer in which he says that the participants in our dream telepathy studies were shown the picture before they went to sleep in our laboratory. But if they were shown the picture, this could not be telepathy. Right? Numerous reviewers of the book pointed out the error. But Wikipedia limits the correction to a statement by me! So an uniformed reader will think that OF COURSE I denied it. The book's second edition made the same mistake, long after the error had been pointed out in other book reviews."

… "The revisions simply made corrections. And the revision included two statements about our work by the Amazing Randi and Ray Hyman, two arch-scoffers. But their statements were very favorable to me and so were not included."

Stanley

The basic point to be made here is that structurally, Wikipedia is the same as it ever was and during the intervening six years there hasn't been any serious attempt to change the culture. The tone deafness is pretty strong. A 2018 article in The Wikipedian asks "Why Aren't There More Wikipedia Editors."[167] In this article are listed many reasons why people aren't getting involved, from not being writers to not being interested in clerical work. In another section they list the barriers to entry, such as complexity and an unwillingness to take criticism. It addresses harassment, sort of, without drawing any conclusions. Frankly, the article whitewashes the topic.

There is almost a tone of condescension towards new editors that they need to try harder and be part of the team. There is one point made in the article to "Stop over-policing contributions and under-policing behavior" which is actually good advice. Wikipedia is terrible at policing behavior. But this too is whitewashed with an admonition to "focus on the edit, not on the editor."

At no point does it get to the meat of the problem: Wikipedia is downright hostile to new editors, especially women. Many editors can't be reasoned with and there is no adult supervision to hold them in check. These volunteers have created a byzantine rule structure, fight any attempt to make the site easier to use and fight any revision to "their" pages. It makes it very unwelcoming to anyone new and as this work is purely voluntary, it is extremely easy just to quit. But it can be even worse than that.

One of the personal outcomes for me in joining in on the Wikipedia "experience" was that I will forever have a slanderous "biography" online attached to me. It's the first thing that comes up when you Google my name.

The site is called RationalWiki and because it's a Wiki with lots and lots of citations, it rises to the top of search results. It lists me first and foremost as an "is an American conspiracy theorist and parapsychology activist, known for posting anti-skeptic rants on the internet. He describes himself as a "psychic healer".

And it goes on to cherry pick various bits and pieces from my 20 years on forums, blogs and other sites on line to paint a very bad picture of me for the world. There is nothing I can do about it. It's not technically libel because it refers to citations of things that I wrote. A lawsuit in the United States would be ill advised.

In particular it pulls an old quote I made regarding 9/11. I'm a general building contractor with over 20 years' experience and while I do not subscribe to any particular theory about how the towers fell, I do know enough about buildings to know that the collapses required quite a bit of help to happen the way they did. It's the kind of thing that requires technical expertise to notice. I'm not interested in who or why.

That is enough to get anyone labeled as a conspiracy theorist whether they subscribe to a conspiracy or not.

The biography goes on to claim that I know nothing about science. It all has the look and feel of a 14-year-old throwing a temper tantrum.

(I am basically self-taught, but well enough to be invited to join the Parapsychological Association.)

You can do this sort of thing to anyone who writes a lot, particularly on controversial topics, and especially if you can pull something from any time in their on-line life. I'm not a public figure and I haven't censored myself as if I were.

By leaving off positive things and loading up on negative ones it's not hard to smear someone. Perhaps the only redeeming quality this has is that it's so over the top hateful that I can't imagine anyone taking it seriously.

While it is certainly no fun to have your name smeared like that, in my case it is utterly unimportant and has had zero effect on my personal and professional life. I work off referrals and personal connections and no one looking for me will care at all about some rant online complaining about me and my book because it's utterly irrelevant to my business and personal life.

This kind of on line trash talking works only in specific situations.

Online I have also specifically targeted skeptics for criticism, so some blowback is to be expected. Anyone who knows of me on the Internet will be unsurprised that I have been targeted and criticized by the people I am criticizing.

Someone who did not fare so well is Tumbleman, who was doxed by Wikipedia editors. He is Rome Viharo in real life. Viharo makes his living online and having his name show up on RationalWiki troubled him because it could affect his professional life. He got on RationalWiki and struggled to make his biography better, but he was not in control of it and, from the looks of it, just ended up getting more of their attention, which is not a good thing at all. His "biography" is huge compared with mine and filled with far more nonsense.

Viharo is arguably even less notable than I am, particularly when it comes to parapsychology and related topics. I, on the other hand, am deeply involved and have this book, my blog and membership in the Parapsychological Association. I've written about parapsychology almost nonstop for 10 years. There is some basis there for them to write about me.

Viharo, though, basically went to Wikipedia, tried to edit Sheldrake's page and got immediately banned. And that was their basis for going after him and trying to destroy him professionally. He really hadn't done much of anything to deserve it.

The motivation for such an over the top attack may have something to do with outing the Guerrilla Skeptics. Sheldrake mentioned them and his bio was attacked, and my RationalWiki bio and Viharo's both highlight how crazy we are for suspecting this group. In Viharo's case it's mentioned in the first paragraph.

> **Rome Viharo** (User:RomeViharo) is a disgruntled ex-Wikipedia editor who was banned and then created an entire website named Wikipedia We Have A Problem to pointlessly complain about his ban and whine about "harassment". Although complaining of being harassed, Viharo does the exact same thing and has doxed Wikipedia editors on his website, while also spreading rumours (e.g. skeptics create articles on Wikipedia by receiving PayPal cash-payments,[1] or RationalWiki "is gas lighting, lying, & covering up cross platform harassment"[2]) and the Guerilla Skepticism conspiracy theory.

For me, it's a subject heading. Note how eloquently they make their case that I'm wrong.

Guerrilla Skepticism on Wikipedia

See the main article on this topic: Guerrilla Skepticism on Wikipedia

In October 2013 Weiler published a blog post titled "The Wikipedia Battle for Rupert Sheldrake's Biography", claiming that Sheldrake's Wikipedia bio was being targeted by a group called Guerrilla Skepticism on Wikipedia.

It wasn't.

Someone sure is trying very hard to convince the world that the Guerilla Skeptics are above suspicion.

Viharo was understandably annoyed. The hardest part of dealing with these zealots is that they get themselves into a position of controlling the narrative and it's very difficult if not impossible (at least in the case of Wikipedia and RationalWiki) for dissent to get anywhere near the same platform.

So Viharo created a website: Wikipedia, We Have A Problem. He has used the platform to out at least one of the RationalWiki editors and document Wikipedia problems and generally be a pain in the ass to the zealots. He was still at it as of November 2018.

Had they just left him alone it would have been a lot less trouble for everyone.

The thing about these "biographies" is that they are unambiguously harassment. They are a direct attempt to intimidate and punish people who have tried to edit Wikipedia in a direction that these skeptic/zealots disagree with. An important distinction here is that this harassment goes beyond Wikipedia itself and is designed specifically to have real world consequences.

In fact, a quick search through RationalWiki reveals that this mechanism for slander is used constantly by Wikipedia editors. A quick search revealed several of these "biographies." Just within 2 months there were 17 of them. At this level of production, they would be slandering and cyber-bullying about 100 people a year. It's conceivable that they've done this to over 500 people.

And this is how low Wikipedia has sunk. In a certain sense, Wikipedia is dying. The statistics for 2018 showed a whopping 10% drop in new editors while the number of active and very active editors basically stayed the same. That is stagnation. Worse, the number of administrators has been declining since 2008. After a high of almost a thousand in 2007, they were down to 515 at the end of 2018. There are about 3,500 very active editors, which, given the size of the encyclopedia is a very small number. (They're the group that counts. Active editors are defined as more than 5 edits in a month.) This is an indication of Wikipedia becoming dangerously insular.

CHAPTER FOURTEEN
MESSY DIVORCE: A TEDX BECOMES AN EX

O ne of the original skeptics to start this mess, Jerry Coyne, took it upon himself to up the ante. On March 22, he put out a blog post criticizing TEDxWestHollywood, in his usual over the top style denouncing it all as "sciencey sounding woo."[168] He encouraged other skeptics to join him in encouraging TED to shut down this independent program. It seems to have worked.

This was the point of no return for TED. What they did next pushed the controversy from a minor one to a major one. It was generally acknowledged at this point that both Graham Hancock and Rupert Sheldrake were actually benefiting from the controversy. Their "banned" speeches were now posted elsewhere on the web and collectively were dwarfing everything else TED had at that time in terms of numbers of views. The speakers were garnering a lot of positive attention and support and, as a result, their reputations were not harmed. But the takedown of TEDxWestHollywood was different. They were about to cause someone real financial harm . . . and for no good reason. I stumbled upon this quite by accident.

On March 27 I was cruising the Hancock TED thread when I saw this comment, on something I had written, from Suzanne Taylor, who was the organizer for TEDxWestHollywood:

Oh Craig – I am such a fan of yours. Every time someone else appreciates you, I want to be that person's friend. You are the best sense-maker.

You don't know the half of it—well, actually you only know half of it. They want to cancel my program. Reason: "We are not comfortable with it." I kid you not. That's all. Repeated over and over on the phone as to why. No more, except there are objections to some speakers, but, "We're not naming names." I must be joking, right? Can an organization have Alzheimer's? Doesn't it know this adds fuel to its fire? Something we don't understand is going on.

Am fighting with TED. More later.

I replied:

Dear God. That is lunacy.

If you like, I can get a blog post out about this and get the word out. I have quite the following these days. It's big news and it will travel fast.

That is, of course, somewhat of a bridge-burner, so it's something to think over carefully before you go that route.

Judging by the flavor of comments I've seen from TED staff on these comments, they seem incredibly tone deaf and arrogant. Businesses normally respond quickly and positively to this much outrage. These are, after all, customers.

Not only that, but the kind of people making a fuss on these boards are not followers, but trend setters. They're the first people to explore new things and new ideas and they influence other, more conservative people around them. That's the worst sort of group to piss off; they take a lot of people with them.

Fortunately, we were in a sub-sub thread that most people would never see. I did not want this to continue to be a public conversation. Shortly thereafter, Suzanne emailed me:

Craig, you are the ally of my dreams. I was praying you would pick up on me. I so love your mind. Where is your body?

This figures to be a huge story. Don't think I don't know that. How to roll it out? Am cautious online right now, and just dropped my little bomb with you as a starter as I await resolution with TED.

We are scrambling to do our event and to Livestream it. We will have a fabulous program if I can hang onto my speakers, and, since my purpose in doing TEDx was to deliver material that would encourage a new worldview, we still can achieve that purpose if we get a large worldwide audience which hopefully the ruckus will deliver. (I can archive it now, so time zones all over the world can get it – something I couldn't do with TED.) I don't want to self-promote to inflate myself, but you don't know me or know how good my program is so let me just tell you I am a Phi Beta Kappa, summa cum laude graduate of NYU, and woo woo is not my game. Outside the box is. You can get a flavor of me from the blog I've been neglecting lately: http://www.TheConversation.org. PS: Graham and Rupert are personal friends.

I'll forward what has taken place in email, in-between phone conversations with Lara at TED. On top of being out to lunch in how they are cutting off heads, on the phone calls they are incredibly nasty.

Suzanne did indeed send me emails she had received from TED, which she said were not indicative of the hostile tone of the phone conversations she'd participated in.

Dear Suzanne,

Thanks for taking my call. As we discussed back in December and again last week, your program plans for TEDxWestHollywood are cause for concern.

TEDx events are supposed to adhere to our scientific guidelines. You have described your program this way: "Brother, Can You Spare a Paradigm?" will deal with the need to change our fundamental value system or worldview to one in which humanity pulls together, superseding the current worldview where whoever has the most toys wins. The new ideation will be based on what science tells us is a quantum universe, with everything being interconnected and interdependent—one organism that needs to function for the good of the whole."

This language alone raises a red flag. (Characterizing the universe as a single organism is really not an accepted teaching of quantum physics.) And when we look at your speaker line-up, we see several people who promote—as fact—theories that are well outside what most scientists would accept as credible. We're not saying all the speakers are off-base. Perhaps you could make a case for each of them individually. But when we look at the program as a whole, it's clear that it doesn't meet our guidelines.

The problem is not the challenging of orthodox views. We believe in that. We've had numerous talks which do that. But we have rules about the presentation of science on the TEDx stage. We disallow speakers who use the language of science to claim they have proven the truth of ideas that are speculative and which have failed to gain significant scientific acceptance.

More than 2000 TEDx events will take place in the year ahead. If your program is allowed to proceed, it will truly damage other TEDx organizers' ability to recruit scientists and other speakers. (Indeed many in the TED and TEDx communities have already reached out to us to express their concern.)

We have reluctantly concluded that your program is not appropriate for TEDx, and we have to therefore terminate your license. You are of course welcome to still hold an event with these speakers. You just can't associate it with TEDx. We are happy to work with you to figure out how to smoothly transition it into an event under a different name. I'll be happy to speak with you directly to facilitate this.

Thanks,
Lara Stein
TED Conferences
Director TEDx & TED Prize

Suzanne responded to this email:

This is not an adequate communication two weeks before a program that has been a year in the making. No speaker in our program is dealing in pseudo-science, and your accusation, to begin to be discussable, needs to have names in it. There is no one on our program who would be an embarrassment to the TED brand, and if you have any specific concerns I'd be happy to discuss them with you.

Physicist Russell Targ, for example, whom you earlier pointed to as questionable, is presenting research on the nature of extra sensory perception. While the subject is controversial, his work has been published in IEEE, Nature, Proceedings of the American Association for the Advancement of Science, and Proceedings of the American Institute for Physics, refereed journals that found it acceptable. This is one of many quotes from the Sheldrake/Hancock dialogues that speaks to the situation that Targ could be thought to be in: "...'science' should not be treated like a religion. 'Scientific truths' are constantly changing. Serious scholars swore that no such thing as bacteria exist, airplanes could never fly, steamships were impossible, we could never get to the moon or survive in outer space, computers were a useless invention, etc etc etc. How many proposals were heavily criticized by leading figures, only to eventually turn into proven realities? Just in the last 100 years, how many inventors and researchers were considered lunatics before their inventions or theories won acceptance?" With TED dealing in ideas worth spreading, wouldn't that include more work that's on the cutting edge than old ideas that are mainstream now?

About your summary dismissal, people don't get sent to jail without being able to defend themselves, and nowhere in my agreement to abide by your rules is there any warning about the possibility of your pulling a program at the last minute. My TEDx is as proposed months ago, with special attention I've paid to vetting the talks, after you expressed concerns, to be certain they didn't stray into unacceptable territory. Not only have my team and I donated innumerable hours to making this an outstanding program, but the fall-out of your dismissal goes well beyond me, with twenty people having been preparing TED talks premised upon the agreement I have with you in which no last minute cancellation was contemplated.

However, if you supply me with the money to rent the space that is being donated by the city of West Hollywood, and cover the expense of putting on my program, I will go ahead and do it without TED. We were operating on a budget of $20,000—$10,000 from sponsors and $10,000 from ticket sales that would become uncertain without the TED brand. So, $20,000, plus the in-kind value of $5,600 that West Hollywood has put on the donated venue, would be acceptable.

At the time, Suzanne was asking for what she felt was a reasonable settlement in order for the show to go forward, which had to occur to protect her professional reputation as an event producer. Were the program to be completely cancelled it could affect who would work with her in the future. This matters a great deal. In public communications, TED stated that this was only one of two programs they ever had cancelled, and with this one being the only one cancelled when it was ready to deliver, the implication was that it had to be a serious failure.

Up to this point TED had made no monetary offers to compensate Suzanne for her very real financial loss. This is something that I just fail to understand to this day. Why not negotiate in good faith, give her a decent settlement possibly contingent on a confidentiality agreement and make the whole problem just GO AWAY as quickly and quietly as possible?

They did not do this and, as a result, Suzanne Taylor did not go quietly into the night.

Suzanne was known as the Crop Circle Queen (an affectionate title). In the late 1980s, she became interested in the crop circle phenomenon and eventually engaged an Academy Award nominated documentary filmmaker to direct her movie, "CROP CIRCLES: Quest For Truth." She went on to make a second film, this time as Producer/Director, "What on Earth? Inside the Crop Circle Mystery," and has affectionately come to be known as "The Crop Circle Queen."

Like pretty much everyone who explores taboo subjects, she had grown highly resistant to the constant bullying, intimidation and aggression of skeptics, so the standard lawyerly tactics that it seemed TED was employing were, by comparison, rather tame. If they thought that they could steamroll Suzanne, they were mistaken.

I made my position clear in an email:

Would it help or hinder you if I publicized your struggles with TED? I am not sure from the answer you gave me what to do. I could read it either way. In any case, **I will do nothing until I am absolutely certain that you want me to proceed. This is totally your call.**

Suzanne was in a crunch and had to decide on a course of action. The deadline for her event was locked in and unchangeable even if nearly everything else was. She had several notable speakers, all of whom had slotted that particular date for her and lining all of them up again might take another year. That drop-dead date was approaching, and she had a lot of work to do. Everything, from a location, to catering, to dealing with all the speakers about the lost license, had to be resolved in very short order. If she wanted publicity, she had to cash in on the notoriety she had received by being banned by TED, RIGHT NOW. I came in as she was attempting to get TED to cover her costs and draw attention to her program. From my perspective, it did look as though she was being forced into a confrontation. She wrote to me:

I look forward to your making this very public—whatever they ultimately do with me—but timing is the question. They have not responded to my email this morning and I suspect now I'm not going to hear, which will be the cue for you. Will try one more email and get back to you. (...)

It appeared that TED was taking a familiar corporate approach to dealing with someone who is asking for compensation. They attempt to put the individual into a financial hole where they will be forced to bargain from a position of weakness.

I was a bit excited at the thought of scooping this. I knew that the post would be big news and I was eager to be part of it. I didn't share this with Suzanne at the time because I wanted to be sure for my own reasons that she came to this decision of her own accord.

On March 28, Suzanne sent me this email:

Craig—Feels like time to go public. You have the exclusive.

Am on my nickel. Marianne and Dossey and Targ are on board in fighting spirits, with Dossey comparing TED's action to a Star Chamber. I need to secure the other speakers. It's important to get viewers for the Livestream.

It was time to write the blog post with the stunning news. It was Thursday and I wouldn't be able to crank it out until the weekend. In the meantime, TED responded to Suzanne with a settlement offer of $10,000 dollars once it was clear that she wasn't going to go away.

This was a fairly significant point of contention. TED only wanted to assume the out-of-pocket costs she had already incurred, not the true cost of salvaging the production she was about to put on. It's hard to interpret the intent of TED in this case. Was this censorship? Or were they merely being cheap?

On the question of withdrawing your license: To recap what Lara shared with you: We have —http://www.ted.com/pages/view/ id/493#speakers—about the content presented on the TEDx stage; the claims presented in our talks need to stand up to scrutiny from the scientific community. As we explained—both on the phone in December and in subsequent conversations—the language in your original program (which I see you have now modified) raised a red flag. And when we looked at your speaker line-up, we saw several people who promote—as fact—theories that are well outside what most scientists would accept as credible. We're not saying all the speakers are off-base. But the program, taken as a whole, was not appropriate for TEDx.

We sought to counsel you over the last few months that the program was raising red flags; you took a hard line in response. As more and more details of the program became public, it finally became clear we could not allow this event to proceed under TEDx branding. This is our curatorial judgment, and we stand by it.

We also have the right to do so. The TEDx rules make it clear that certain types of content are disallowed at TEDx events. The license you signed as a TEDx organizer makes it very clear that you need to follow the rules, and explicitly explains that a license can be revoked for such a breach. If you review the license— http://www.ted.com/pages/tedx_license_agreement—you'll see that TED also has the right to terminate your license, at our sole discretion. **We don't take this decision lightly**, but it is well within our rights.

Suzanne had been planning and working with TED for about a year at that point, well before the new rules came into effect. In my opinion, TED would have been entirely justified in grandfathering her program in and, while the skeptics would have squawked about that, TED's reputation wouldn't have been damaged. Previously, the agreement TED had with Suzanne was that TED would not put any speeches they found disagreeable up on their main video site. Up until her program was cancelled, it was Suzanne's understanding that this was her only jeopardy.

With regards to the money, Suzanne eventually decided against a legal battle as the cost and the risk of such were too high. The clause in their license that says they can cancel a program for no reason is superseded by ordinary contract law which prohibits acting capriciously, which TED was certainly guilty of. Nor was Suzanne in violation of any of the rules despite TED's characterizing her program as unacceptable. Just as Rupert and Graham were not in violation of TED's tenets, neither were Suzanne's speakers.

If a speaker has peer reviewed, scientific research that they've published in science journals, then by definition it is not pseudoscience. Further clouding the issue is that TED had no idea what the speakers actually were going to say. They were merely relying on a vague understanding of the speakers' general area of expertise. TED never checked into the actual talks that were going to be given. Scientists tend to couch their language in neutral objective terms and be very conservative about their word choices; they are not likely to outright promote a point of view, but rather say things such as "the evidence points to," and, "it appears that." A person speaking in this manner is sharing ideas, not promoting an ideology. That's not an insignificant difference. And it is puzzling as to why Marianne Williamson was on their questionable list since she isn't a scientist, doesn't speak about science, and, in fact, a few weeks after Suzanne's event she went on to do a TEDx talk at another venue.

Suzanne was also accused of taking a hard line, which underscores the cultural differences at play. TED was taking the skeptical position that mainstream science rejects these ideas as not credible . . . etc. Suzanne on the other hand, is someone who has seen first-hand that the mainstream position isn't always credible itself, so she naturally pushed TED to explain exactly what was wrong with her speakers. Skeptics typically don't like their core assumptions challenged so this was probably seen as a "hard line" that Suzanne had drawn.

Suzanne replied to this email with her usual directness:

Thank you, June, for your kindly tone, which is different from other people's communications. TED needs to send some people to charm school.

But, I don't want to play on your terms and don't want to have to rehash the reasons why. You speak naively as if not understanding the tremendous power of TED and the desirability of association with it. If you think you can get the city of West Hollywood to give me their $5,600 venue, you are out of touch. And, I wouldn't have produced an event without TED—it's been more than a year where this has been my major focus, all done as a volunteer to be part of the TED family, as just one example of what goes beyond simplistic ideas.

I don't think what TED has done to me will hold up to any scrutiny. To yank a program so close to its delivery, making it herculean to deliver anything in its stead even if the producing entity (me) had any desire to deliver anything aside from a TEDx event, I believe would be considered unconscionable. Your tax exemption, if like mine, is based in language that makes you treat everyone fairly or risk losing the exemption, and what you are engaging in is punitive treatment of me. There never was a risk expressed to me of the program being pulled, and every directive I got I conformed with. In fact, I was told that if TED didn't like my talks they wouldn't be on the YouTube Channel—with no intimation that the program could be cancelled. If TED is sorry they created me, in my opinion they need to take responsibility for their foolishness.

There were emails between Suzanne and TED on the 29th as it became clear to TED that this problem was not going as planned. After Suzanne produced the relevant section of California law that TED was violating, TED upped its offer to $20,000, including a confidentiality agreement, and offered to mention the Livestream of the show on their blog.

Hi Suzanne,

Yes, I believe there may be a similar clause in NY law, and in any case, these are fine words for any business to live by! We do, actually believe strongly in upholding a covenant of good faith and fair dealing. And as I mentioned in my last brief note, I do truly appreciate the effort and energy you've put into the program over the last year. I hear where you're coming from on that, and on the impact of hosting a non-TED vs. a TED event.

On the money side it was your typical corporate maneuver. Offer a little, offer a little more, constantly assert that you're being very reasonable.

So, given what I saw here, I did a late-night conference with the team, and I'd like to propose a solution: We're willing to offer you $15,000 flat for your sunk costs. This is on the generous side, based on your budget, but would give you some leeway around the fluctuating costs, like catering. Then we'd cover up to $5000 *more* for the venue. But we'll need to see the invoice for that, after the fact. This would take you to a total of $20,000.

This is what you would normally expect a business to do in this situation; parsimonious negotiation is just how business is done. However in this context, with the Sheldrake/Hancock controversy going full bore, the bad publicity was going to be huge if this gambit failed. This is something that they should have foreseen.

Graham Hancock, who had been party to these emails, had this comment:

Hi Suzanne

Very interesting development. So it's worth $20,000 to them "to officially put an end to the matter (and I know we will both be grateful for that). So, as awkward as these are, it would have to be a standard legal settlement, with standard settlement terms, like release of claims, confidentiality, non-disparagement. We can come up with some workable language for publicly explaining the split with TEDx."

Emphasis on "confidentiality". They quite badly—$20,000-worth—want to silence you and negate in advance any negative fallout for them. This is like one of those companies that pollute and kill and then do out-of-court non-disclosure deals with the victims to keep them quiet.

Again, and again TED present themselves as champions of truth and light and behave like the biggest, most harmful corporations.

The more I learn about TED the less respect I have for them.

Lots of love
Graham

At this point, any doubts Suzanne had about going forward with publicizing the removal of her license were no longer preventing her from going public. On March 29, we focused on the final revisions to the post and I waited to post it until she got a donate button up on her site. On Saturday morning, I hit send and the post went on line:

TED Not Satisfied With Current Censorship: TEDxWestHollywood is Taken Down

TED, the parent organization, *is removing the license* of TEDxWestHollywood only a couple of weeks before their planned event "Brother, Can You Spare a Paradigm" after they had spent more than a year preparing. Tickets are already on sale. After summarily dismissing the program with no recompense at all for monies that had been expended, they amended their stance to offer a fraction of the operating costs in compensation and all because they deem the program to be . . . wait for it . . . unscientific. Does this sound familiar? It does indeed. This is the same charge that was leveled at Rupert Sheldrake and Graham Hancock when TED first pulled their videos. (Link here.)

In an email to Suzanne Taylor, the organizer of TEDxWestHollywood, a representative of TED outlined the objections:

(...) And when we look at your speaker line-up, we see several people who promote—as fact—theories that are well outside what most scientists would accept as credible. We're not saying all the speakers are off-base. Perhaps you could make a case for each of them individually. But when we look at the program as a whole, it's clear that it doesn't meet our guidelines. The problem is not the challenging of orthodox views. We believe in that. We've had numerous talks which do that. But we have rules about the presentation of science on the TEDx stage. We disallow speakers who use the language of science to claim they have proven the truth of ideas that are speculative and which have failed to gain significant scientific acceptance.

More than 2000 TEDx events will take place in the year ahead. If your program is allowed to proceed, it will truly damage other TEDx organizers' ability to recruit scientists and other speakers. (Indeed many in the TED and TEDx communities have already reached out to us to express their concern.)

We have reluctantly concluded that your program is not appropriate for TEDx, and we have to therefore terminate your license. You are of course welcome to still hold an event with these speakers. You just can't associate it with TEDx. We are happy to work with you to figure out how to smoothly transition it into an event under a different name. I'll be happy to speak with you directly to facilitate this.

This line in particular is telling:

Perhaps you could make a case for each of them individually. But when we look at the program as a whole, it's clear that it doesn't meet our guidelines.

It's basically an admission that the parent organization is not prepared to argue their case factually. As science is, at its most fundamental level, about the facts and details, it's rather curious that they would make a case for being on the side of science, but avoid addressing the science. It's the same thing they're doing with the Sheldrake/Hancock controversy. Sheldrake has asked for an opportunity to debate, but has been met with silence.

So what is the fuss all about? (here is her lineup of speakers.) Although TED refused to "name names" in their dismissal, whereby an argument could be made, it surely has to do with three of the speakers who are scientists, about whom they earlier had raised eyebrows asking for justification for their place on the program with the caution that if they weren't pleased with the end results they would not post the talks on their

YouTube page. Pulling the program was never brought up. The three are: Russell Targ, who will talk on the reality of ESP and Larry Dossey, who will talk on the revolution in consciousness and Marilyn Schlitz, who is a social anthropologist and psi researcher, speaking on "How do we shift our paradigm." All three have the proper credentials along with ability to speak to the evidence and present their views using credible science. They, more than the other speakers, represent the real threat to the materialists/skeptics at TED. However, in addition, TED also had objections to Marianne Williamson and Paul Nugent although neither was giving a science talk. This is the pertinent email to Suzanne Taylor:

> We will be especially interested to hear about the ideas that Marianne Williamson, Russell Targ, Larry Dossey, Paul Nugent, and Marilyn Schlitz will be presenting. We feel that the pseudoscience struggle is an important one. TED and TEDx cannot be platforms that give undo legitimacy to false evidence and selective logic—regardless of brilliant packaging.

You can now add these speakers to the growing list of people that TED is using its influence to censor via withdrawing their support.

My best guess is that TED intends to take down the Sheldrake and Hancock talks at the end of the debate, but would not have much of a case if they went ahead and allowed the lineup of the TEDxWestHollywood event. Allowing Larry Dossey and Russell Targ, but censoring Sheldrake and Hancock would not make any sense at all. They seem to be on a slash and burn campaign dedicated to preserving their materialistic point of view, even though it has become increasingly indefensible over the years.

From a business standpoint, TED is destroying their brand with this nonsense. With their motto, "ideas worth spreading" it looks like the worst sort of hypocrisy to the people who disagree with them. It is a bad idea to piss off such a large section of their audience. This part of their audience by the way, is the demographic that seeks out novel ideas and experiments with new things. They are early adopters; the trend setters. This group, that TED is antagonizing, is the absolute sweet spot of marketing. If they abandon TED, the company will suffer disproportionally for their loss. And for what? To defend an ideology? It's madness.

What these actions by TED mean to the large group of people, including myself, who support these ideas about consciousness and physics, is that we are being totally disrespected. Our ideas are deemed unscientific for essentially nonsense reasons; we're labeled anti-science, woo or other similar derogatory terms; they censor our popular speakers and won't even defend their position. The completely reprehensible action that TED is taking against TEDxWestHollywood is the most egregious example of this. We have enough influence and power right now to make them regret this and this is a good place to draw that line in the sand. We don't have to take it anymore.

(For the print edition, blog post and its links can be found at weilerpsiblog.wordpress.com)

This particular piece of news was huge. I got more views on my blog in a single day than I had in any previous month. The news travelled quickly around the web with many more bloggers passing along the news.

Now, Sheldrake and Hancock had company: Larry Dossey, Russell Targ, and Marilyn Schlitz who wasn't even going to talk on the subject of parapsychology. (As it turns out, Marilyn Schiltz dropped out of the program for unrelated reasons and did not want to be part of the controversy.)

Just putting the post up didn't mean that we were done. I knew that my own blog would not get the story very far even with the enormous amount of traffic it was generating. It was not enough oomph to get the story big enough for the mainstream press to get interested.

So, I started writing to whomever I thought might be sympathetic. With large news organizations, my attempts to get some traction went into a black hole. Suzanne, who seems to know everyone in the whole world, sent Arianna Huffington a missive to try and generate interest. No response. I even tried Oprah Winfrey. Hey, why not? Reality Sandwich did pick up on the story and so did The Daily Grail but these are not mainstream publications. From there, my efforts went cold in making it a bigger story.

And, across the hall in the irony department, the single biggest contributor to the spread of information about the TEDxWestHollywood takedown was skeptic Jerry Coyne, who basically just copied my blog while adding comments that were very disparaging to Suzanne and her event, and *got into the top ten blogs on Wordpress.*[169] I was linked as "an angry pro-PSI blog, " which is a very petty and biased way to cite the person whose work you're basically copying.

I've been coming to the realization that it will take some time for the full import of this story to be recognized. This was an entirely irrational act on the part of TED because it wasn't based on the science that they purported to support.

We did get some mainstream interest, but no one really grasped the significance of what was going on. *LA Times* reporter Chris O'Brien published a relatively neutral piece in the business section (because this was a local issue) and some British papers wrote pieces, but TED escaped any widespread criticism due to the complexity of the issues involved. Online, many pro-psi blogs picked up on it, as did many skeptical ones, but while each person might contribute something worthwhile to the discussion, all were preaching to their choirs.

Some notable people picked up on the story on their blogs, like Ray Kurzweil,[170] who is famous for his work in artificial intelligence, who understood the situation and wrote very favorably to our perspective. And Deepak Chopra was joined by several prominent scientists, including Nobel Prize winner Brian Josephson, in a condemnation of TED' actions for a blog post on The *Huffington Post.*[171]

Support also came from other quarters, like Steve Allen Media, who specialize in PR with a conscience and donated their efforts to help get the word out.

The basic problem with the mainstream media was that they saw the story on the surface, "TED axes one of their programs for pseudo-science" and didn't look any further. Had they scratched the surface, they would have discovered that TED actually had no reasons at all for taking down TEDxWestHollywood. But this was complicated and led down a rabbit hole, which no mainstream journalist had the time to travel. The TED controversy marked the beginning of the end for materialism. Their best argument was no argument, so that battle was lost. It also marks the beginning of new era for science, but that is a different story.

On April 1, TED put out a blog post on the withdrawal of the TEDxWestHollywood license, which followed the by now familiar path of saying a great deal while explaining almost nothing. "Our assessment was that it didn't meet the TEDx guidelines for solid science."[172] was about as close as it got. The TED staff opened up another comment section to discuss this, but it seems as if the pressure of all the negative responses was getting to them and they closed it a week early (which was a week before the ExTEDxWestHollywood program was going to take place) rather than endure the blowback.

> This topic is being closed one week early, due to an overwhelming level of personal attacks and other violations of our community rules.[173]

To a certain extent, this was true, although those personal attacks were mostly coming from TED supporters, not the other way around. One person, who went by the name John Hoopes, engaged in some of the most prolific and professional grade skeptical trolling I've ever seen. Suzanne naturally went to that comment thread to defend herself and Hoopes went after her. In the span of a week he posted 270 comments on that thread (all comments totaled 1,274) and 590 in total in the eleven days in between March 27, and April 8, solely on the TED controversy and never discussed anything else on TED ever again.[174] For comparison, my comments totaled 54 for the same topics, which spanned thirty days beginning March 8, and ended on the same date as Hoopes.[175]

Hoopes appeared to have administrator rights (which would mean that he was a plant by TED) because it was confirmed that he was able to post a website link that no one else could. (This means that his privileges were different from everyone else's.) Some claimed that he had modified some conversations, however no one was able to provide proof. He sided with TED in every situation and engaged in nearly every argument. If he wasn't mucking things up on behalf of TED, he did an excellent imitation of it.

On April 9, Ken Jordan of Reality Sandwich posted this often re-posted letter on their website:

An Open Letter To TED's Chris Anderson

Dear Chris,

I'm one of the many who in recent years discovered new and noteworthy ideas thanks to TED. You've grown TED into an important platform for the introduction of innovative thought to a popular audience; it's a wonderful vision and your achievement of it is widely appreciated. TED's prominence has made it, perhaps inadvertently, into a forum that validates worthy intellectual progress. If a good idea gets momentum, it will most likely end up, one way or another, presented by TED or one of the TEDx offshoots.

That's why the censure of the TEDx talks by Graham Hancock and Rupert Sheldrake is so dismaying. As you must know, to many of us the reasons behind their removal from the TED YouTube site are just not clear. On behalf of the Evolver community, I'd like to extend an invitation to you to help us understand the reasoning that led to TED's actions, because we suspect that behind your decision is an uninformed prejudice against groundbreaking research in a critical area of study, the possibility that consciousness extends beyond the brain.

The cause of our concern: while the original criticism against Hancock and Sheldrake was later retracted—literally crossed out on the blog page—after the speakers rebutted it, the initial decision to remove the videos still held. Statements from TED staff implied that the presentations were "pseudoscience" but no specific allegations were made. Both Rupert Sheldrake and Graham Hancock offered to debate a member of the anonymous science board, or any other representative, about actual criticisms, but got no response. To an outsider, TED's actions are baffling.

In your personal statements you say that TED is not censoring the videos, since they are available on a back page of your site, and technically that may be true. But by relegating them to obscure blogs that are not indexed as part of the regular pool of TEDx talks, the unequivocal message is that these talks are not fit to be seen among the thousands of other presentations that TED offers through YouTube. Somehow they were mistakes that slipped through and need to be quarantined from the "good" TED talks, to keep them from contamination. Given TED's influence, this treatment is unfairly damaging to the reputations of the speakers singled out.

The subsequent cancellation of TEDxWestHollywood, apparently due to the involvement of three of its speakers, who were named in a letter from TED staff, seems to be a continuation of the same baffling behavior. Again, the only reason given was a vague reference to "pseudoscience." But why these speakers? What had they done to justify reprimand—especially since TEDxWestHollywood had been in development for a year and was only two weeks from taking place?

The five people identified as problematic by TED work in different fields. Rupert Sheldrake is a biologist. Graham Hancock is a journalist who has written about archeological ruins. Larry Dossey is a doctor. Russell Targ is a physicist. Marilyn Schlitz is a social anthropologist and consciousness researcher. The one subject they all have in common is a shared interest in the non-locality of consciousness, the possibility that consciousness extends beyond the brain. Each speaker has devoted many years to the rigorous study of consciousness through the lens of their respective disciplines, and they have come up with provocative results.

Through its actions, TED appears to be drawing a line around this area of investigation and marking it as forbidden territory. Is this true? In the absence of any detailed reasoning in TED's public statements, it's hard to avoid this conclusion. It would seem that, despite your statement that "TED is 100% committed to open enquiry, including challenges to orthodox thinking," that enquiry appears to not include any exploration of consciousness as a non-local phenomenon, no matter how it may be approached.

This in turn leads to more questions, such as: Can we expect that other TED talks referring to the possibility of nonlocal consciousness will also be removed from YouTube? Should future TEDx organizers steer clear of any speaker who is associated with these investigations?

That would be a shame, since rigorous research in this field is producing intriguing results, and evidence for the non-locality of consciousness keeps growing.

What is the official position of TED? We invite you or a TED representative to an online forum where you can speak candidly about what TED means by "pseudoscience," and in what context a discussion about consciousness as a potentially nonlocal phenomenon might take place. This would be an opportunity for TED to clarify the criteria it uses to decide what does or does not belong at a TED sponsored event, and to address criticism that the decision to distance TED from particular speakers was based not on lack of knowledge, but on informed opinion.

Yours,
Ken Jordan
Publisher & Editorial Director, Evolver/Reality Sandwich

Because of my own involvement in the story, Ken asked me to re-post this letter on my website, which I did, with a link to his. (You can search Reality Sandwich or weilerpsiblog.wordpress.com to find the original speech and links.) All those who were following the controversy had the same sorts of questions, none of which were getting answered by TED.

CHAPTER FIFTEEN

PARAPSYCHOLOGY: THE RODNEY DANGERFIELD OF SCIENCE

Parapsychology, to quote the above-named late comedian, "can't get no respect." Resistance from the scientific establishment to psychic research is very vocal and persistent. The effect it has had is to starve this area of science for research funding to the point that, at least in the United States, parapsychology relies almost entirely on private donations. In the world at large there are probably only fifty people who count parapsychology as their profession. It's not that there is a lack of interest in and even pursuit of this area of science; it's that it is a career killer to demonstrate an interest in it.

On an FAQ for the Parapsychological Association they say this flat out:

> ... as noted by Dean Radin in a talk for Google, there is a real taboo in academia about studying the paranormal. Many researchers are afraid to work or publish in the field for fear of ostracism by their colleagues. Some may even be demoted in their departments or lose their chance for tenure if they publicly speak up about their interest—even if they

are only reflecting the feelings of the public majority. To put it bluntly, their reputation and careers are at stake.[176]

Dr. Ian Baker, a parapsychologist, had this to say in an article on his website:

Many of the "successful academic parapsychologists" (i.e., those who get paid!) that I know were able to get jobs in academia by *not* talking too much about parapsychology.[177]

John Palmer has managed to make a career out of parapsychology by moving to wherever a grant was available. On acquiring a professorship he states:

I also became aware early in my career that parapsychology is frowned upon by academic scientists in mainstream disciplines, especially in my own field of psychology. As a result, I have never bothered to apply for University professorships other than the very few involving parapsychology, ...[178]

Dean Radin has this advice:

In terms of realistic career advice, you must realize that parapsychology is considered "marginal" at best by mainstream psychology, at least within the US. If your goal is to achieve a tenured faculty position at a major university, with plenty of time for research, then any degree with an emphasis in parapsychology will not be looked upon with favor (to put it mildly).

In the United States and Great Britain, you cannot get a degree in parapsychology despite its continuing popularity. It simply isn't offered, and all of the advice recommends that anyone interested should get a degree in something else with statistics, such as psychology or physics.

The resistance to parapsychology occurs in ways that are not generally visible to the public. Its researchers are unlikely to receive appointments, tenure or position at universities; most prestigious journals do not publish parapsychological research; and major funding sources, such as the National Science Foundation, are unavailable for parapsychological research.[179]

A very telling example of this resistance comes in the form of a 1988 report by the National Academy of Sciences that concluded: "The committee finds no scientific justification from research conducted over the last 130 years for the existence of parapsychological phenomena." The conclusion was published by Ray Hyman, an original member of the radical atheist skeptic organization, the Committee for Skeptical Inquiry. There were no parapsychologists involved in writing the report. Parapsychologists did not take this lightly and protested these findings. The accusations of bias led U.S. Senator Claiborne Pell (D., RI, 1960 to 1997), who sympathized with parapsychological causes, to request an investigation by the Congressional Office of Technology Assessment (OTA) with a more balanced group.

In a one-day congressional workshop which included parapsychologists, critics, and experts from related fields, the report concluded that parapsychology needs "a fairer hearing across a broader spectrum of the scientific community, so that emotionality does not impede objective assessment of experimental results"[180]

Although this was over twenty years ago, not much has changed. The skeptical talking point that "there is no evidence for psychic ability despite 130 years of research" is still very much in play. As late as 2012, this talking point could still be found at Discover.com where CSI employee Ben Radford wrote an article on an experiment by Daryl Bem.[181]

The scientific community reacts to parapsychology with all of the dignity and maturity of a clique of popular tweeners organizing a dance at middle school. Cleve Backster, who gained fame in the 1970's for his research into plant consciousness, related a story about defending his research at a 1975 meeting of the American Association for the Advancement of Science. No stranger to controversy, Backster had put together 400 packets of information that included his published report, *Evidence of Primary Perception in Plant Life*, a lengthy bibliography, and some related research. He took only 200 of them to the AAAS press office and left the remaining copies in his hotel room.

When the time came for the press conference, the day before my symposium's scheduled working session, I was told by the AAAS staff that they had misplaced the 200 packets I had delivered. They did provide those in attendance a brief one page blurb not at all favorable to my research.[182]

Backster went to his hotel room, got his additional copies and distributed them. Afterwards, the AAAS staff somehow found the copies that they had misplaced.

Psi researcher Dean Radin was invited to a conference about the frontiers of consciousness at the United Nations some years ago:

> Someone chickened out when they discovered that I actually study this topic rather than think about it, and so I found myself disinvited. I discovered this only after asking the organizers several times for more details about the venue, conference dates and speaking schedule. Apparently no one thought it necessary to inform me.[183]

The same sort of treatment was afforded Nobel Prize winning physicist Professor Brian Josephson for the same reasons, although the ensuing uproar resulted in his invitation being reinstated:

> Last week, any veneer of serenity was shattered. Conference organiser Antony Valentini, research associate in the Theoretical Physics Group at Imperial College London, wrote to three participants to say their invitations had been withdrawn ...

> Brian Josephson, head of the Mind-Matter Unification Project at Cambridge, was rejected on the grounds that "one of his principal research interests is the paranormal".[184]

One of the petty ways in which mainstream science keeps out frontier sciences is to not list them on the Web of Science, which is an online citation resource. While the *Journal of Parapsychology* and *Journal of Consciousness Studies* are listed, the more popular *Journal of Scientific Exploration* is not, even though they use the same peer review process as the others. It's unfortunate that they marginalize such a worthwhile publication that prints things like a study done by William Bengston that showed amazing replicated results for using hands-on-healing to *completely cure* lab mice of a type of *incurable breast cancer.*[185]

One of the ways in which the field of parapsychology has been held back is the diversion of funds that actually have been intended for that purpose.

Three universities, Harvard, Stanford and Clark, received large donations in the early twentieth century for the study of psychic phenomena. At Clark, no research was ever done, and the money was hijacked for the psychology department. Stanford and Harvard both produced some parapsychology research, but, after a short time, the money was diverted to other purposes.

At Uppsala (the Sydney Alrutz bequest), Freiburg (the Asta Holler fund), and at Lund more recently, money intended for psi research has been shifted into the psychology departments. Funding has also been diverted to skeptics.

> **Yet much P-W money** [Perrott-Warrick] has also been given in the past to self-declared sceptics including Susan Blackmore, Richard Wiseman and Nicholas Humphrey, whose three years' funding (an estimated £75,000) produced no original research at all and a book, *Soul Searching*, notable for the absence of any reference to any published psi research. Clever exploitation of loopholes in the wording of the P-W bequest has enabled opportunistic sceptics to get away with this kind of thing.[186]

Money from a grant by Arthur Koestler was properly used for almost twenty years at Edinburgh University until the death of parapsychology chair Robert Morris. After that the shenanigans started, beginning with a rejection of seven qualified applicants, continuing with the acceptance and then, after a predictable furor, rejection of four unqualified applicants, with the end result being that the university ended up with two empty chairs for parapsychology, with a minor amount of the funds being used for two lecturer appointments in the area of parapsychology rather than one professor.[187]

The most odious part of the diversion of funds is that some of it ends up in the field of Anomalistic Psychology, which is the study of why people are crazy enough to believe in psychic phenomena.

CHAPTER SIXTEEN

THE ANTI-CLIMACTIC CLIMAX

Before TED made its final (and very predictable) final decision on the two speeches, Larry Dossey and Russell Targ added their comments to TED's process. These are the comments as they were originally sent to me.

Larry Dossey

I can add my name to those of Rupert Sheldrake and Graham Hancock as speakers who find themselves in TEDx's crosshairs.

I was scheduled to speak at the West Hollywood event. But my scientific credibility was questioned by TEDx's science advisory board in their decision to withdraw support and revoke the license of TEDxWestHollywood. I've lectured at dozens of top-tier medical schools and hospitals all over the U.S. for two decades. Although my colleagues don't always agree with my points of view, this is the first time my scientific credibility has ever been questioned.

My TEDx talk would have dealt with the correlations between spirituality, health, and longevity, for which there is immense evidence; and recent experimental findings that point toward a nonlocal view of consciousness for which, again, there is strong and abundant support. In view of our lack of understanding of the origins and destiny of consciousness, and considering the demographics of the TEDx followers, I thought this information would have been of considerable interest.

As a board-certified physician of internal medicine, former chief of staff of a major hospital, author of twelve books and scores of papers on these subjects published in peer reviewed journals, a recipient of many awards, a frequent lecturer at medical schools and hospitals, and executive editor of the peer reviewed journal, Explore: The *Journal of Science and Healing*, I'd be interested in knowing from TED where I came up short.

"A clash of doctrines is not a disaster, it is an opportunity," Whitehead said. It should not be a reason for censorship.
~ Larry Dossey, M.D.

Russell Targ

In cancelling the TEDx event in West Hollywood, it appears that I was accused of "using the guise of science" to further spooky claims (or some such). People on this blog have asked what I was going to talk about. That's easily answered. I was co-founder of a 23-year research program investigating psychic abilities at Stanford Research Institute. We were doing research and applications for the CIA, Defense Intelligence Agency, Air Force and Army Intelligence, NASA, and others. In this $25 million program we used "remote viewing" to find a downed Russian bomber in North Africa, for which President Carter commended us. We found a kidnapped US general in Italy, and the kidnap car that snatched Patricia Hearst. We looked in on the US hostages in Iran, and predicted the immanent release of Richard Queen, who was soon sent to Germany. We described a Russian weapons factory in Siberia, leading to a US congressional investigation about weakness in US security, etc. We published our scientific findings in Nature, The Proc. IEEE, Proc, AAAS, and Proc. American Institute of Physics. I thought a TED audience would find this recently declassified material interesting. And no physics would be harmed in my presentation.

Remote viewing is an ability that many people can easily learn. It is a nonlocal ability, in that its accuracy and reliability are independent of distance. Dean of Engineering Robert Jahn has also published extensively on his experiments at Princeton, (Proc. IEEE, Feb 1982). I am not claiming it is quantum anything. It appears to possibly make use of something like Minkowski's (8 dimensional) complex space/time that he described to Einstein in the 1920s, and is now being re-examined by Roger Penrose. This is not necessarily The answer. But the answer will be some sort [of] similar nonlocal space/time geometry. We taught remote viewing to 6 army intelligence officers in 1979. They then taught a dozen other officers, and created an operational army psychic corps at Ft. Meade, which lasted until the end of our program in 1995. You can see two examples of real remote viewing on my website, www.espresearch.com. One with Hella Hammid is double blind, live on camera for a 1983 BBC film, "The Case of ESP." available on Google.

I want to call attention to the clarity of the ideas expressed here, the concise prose and attention to detail these men provided. How different this is from everything that came out of TED. Sheldrake, Hancock, and now Dossey and Targ provided the clarity and exposition in their arguments and explanations that should have been coming from Chris Anderson and the mysterious science board.

Many skeptical comments over at the TED blogs guessed at TED's reasoning, but since none of them actually spoke for TED, what they said was irrelevant, and, at that point, I mostly stayed out of those discussions. In shutting down TEDxWestHollywood, TED telegraphed what their final decision was going to be about the two videos. Sure enough, on April 2, the official word came down: The videos would remain on TED's website stored away in obscure blog posts, unsearchable through TED.

The actual judgment handed down by TED was anti-climactic. I wrote at the time of the decision:

TED Makes a Decision: Not Technically Censorship (Plus a recap)

In a move that surprised absolutely no one, TED has come to the conclusion that the videos of Rupert Sheldrake and Graham Hancock can stay in quarantine where they are searchable by Google and barely searchable within the TED site. As Chris Anderson put it in his messsage: (link.)

Some asked whether this was "censorship." Now, it's pretty clear that it isn't censorship, since the talk itself is literally a click away on this very site, and easily findable on Google.

(You can find the talk here.) Since this message is identical for Graham Hancock, here is his video as well.

This message in its entirety is an amazing package of . . . nothing. Here's another sample:

> A number of questions were raised about TED's science board: How it works and why the member list isn't public. Our science board has 5 members—all working scientists or distinguished science journalists. When we encounter a scientific talk that raises questions, they advise us on their position. I and my team here at TED make the final decisions. We keep the names of the science board private. This is a common practice for science review boards in the academic world, which preserves the objectivity of the recommendations and also protects the participants from retribution or harassment.

It's very questionable whether the science board would have received retribution or harassment. From whom? But that wasn't the real issue. Their names weren't nearly as important as what their reasoning was. And we have no idea what that was. Why weren't the talks re-instated? For that matter, why were they left in quarantine? What specific problems from these videos did the science board object to? Where is the science?

This becomes even more glaring in his next paragraph:

Finally, let me say that TED is 100% committed to open enquiry, including challenges to orthodox thinking. But we're also firm believers in appropriate skepticism, or critical thinking. Those two instincts will sometimes conflict, as they did in this case. That's why we invited this debate. The process hasn't been perfect. But it has been undertaken in passionate pursuit of these core values.

What open enquiry? What critical thinking? Where is the appropriate skepticism? Is it a secret? An endeavor can hardly be called an open enquiry or even a debate if none of the important questions are ever answered. So what are we left with? Nothing much. It has all the content of a BP press release right after the oil spill. I suppose I could go on criticizing them, but what's the point? The fact that they're not even trying to defend themselves pretty much says it all.

After TED revoked the license, it was a foregone conclusion that these two videos weren't ever going back up on the main page, so from there it was just a waiting game to see how long it would take for this predictable decision to be made. (...)

(To see the original blog post and relevant links, visit weilerpsiblog. wordpress.com)

And so the portion of the controversy between TED, Rupert Sheldrake and Graham Hancock ended as it had begun . . . with nothing. Like the Internet meme video of the rambling, emotional soliloquy about a double rainbow in Yosemite National Park, we're left asking: What does it all mean?

Well, for starters, it means that if there was anything wrong with the two videos or with TEDxWestHollywood, then no one ever clearly stated what they thought that was. I don't think it's out of line to conjecture that if Chris Anderson, the TED science board, or anyone else had truly found a problem with the videos, they would not have hesitated to speak up.

It means that all previous arguments put forth by Jerry Coyne and company had to be discarded because they would not hold up under scientific scrutiny. To put this in the vernacular; they were all hat and no cattle.

Perhaps most importantly, it means that the *mere charge of pseudoscience* was enough justification for TED. That had to have come from a belief system and not from a rational thought process.

And therein lies the great hypocrisy not just of TED's, but of the entire skeptical movement, scientists included. Science is about proving your assertions with evidence. By not explaining exactly what was wrong with the two talks or with TEDxWestHollywood's program, TED, like the skeptics it was relying on, was promoting views held by materialists. That is a philosophical viewpoint not a scientific one. TED's position could only be scientific (and tenable) if they provided evidence to support it, which they did not do. In other words, TED was flat out unequivocally guilty of the very thing it was critical of: pseudoscience.

The whole TED controversy could turn out to result in the death of materialism as the way of science. Graham Hancock made this comment:

> The whole process of grappling with TED has been extremely painful, time-consuming and energy-draining but this is a small price to pay for the many good things that are going to come out of it. These strange events in which we are all caught up will, I think, prove to be of the greatest significance in the long run—the first serious breach in the dam of rigid materialist thinking that has become such a major block to human progress.

That's been my take on the situation as well. Something important just happened.

The parapsychologists and the parapsychology community totally get this. They are excited because the massive scientific belief logjam is starting to break up. It's a good thing for science, obviously, to embrace evidence over beliefs.

Just before the TED ruling came down, I expressed my thoughts about the meaning of the TED controversy in this blog post:

The Loud and Clear Message that the TED Controversy is Sending

> TED talks is actually pretty cool. Although I've been talking nonstop about the TED censorship for the past couple of weeks, I don't hold a grudge against that organization. Truth is, they've been pretty good to me. They've helped me increase my site views by 500% over this past month and pushed my blog into the top 5% of internet blogs in general, by views. What's not to like? They have picked sides in a growing controversy, which has galvanized the pro-psi camp in ways that have never been seen before. Indeed, a lot is happening that has never been seen before and I'm delighted to be in the middle of it. My battle was never with TED: it's with the skeptics pulling the strings behind the scenes at TED.
>
> Which brings me to my point. The loud and clear message that has been sent is that there IS a major scientific controversy brewing and institutions, from TED to all of academia and the media, need to stop

taking sides. They need to step out of the way and let the controversy play itself out or suffer huge PR damage as a consequence. The new thing that is happening is that change isn't coming from within the hallowed, starched halls of academia and within the confines of scientific conferences, but from the outside. The ideas that skeptics so quickly dismiss are gaining mass acceptance and are starting to redefine the power structure. From what I can see, this is very confusing to everyone on the skeptical side of the debate.

(For those not familiar with the debate, it can be oversimplified thusly:

On the one side we have materialists/reductionists/skeptics who see the universe as a lifeless machine that can be understood by figuring out its mechanics. On the other side we have Biocentrists, for lack of a better term, who see consciousness and life as being fundamental to the universe. In other words, they see the universe as a giant thought. You generally won't hear much about the second theory, but the evidence is much better than most people realize. Mainstream science does not acknowledge this fact, which is pretty much why there's a big controversy.)

Science, after all, is decided by scientists, right? What gives the ordinary rabble the right to intrude on discussions about the fundamental nature of the universe? This needs to be decided by people with advanced degrees who have studied these matters during their whole adult lives. Surely only they have the requisite knowledge to decide? That certainly holds true for most areas of science; the public is more than willing just to accept what they are told. What makes the psi debate so different? What the heck is *happening*?

In a word, this particular area of science is being crowdsourced. While people obviously aren't out conducting experiments en mass and publishing them in scientific journals, they are able to substantially verify scientific claims such as "there is no evidence for psychic phenomena." If this phrase is uttered by a scientist and turns up in a mainstream news article it is a relatively simple matter to browse the comment section to find more substantial sources of information. Often these days, links with real scientific information will be shared by a knowledgeable person, effectively demonstrating that the statement was false. This scenario has become pretty common.

It's precisely this kind of thing that has sent TED reeling these past couple of weeks. Just a few short years ago, this problem with Sheldrake and Hancock would have been easily managed. Drop the speakers, ignore the few protest emails and proceed as if nothing had happened. It would have been over before most of the public even knew what was happening. What happened a few weeks ago, however, is something that will play out more and more in the future. The two videos were taken down for the usual skeptical reason of being unscientific. People who were well- informed about this topic showed up for the debate, but it also started to draw attention, largely due to the fact that word spread about what had happened. Someone mentioned it on the parapsychology blog/forum? that I hang out on and I blogged about it. I sent a link to parapsychologist Dean Radin; he posted a link on his blog; it got picked up by The Daily Grail and took off from there.

Now, all eyes were on TED and they were forced to back down from their original position due not only to the outcry, but also the obviously well informed logic behind it. Anyone who saw that comment thread objectively could see the weakness of skeptical arguments, the irritating nature of paternalistic drive-by comments by TED staff, and, well, *everything.* This is the new reality; everyone gets to share and see what everyone else is sharing.

One outcome of this is that skeptics are being forced into the intellectual debates, which expose the weakness of their arguments and, more importantly, their arrogant attitudes. One of the hardest things to convey to other people not familiar with the debate is the unreasonableness of skeptics, but in these comment threads it's there for everyone to see. TED and its skeptics have not recognized the impact of this, yet, and do not understand how much this is changing things. This crowdsourcing is increasingly going to force intellectually honest discussions, which will ultimately force change that companies and institutions like TED and its skeptics would rather not deal with. They are operating according to an old paradigm in which they believe that they can make whatever decisions they please, irrespective of pesky comments. That era, though, is fast coming to a close. The tail is wagging the dog.

Academia will surely be the last bastion to fall under the new order, but ultimately it answers to the public and if that public is well informed and communicating constantly with each other, as they now do, then fall it will. The basic problem—that they are ignoring important evidence—is exactly the sort of thing that will put a target on their back. An energized public can award power and prestige to some, while taking it away from others. Universities aren't blind, deaf and dumb. If they start losing money and grants because their skeptics are putting people off, they'll do something about it. I'm fairly sure that's what it would take.

I've been following the psi wars for a number of years and I can see two things: First of all, this is not a debate over science, despite what skeptics claim. The body of evidence supporting the marriage of consciousness and physics is simply enormous and utterly convincing by any sane scientific standard. (and here) The science, in other words, is settled. The TED controversy deeply underscores this point: TED has never clearly defined their reasons for censorship; they have never taken Rupert Sheldrake up on his offer to debate the TED science board; the reasons for axing TEDxWestHollywood have never been convincingly laid out; Jerry Coyne, in his blog, (which unwittingly helped to raise the profile of the censorship issue considerably) has never scientifically spelled out his objections either. They all act as if it's a problem with a solution so obviously in their favor that it doesn't need discussion. Thus, they never engage the evidence in any meaningful way. The lack of meaningful discussion highlights a very significant point. The controversy isn't a scientific one: it's a social one.

Second: The internet has given the opposing side two tools that it has never had before; we now have an easy way to find each other and we have a way to spread scientific information that skirts the normal walls that science builds around ideas it doesn't like. Typically, the mass media goes along with this wall and tends to avoid publishing controversial topics as truths because they are far too technical and it's easier to trust mainstream scientists than to go out on a limb. But the internet skirts around mass media as well. A community has developed that spreads the information through an informal chain of blogs that together have the reach of lesser forms of mass media. It's hard to judge exactly, but I would guess, based on the interest that this topic has generated, that news of the axing of TEDxWestHollywood has probably reached 100,000 people with *no mass media intervention*. (My blog post alone would account for about 12% of that traffic.)

This community contains parapsychologists and other people with advanced degrees, as well as a very large number of well read individuals, such as myself, who can see the evidence and decide for themselves. These scientists, by the way, no longer need to rely on academic and scientific institutions to forward their ideas and evidence and make rebuttals to obvious smears: They can take to the streets, so to speak. It has taken several years for this community to form because much of the information has not been on line and people needed to get used to this new format of communicating. People, such as myself, needed time to develop a portfolio of work and build a reputation, which is just now coming to good use. As these blogs have developed, people needed to find them and set the groundwork for this loosely connected network of like- minded people. There have always been far more of us, than skeptics, so the issue hasn't been persuading people, but merely getting them together and making them properly informed.

Now that the network is in place, and this group has had time to settle in and grow in numbers, an attitude change has taken place. With the scientific evidence on its side and a firm sense of being right, this group has gone increasingly on the offensive, pushing back at empty skeptical claims and denouncing obvious lies and half truths. The message is fairly simple and straightforward: "Don't suppress this stuff." This is where we are now: pushing back. The controversy, which is social, is getting a social solution and it's starting to have a pronounced effect.

The effect has been to cause the skeptics to polarize the debate and to send them into a furious campaign to put the genie back into the bottle. There is no longer any pretense of being nice about it and, in the near future, it is this frenzied activity by the skeptics that will create the change more than anything we do. The skeptics are to science, what the far right wing is to Republicans. They're on the same side, but their radicalized beliefs present both a solid base of support and send moderates running in the other direction. You can see what has happened to TED as the skeptics have gained control. Their heavy-handed attitude is having an impact on the TED brand (it's too soon to tell just how much), and they are so consumed with their small battles that they are losing sight of the war, which they are losing.

The parapsychological sciences that are shunned by mainstream science have always been very popular with the public. This huge gap in acceptance has always existed and it has led to a sort of running 140 year battle between the mainstream sciences and parapsychology. The skeptics in academia have always succeeded simply by shutting out both the scientists and the public interest, but they can't do that anymore. Their main tool, control over information, has been taken away from them. As the TED drama has shown, they have no ability to fight on open ground. It is just the beginning of an ideological clash that will spread all over the world and eventually force a change.

The wall that the skeptics have put up is like a shaky dam with a rapidly growing river behind it. They will hold sway for a while, and it will look as though they are succeeding because so little gets past them; but it is an illusion. The broad network of people supporting an alternative view of the universe, backed by solid evidence, is still growing and becoming increasingly aware of its power. Everything will be fine in Camp Skeptic until it isn't. Once institutions realize that taking sides in the debate is harming them more than helping, then, change will come swiftly and the sciences will be fundamentally altered forever.

(For the print book, this blog post and relevant links can be found at weilerpsiblog.wordpress.com)

The issue about why parapsychology has not been accepted has never been about the evidence. J.B. Rhine published enough evidence in the fifties to meet any sane scientific standard. The problem has always been one of belief. The media and the mainstream scientific community simply don't believe it. This has allowed skeptics to gain prominence not by careful rational thinking, but merely by playing on existing prejudices and reinforcing beliefs through bold, definitive statements.

CHAPTER SEVENTEEN

THE ARGUING MACHINE

The Internet has dramatically changed our intellectual landscape worldwide, as this controversy with TED so dramatically demonstrates. The exchange of information has always been with us and it has been getting successively faster and faster. It has changed the nature of conversation from small town square discussions in small villages to enormous debates, with hundreds and sometimes thousands of people at a time, spanning the globe. The history of this is fairly straightforward with each technological improvement providing more information faster and faster. Where communication between towns was once accomplished by runners, then by horse, then telegraphs, we are now so completely interconnected that we can have a fully documented written debate complete with bibliography, in a matter of hours, with anyone in the world. As long as everyone can write in the same language, they don't even need to speak it.

But while the speed with which we can communicate has advanced thousands fold, our ability to communicate effectively from person to person has not changed much. A person from five hundred years ago would have been no less able to write coherently and effectively than a person today. People are still just people no matter their technology.

What's particularly difficult is that where, before, we were all able to have our little groups where everyone basically shared similar belief systems, that is no longer possible. People with every different belief system have been thrown together to hash it out on the largest communication network mankind has ever known.

While we were all marveling at our shiny new Internet, a monumental social change has snuck up upon us in the last five years or so. We have entered the Age of Debate. We are all essentially standing in the same town square. It's completely new territory for mankind. All those different belief systems now have to hash it out with each other in a kind of giant free for all.

It is so new that its impact hasn't yet been fully felt, but the TED controversy gives us a peek at things to come. It is quite possibly the biggest threat to the status quo there has ever been. The keepers of the old ideals are getting mightily unnerved by it. The most recent example is *Popular Science* magazine, which is shutting down its comment sections entirely, citing trolls and spambots as part of the problem, but not the whole thing.[188]

They cited the problem of negative comments damaging their ability to portray scientific articles properly. And they have a point. Studies have shown that strongly worded comments polarize readers even when they are civil.

But here's something else *Popular Science* had to say:

> A politically motivated, decades-long war on expertise has eroded the popular consensus on a wide variety of scientifically validated topics. Everything, from evolution to the origins of climate change, is mistakenly up for grabs again.

Evolution and climate change are indeed under attack and always have been. What *Popular Science*, TED and many other organizations are grappling with, now, is the idea that the very platform, which they use to *influence* public opinion, is being subverted either for promoting ideas that they don't agree with or casting doubt. After the article is written or the decision is made the argument isn't over anymore. It's just beginning and there is no hiding from it.

Popular Science will almost certainly re-institute comments once they find out how much money they're losing. Comments drive up pages views by a lot. From a commercial perspective, they are indispensible. People stay on the page longer, they refresh the page to see more comments and thereby are exposed to more ads while increasing the number of pages views. It can double the ad revenue of an article.

Suppressing the voices of the unwashed masses comes at a very high price. Literally.

Another attack by the status quo is underway in Britain right now where legislation is being proposed that might block spiritual content on the Internet there. Through the usual ploy of attempting to block child pornography, legislators are hoping to remove all sorts of "esoteric" material.[189] Read: spiritual content. Other countries considering similar moves are Canada, France, Australia and China.

These moves are largely occurring because we are now in the Age of Internet Debate. The top down information model is starting to disappear and, in its place, information is coming in from every direction. It's bad. It's good.

On the one hand it's too much information and it can be confusing. It's nice to have experts simply give you the short story and not have to worry about whom to believe. But, on the other hand, if you're not convinced that an expert is right, or if there are differing expert opinions on something that you care about, you have the option of exploring almost any subject more fully. Whatever it is, someone, somewhere has probably blogged about it and, in the process, made themselves the world's expert on some obscure set of facts or situation. It's just a matter of finding them.

The Age of Internet Debate also means that it is getting harder and harder to control a point of view or suppress a controversy. China is discovering this, and many other countries as well. You can't stop everything.

When it comes to the sciences, everyone has to rationally defend their actions and their philosophical positions. And, if your position is unsupportable, then you will suffer for it.

A spectacular example of this occurred recently in The *New Republic*. Jerry Coyne was somehow allowed to repost one of his blog articles with all the usual histrionics. Titled: "Pseudoscientist Rupert Sheldrake Is Not Being Persecuted And Is Not Like Galileo."[190] The article was, of course, over the top biased and unfair. It was just the sort of publication and article to bring out the intellectuals and when they started commenting they tore into Coyne's article.

The commenters quickly pointed out how bad the article was and had no trouble refuting its main point, that Sheldrake was a pseudoscientist. If Coyne had intended the article as a rallying point for skeptics to smack down the "woomeisters" he must have been disappointed. He had done such a poor job of supporting his arguments that his detractors had no problem in refuting them. Instead of making his point, the article now stands as an excellent example of the worst sort of skepticism and draws favorable attention to Sheldrake.

The social aspect of this is that people who disagreed with Coyne could not only add their comments, but they could see other people's comments as well. Commenting has allowed like-minded people who share the same views to find one another and share information. This is very powerful. A good, well-articulated critique with sources can make a huge difference. If you read the article, but you knew nothing about Sheldrake or Coyne, you could read the comment section to get a sense of the controversy and learn what the counter arguments were. Commenting on articles, at its best, functions as a sort of peer review. This is especially important for those subjects which are not part of the mainstream.

The article was basically designed to preach to the skeptically converted, not to the world at large, and, as a result, only the most hard core skeptics showed up in the comment section to defend Coyne, which led to very poor skeptical arguments.

I had submitted an article refuting Coyne, but The *New Republic* never responded. I was, however, able to make my main points in the comments section.

It's the sort of situation where no one incident matters, but, as they build up over time, they sensitize people to the idea that the situation is not what the mainstream media makes it out to be.

TED, *Popular Science* and other periodicals are facing an unprecedented situation; it's no longer possible for them simply to assert their position and then call it a day. Everything has to be argued over and over again, whether they're right or wrong. *No one ever really wins; there is always more disagreement.*

The general public will have to get used to this new social situation: information will nearly always have conflicting viewpoints, and there isn't a definitive authority that sorts it all out.

It's a state of affairs all too familiar to parapsychology and now the rest of the world has to deal with it as well.

In the Age of Internet Debate, you can achieve status, even if you have no accreditation, solely on your ability to create good content or share the content of others effectively. Specialty bloggers, such as myself, are being taken more seriously than ever before. Our credibility comes, not from being an accredited expert in a particular field, but from having done a superb job of sourcing and commentary.

When other people can see your sources, they can evaluate the quality of your work for themselves and no longer need to rely on expert opinion.

Seen from a certain perspective, the Internet is one huge debate factory.

This massive fact sharing is a crucial part of debate. It's a crucial change that moves the conversation from what people can remember in their heads or save in a drawer or remember from a book they read, to being able to search-and-share the relevant sources, which can also be debated. This is important because debate has moved from an exchange of ideas to an exchange of ideas backed by evidence. I have used this myself to great effect on occasion by providing links that unequivocally demonstrate the falsehood of the statement "there is no evidence for psi."

Another change, which I've seen on the Internet, is that the book is no longer the king of sources. They have been replaced by the 1,000 to 2,000 word article. That is the general article size in mainstream media and it's pretty near ideal for sharing some specific information in a link.

In the beginning, it seemed like a great idea for people to be able to be anonymous on the Internet and to speak freely. It was a grand experiment that failed. It has allowed rude behavior to flourish, which greatly dampens intelligent conversation and chases away thoughtful commentary. Some people act in ways that would be regarded as deranged in real life, which has spawned a whole new creature: the Internet troll. Rudeness and idiocy abound on unmediated comments and forums and it's very hard to get rid of it. While the worst offenders are usually quite easy to spot, others have developed the minimal skills needed to avoid the banhammer while still being obnoxious.

Here's how bad it is: in August of 2013 the *Huffington Post* stopped allowing anonymous comments altogether. If you want to comment, you have to give them your identity. The hope is that the loss of anonymity will force people to behave. They receive a staggering nine million comments a month, but three quarters of these are either spam or trolls. It places a tremendous burden on their forty-plus team of paid moderators to deal with that.

> Trolls have grown more vicious, more aggressive, and more ingenious. As a result, comment sections can degenerate into some of the darkest places on the Internet.[191]

It is a great human experiment in how to make people get along with one another and have civil conversations when literally everyone in the world is invited. It is a problem on Wikipedia, on the *Huffington Post* and YouTube. It's pretty much everywhere that you find enough people to engage in commenting and other discussions. The people who are most likely to participate are often the most opinionated. On my own blog this is rarely a problem, but, at the height of the TED controversy, when TEDxWestHollywood was taken down, the traffic on my blog site was so high that I finally started seeing some trolls (both skeptics and proponents) and I had to devote some time to dealing with them. I can say from personal experience that it is often a tough call. Is this a troll? Or just a snarky comment? Sometimes I didn't know.

Provided you can keep the trolls at bay, two polite and informed commenters with disparate views having a discussion can be immensely interesting. It gives both sides insight into how the other one thinks.

Intelligent statements are what most people look for when they go through comment sections. Certainly at TED, that's what people were expecting when they perused the Sheldrake and Hancock comment threads. It was one of the best examples, at least for a while, of intelligent and polite conversation between people who disagree.

This new Age of Internet Debate is forcing us to think about what we want. Do we want to hear from everybody with no sense of order? Or do we want someone to choose the best stuff for us so that we don't have to search for it? And who decides? How would that work if an organization like TED found that they could manipulate the comments to push their favorites to the top while pushing down disagreement? That's what happened on reddit, where the ideologues pushed everyone else's opinions out of view. That idea isn't all that great.

YouTube is currently experimenting with anti-troll commenting software, but it remains to be seen if the trolls can figure out a way around it.[192] TED has a very good system, but even it has some faults. The main problem of almost all commenting systems is a human one. There is almost no way for the most intelligent commenting to rise to the top while suppressing trollish or ignorant comments without human intervention. Rating systems do not work. They merely tell you what the ideologues want to see. That crowd is far more likely to go to the extra effort to promote their point of view by upvoting comments they agree with and given the chance, downvoting the comments they don't like.

It is also necessary to pay attention to who is moderating the comments. While paid employees are generally pretty impartial, it is also very labor intensive. While community moderators are free, they are often ideologues because this gives them an opportunity to push their point of view and suppress those whom they disagree with. This degrades the debate experience and reflects badly on the organization hosting the comments. It comes down to this: we are all still learning how to argue on the Internet. It's not an easy task.

Old philosophical tools have been dusted off and find themselves repurposed for the Internet. The straw man argument, the ad hominem and appeal to authority are the logical fallacies that were half forgotten before the Internet, but now they're getting mentioned quite often.

Pretty much everyone is learning how to communicate this way on the fly. In real life, now, we are not just reading articles, but we are interacting with them. With that comes learning how to be a good communicator through years of repetition. We have to think, and then write over and over again to participate. This process produces better thinkers over time because we will be challenged every now and again to support our statements. Sometimes we'll look like idiots, but we'll learn.

I've gone through this process myself. My early comments were frequently nothing to be proud of and I certainly lost my temper on occasion. I also learned a little philosophy along the way when I was accused of committing some logical fallacy or another. I also had a few times when I acted like the worst ideologue, arguing all over the place on an issue I felt passionate about. But, after I had some time to reflect on the idiocy of doing that, I changed my behavior, eventually learning to change my tone and be much more neutral. I don't think my path was all that unusual.

Perhaps the biggest social change, which the Internet is creating, is a great dialectic on a scale never dreamed of by philosophers.

The Dialectic

The dialectic is a philosophy term. It refers to the most basic form of argument: thesis, antithesis and synthesis. It sounds confusing, but just think of it as: assertion, rebuttal and resolution. Arguments begin with assertions, such as "global warming isn't happening." It's a statement that someone is putting forward as fact. In an ordinary argument someone else will rebut this statement ("Yes it is.") and there will be a back and forth of both parties showing their evidence and delving into the argument more deeply. In a perfect world, one person will concede that the weight of evidence is against him. (Or both may simply agree to disagree.) That is the resolution.

Individual arguments are seldom resolved on the Internet. Human nature being what it is, those who are losing arguments either fail to respond or switch tactics, depending on their personal traits. However, taken as a whole, there can be overall shifts in behavior as controversial topics get hashed out on a large scale. These things are kind of difficult to pin down and quantify scientifically, but I have noticed trends over the years with regards to parapsychology. As I mentioned earlier, the use of the JREF million dollar challenge as proof that psychic ability doesn't exist seems to have diminished greatly in recent years and has now come to an end. It's a sign that, overall, skeptics have been forced to drop their most simplistic, easily disputed arguments.

What I've also noticed is a gradual increase in the number of people willing to argue in defense of parapsychology on scientific grounds. That requires a considerable amount of sophistication, but it has occurred because more credible sources have become available online.

I'm also not seeing the same kind of confidence in the skeptics that do get online and argue. They seem to have lost some of their mainstream appeal and, with it, many of the sorts of people who can engage in truly polite conversation. It's not that I see more obnoxious and ruder comments than I used to, but rather less of the more even-handed type of skepticism. Skepticism seems to be losing the middle ground.

One thing I expect to see as a result of this change is more favorable mainstream journalism. It seems to have already begun in fits and starts as the mainstream becomes gradually aware that there are two sides to this issue. I've noticed articles occasionally that favor psi research without excessive skeptical input.

The proliferation of bloggers and alternative news sites, constantly pushing the evidence to front and center, is forcing the dialectic, which will embolden more and more scientists to question the status quo until, finally, the skeptics will find themselves left behind. As I said, the arguments never end, it's just that the tide shifts in another direction.

The TED controversy illustrated this problem quite well. If you can't find a way, legitimately, to defend your viewpoint, you're going to suffer for it. TED was explicitly asked both to state clearly their position and, in lieu of that, to engage in a debate by both speakers. The fact that TED never did either showed some neutral observers that something was wrong with TED. This is a process that is likely to be repeated over and over again in various forms, on stages larger and smaller as time goes on. It puts pressure on mainstream journalism to start conforming to the new reality.

TED lost some credibility in 2013. They made some enemies, got some bad press in the world of alternative science and medicine and are regarded by some people now as being reactionaries.

CHAPTER EIGHTEEN

EXTEDXWESTHOLLYWOOD ... THERE'S NO BUSINESS LIKE SHOW BUSINESS

A mean-spirited turn of the knife

The now ExTEDxWestHollywood event was to be streamed live and an account was set up with Livestream.com to accomplish this. However the account that Suzanne Taylor used still had TED in the name. With two days to go and advertising underway, TED twisted Livestream's arm and got Suzanne's account terminated. What was especially galling was Livestream's refusal to even provide a link to the new account when it was set up. Everyone had to scramble to explain the situation and provide viewers with a new web address at the last minute.

Since TED had yanked a license for a program at the last minute that they had previously green lit and never given any legitimate reason for doing so, this was more than a little mean spirited.

Suzanne Taylor Takes a Hit

Suzanne Taylor had been working for a year to set up her program. TED's agreement, according to her license, was that TED could refuse to post any talk they didn't like. As a TEDx event producer, she had secured a site, lined up sponsors and gotten all of her speakers. It was an enormous amount of work to put this together and when TED removed her license she also lost her venue, the West Hollywood public library. She also lost her TED backed sponsorship and had her speaker line up thrown into uncertainty. (Her event was now "controversial" and speaking there might damage one's reputation. Four people backed out.)

Her TEDx event consisted of a whole team of volunteers who had given many hours over the year and now all their hard work was in jeopardy.

Many of Suzanne's speakers, though, having long ago become accustomed to this sort of over-the-top skeptical behavior that TED was displaying, simply rolled with it and stayed with the program. If anything, it created a sense of camaraderie. Besides that, the show was being live-streamed. The videos would stay up for a long time and would be viewed by thousands of people. Most of the speakers were aware that the public whom Suzanne was going to reach were not the sort that required TED's stamp of approval.

No matter what, though, the show had to go on. The final two weeks before the show had been intended as time to coach the speakers on their talks, but this fell by the wayside in light of more serious problems. The most pressing of Suzanne's concerns was getting a new venue and then advertising it in the very short time she had remaining. Having the TED name would have meant an automatic sell out, but without the TED name and on such short notice, filling even a small house was an iffy proposition.

She called her production ExTEDxWestHollywood, to help bridge the transition and to draw attention to the controversy surrounding her production. The furious scramble to secure a new venue succeeded against all odds. She found a simply incredible location, The Vortex Dome on the lot of Los Angeles Center Studios, a 20 acre TV and film studio campus. Suzanne had to put up $30,000 of her own money, but the show would go on.

I Travel to L.A.

The TED incident had increased my profile tremendously, and the first thing to come out of it was the opportunity to go to Los Angeles to participate in the West Hollywood ExTEDx production. I had offered to do a sort of pre-speech to cover the whole TED controversy, but hadn't gotten confirmation about that from Suzanne. The show was to take place on Sunday, April 14, but I was to arrive on Friday. My wife loaned me her Prius and I made the four hundred mile drive from the San Francisco peninsula down to Los Angeles Friday morning and arrived in the afternoon.

I met Suzanne for the first time when she came out to let me through her gate. She was very warm and genuinely friendly, and from the first instant I immediately liked her . . . a lot. She is full of energy. She welcomed me in and had me greet her two guests who'd already arrived and were sitting at the dining room table, talking. She went off to make some coffee while we made introductions.

Meeting Larry Dossey and Russell Targ

One of the gentlemen at Suzanne's table got up to greet me. I recognized him immediately: Dr. Larry Dossey, a distinguished Texas physician. Dossey was a battalion surgeon in Vietnam, where he was decorated for valor. He's written nine books, is a former executive editor of a medical journal and teaches and lectures on alternative medical therapies all over the world. The other gentleman was physicist Russell Targ. A pioneer in laser development and co-founder of the Stanford Research Institute, Russell began his investigations into psychic ability in the 1970's. He's a retired senior staff scientist from Lockheed Missiles and Space Company where he developed airborne lasers to detect wind shear and turbulence. He's also the author of nine books on scientific investigations of psychic abilities. I'd been reading and writing about these two guys for years, and now here we were, just the three of us sitting around a table in the afternoon. I could feel the fanboy in me getting excited, but my years of professional experience talking to people kicked in and, after a couple of moments, my composure returned. There was a rehearsal that night, so we would all be driving to the location. While I don't remember the conversation, we did talk about TED and the situation with parapsychology. I do remember that it was great to be around other people who knew more than I did. Parapsychology is such a tiny field, with very few people who study it in any depth, and these two men were real experts.

We went to the rehearsal in Suzanne's car, with the long-legged Russell up front, and Larry and me squeezed into the back. As it was Friday night in Los Angeles, there was no point in taking the freeways so we went on the side streets with stuff crammed into every free spot of the car for what we'd need on Sunday. I mostly just hung out when we got there. It was a wonderful space.

The Vortex Immersion Dome at Los Angeles Center Studios is an actual geodesic dome with a metal frame supporting a domed canvas shell. The entire curved space acts as a projector screen allowing for spectacular visual effects that take up the whole domed ceiling. As I was oohing and aahing with everyone else, Suzanne came up to me and showed me the program for Sunday. I was the first speaker.

I was quite surprised, but I rolled with it. I'm a very experienced speaker. I'd brought some good clothes and was confident that I could do a good job. This, also, was a technical rehearsal. Anyone who has done theater knows what that is. It's when you sort out all the equipment and make sure that all the workers know what they are supposed to do so that all technical aspects of the show work properly. Many speakers had slide shows, there was a Dome show for intermission, and the event was being livestreamed to the world. It was going to be a long night.

Even something as simple as my talk, which had no slideshow, had its own technical aspect to it. The sound person had to listen to me talk—I'm naturally loud. I'm used to projecting my voice without a microphone, so they had to adjust for that. I also use the whole stage, walking around, and I talk with my hands, so the camera person had to know not to zoom in too close. These are not things you want them to discover when the show is live. I did a quick two minutes of talk, they saw how I moved and spoke, and that was all it took. They had me figured out. For my part, I had to know where the countdown timer was. My speech was going to be improvised and I would be depending on the timer for pacing. Some of the speakers had trouble with the lighting. The dome was going to be pretty dark inside to allow for the visual effects of the projections on it, but the show being filmed meant that the speakers had to be pretty brightly lit. Having a bright light constantly shining in your eyes is one of those things about being on camera that takes a bit of getting used to. It also made it harder to relate to the audience because everyone was in deep in shadow.

Tech rehearsals tend to be chaotic. Microphones don't work, software glitches screw up PowerPoint presentations, stuff gets out of order, and many small problems pop up that have to be dealt with for the show to run smoothly. They also tend to be very time consuming. A six-hour tech rehearsal for a two-hour show is pretty normal. The crew that Suzanne had hired was a first rate professional outfit and they were extremely competent. It was a long night, but a successful one. All the technical problems were dealt with by show time.

On Saturday, Suzanne had a full house, including a filmmaker who came to document as much as he could about the event. I met a lot of people and told my story. Of particular personal interest was the fact that everyone knew who I was because of my blog. Up until that point I'd never run into a single person who'd read it. After a morning full of talking, I took some time in the afternoon to practice my speech. I don't normally talk a lot and I was starting to strain. That evening, I got a call from the program director who asked me not to bash TED in my talk. I hadn't intended to anyway, but it did suddenly inspire me as to the direction that I wanted to take my talk. I threw out all the notes I had made, but there was no time to create new ones. I was going to be completely winging it.

Sunday morning went quickly. Because of the amount of stuff that Suzanne had to bring, I ended up driving both Larry and Russell in my car. I had a GPS, so everyone else followed me.

And Away We Go

My speech was added as a pre-talk, before the formal start of the previously scheduled program for people who came on time during the customary half hour or so between the stated start time and the actual start time of an event. But with Suzanne having gotten the word out for people to come early to hear me, we had a pretty full house by the time I spoke. I was asked one last time not to bash TED before I went on and to make sure that I didn't say anything libelous, and I assured everyone that I would not do that. My voice was extremely hoarse, but, rather than panic I took it as a blessing. When I am amped up and excited I tend to talk too quickly. Being forced to slow down would make me a better speaker.

The house lights dimmed, Suzanne came on stage to give a welcome, and from the darkness at the side of the stage I stepped up into the bright lights and all eyes were upon me. Suzanne gave me a wonderful introduction and she stepped off the stage. There was a moment of silence as I looked out past the bright lights at the shadowy faces seated in the house. Everyone was waiting. A couple of seconds felt like ten times that long. This was the most important speech I had ever given, but many years of speaking in Toastmasters had prepared me for it. It was show time. I just started talking and the speech began to flow coherently as I trusted it would.

I started with a brief history of parapsychology, to help show the context of what TED was doing, and, when I hit the ten minute mark, I switched over to talking about TED and what had happened. I started wrapping up with about two minutes to go and as the timer was winding down I began looking for a way to wrap up. When I hit just the right note for a strong ending, I just stopped. I finished up about a minute early. That's something about speaking that you learn with experience. It's better to close on a strong ending a bit too early rather than try to fill all of the available time. I got my applause and I left the stage. My part was done and now there was nothing to do but sit back and watch the show. As I got feedback for the speech later, it became clear to me that the primary goal of giving a good, TED centered speech had been met. I had set the proper tone for the show and gotten the TED controversy reported about without being overly negative. After I got a congratulatory text from my wife, who had seen the Livestream from Northern California, I knew I had done well. No one gets a compliment from her who doesn't deserve it.

The Vortex Dome was really cool with the way things were projected onto the walls and ceiling; Marianne Williamson, Russell Targ and Larry Dossey gave the excellent speeches one would expect of them and the other speakers, all experts on their topics, also had interesting things to say.

I had loaded my stuff in the car already and, when it all ended, I left for Northridge, where I would be staying with a friend. I made the long drive home the next morning. All the main aspects of the TED controversy had now come to a close. It was over.

CHAPTER NINETEEN

DEEPAK CHOPRA

JOINS THE FUN

The fallout from the controversy continued to plague TED. On April 18, a group of scientists took it on by publishing a blog post in the *Huffington Post*.[193] Deepak Chopra, MD. FACP; Stuart Hameroff, MD; Menas C. Kafatos, Ph.D.; Rudolph E. Tanzi, Ph.D.; and Neil Theise, MD all took TED to task for their censorship. I wrote this about it:

TED Psi Wars Double Bonus Round: Chopra Smacks Down Anderson

This post is a variation of a theme I've already covered, but this is such a good example that I have to share.

In a *Huffington Post* blog article, Deepak Chopra, MD. FACP, Stuart Hameroff, MD, Menas C. Kafatos, Ph.D., Rudolph E. Tanzi, Ph.D., and Neil Theise, MD, all took TED to task for all the same things that have already been covered by what seems like a thousand people. There was nothing particularly unusual about that; consciousness research is in their wheelhouse and this was a choice opportunity to take some shots at the intellectual equivalent of a training dummy. Chris Anderson and TED have gone a course that is built upon an easily discovered lie and it is no great matter to point out that lie and get down to the business of delivering a good smackdown. There have been several incredibly eloquent examples of this. (Ben Goertzel.); (Charles Eisenstein.); (David Metcalfe.)

In choosing to quash the mountain of consciousness research and all the people who support it, TED has instead given them a platform upon which to build their case. It's a very easy thing to use TED as an example of the legitimacy of consciousness research because all anyone has to do is ask TED to explain its reasons for pulling the videos and TEDxWestHollywood and point out how vacuous the reply is: the response is always the same:

"I got nothing"

What set this encounter apart from the others was that apparently Deepak Chopra et al. blogging on the *Huffington Post* was enough to goad Chris Anderson into responding with the same rather poor logic that he has been using all along.

Is TED under the thumb of "militant atheists"?!

That's another simple no (and a chuckle). We certainly have talks on our site from prominent atheists like Richard Dawkins and Sam Harris. We also have talks by religious leaders, including Pastor Rick Warren, Imam Feisal Abdul Rauf, Buddhist monk Matthieu Ricard and His Holiness the Karmapa, among many others. Religious scholar Karen Armstrong won the TED Prize in 2008. Benedictine Monk David Steindl-Rast will speak at TEDGlobal this June. When it comes to belief in God, and the practice of spirituality, a broad swath of beliefs are represented on TED.com, and also in our organization; our 100-person staff includes observant Buddhists, Bahai, Catholics, Quakers, Protestants, Jews and Muslims, as well as agnostics and atheists.

Militant atheists aren't bothered by religion, which they regard as simply the woo of belief in the bearded sky daddy. They are, however, threatened greatly by serious consciousness research, which undermines their belief that science—which they consider to be the only source of truth—is firmly on their side. Although this distinction is glaringly obvious to everyone who follows this stuff, Anderson just glosses it over.

Should TED have a policy of asking its TEDx event organizers to avoid pseudo-science?

> Your note implies we should not. We should allow "any speculative thinking ..." and just let the audience decide. I wonder if you've really thought through the implications of that. Imagine a speaker arguing, say, that eating five Big Macs a day could prevent Alzheimer's. Or someone claiming she was the living reincarnation of Joan of Arc. I'm sure at some point you too would want to draw the line.

A humble college freshman could point out the flaw in this statement: it's a straw man argument. Anderson has completely side stepped the hard problem of dealing with the evidence for nonlocal consciousness by comparing that research to the reincarnation of Joan of Arc and Big Mac research.

> But he or she should expect to face a robust standard of proof before their ideas take hold. And for every Galileo, there are thousands of people who just have bad, unscientific ideas. That's why in our guidance to the thousands of TEDx organizers around the world, we ask that they steer clear of talks that bear hallmarks of unsubstantiated science.

Another straw man. He is not talking about consciousness research because that meets a robust standard of proof. Anderson again steps away from the hard problem of the evidence by simply pretending that it doesn't exist.

Anderson isn't saying anything here that he hasn't already been said before; that is to say, copious amounts of nothing. All he has given here are ridiculously vague statements that never specifically deal with the reasons for TED's actions. To claim that someone is practicing pseudoscience is, itself, a claim. You have to provide proof for your statement otherwise all you have is this:

"Yeah, well, that's just, like, your opinion, man."

The point here, is that criticizing TED is ridiculously easy and, when Anderson replies, Chopra responds in the best way possible: he lets others do the talking for him. I found this one the most compelling:

> As a psychologist and professor who has spent years studying and teaching about consciousness at a public research university, I am alternately shocked and amused at the lengths people will travel to preserve an outmoded, materialist belief system in the face of overwhelming evidence to the contrary. I have colleagues who know nothing about the complexities of consciousness studies yet who, in their ignorance and arrogance, snidely condemn it as "pseudoscience", much as TED and its "anonymous" scientific advisory board have done. In response I have trained myself and my students to ask "What specific studies and data are you troubled by? What experimental procedures are you questioning? Have you read Thomas Kuhn's "The Structure of Scientific Revolutions?" Invariably the answer is silence.

> The kind of backlash exemplified by TED has occurred again and again since Giordano Bruno was burned at the stake in 1600 for proposing what astrophysicists now call "the multiple worlds theory", and it is always is at its most vociferous and vicious as a new way of thinking is emerging. But, as Thomas Kuhn reminds us, the old guard eventually and inevitably gives way to the new. I am currently teaching an upper-division undergraduate course entitled "Consciousness, Ethics, and the Natural World." Among other works that we are reading is Rupert Sheldrake's "Dogs that Know When Their Owners Are Coming Home." Yesterday I asked my students what they thought about TED's censuring of Sheldrake. Here are some of their thoughts:

> "TED is starting to exclude the very minds that it was created to gather."
> "TED is behaving in a very immature way ... just like middle school cliques."
> "TED has become a synonym for censure."
> "To which special interests will TED bow before next"?

"The scientists who pressured TED into censuring Sheldrake are afraid that accepting his perspective invalidates their own work and that they'll be pushed aside. They don't realize that there's room for everyone in the Multiverse."

These are students at a mainstream research university for whom Sheldrake's ideas are common sense rather than "pseudoscience." Clearly, this latest scientific revolution is upon us.

Kathleen D. Noble, Ph.D.
Professor of Consciousness
School of Science, Technology, Engineering, and Math,
University of Washington – Bothell

The kids have this one figured out.

I keep emphasizing how easy it is to criticize TED and Chris Anderson because I want to demonstrate something important that has shifted in the Psi Wars. There is nothing to fear from the skeptics. I used the analogy of a training dummy earlier because they hit back with all the force of a four-year-old boy. Once you get past their invective, insults and bad arguments you're left with nothing. They have no intellectual position to stand on; they can't prove that they're right and they can't prove that we're wrong. If you look at it from this perspective, you'll see what I see: Chris Anderson has closed the gates and walled himself up in his castle because his arguments are too weak to march into battle. As anyone who understands warfare will tell you, if all you can do is defend, then you have already lost; it's just a matter of time.

It's as if the skeptics have been viciously attacking us and we cowered at first, but then suddenly realized that they can't punch hard enough even to bruise us.

You can see that happening here. Deepak Chopra et al. have no fear of Anderson or TED. They know that the skeptics have no answer, no legitimate argument; no science to fall back on. Everyone can march right up to their gates and debate them with only the most feeble responses in return. Sheldrake and Hancock knew this when they challenged the science board to a debate. Everyone knows what cards the skeptics hold: They've got nothing. They can't give a good explanation of their actions; they can't debate Sheldrake or even Hancock; they won't respond to the open letter by Ken Jordan and they have no real answer to Deepak Chopra's criticism beyond bland corporatese assurances that say all the right things but have no substance at all.

What I've presented here is a way of looking at what's happening. We can either be upset by the intransigence of skeptics and complain about how they distort everything or we can choose to view them as making desperate moves to shore up their defenses against rising tides. The former is a defensive position that plays right into their hands, the latter acknowledges that we are taking the field and driving them back and forcing them to operate with a diminishing number of supporters and a shrinking space in which they can say what they please without having their poor arguments exposed. As far as I can tell, this is what winning looks like.

(Blog post and relevant links can be found at weilerpsiblog.wordpress.com)

Since the TED controversy, the battle has been slowly heating up, mostly on the backs of Rupert Sheldrake and Deepak Chopra, two figures who have gotten more than their fair share of attention from ideologue skeptics over the years. It's created an unusual situation where skeptics have been on the defensive, having to justify their actions rather than just having their way. What I've seen so far is that they tend to make more mistakes, such as the recent article by Jerry Coyne smearing Rupert Sheldrake and Deepak Chopra that was so over the top that it actually backfired.

There is a very positive development. In the middle of May, Reality Sandwich launched a Kickstarter campaign to raise $40,000 with a month to do it. While things looked dicey going into the last week, donations suddenly surged and kept surging right on past the goal and all the way to $56,360.[194] Money is finding its way into the hands of people who are reporting on and documenting the coming changes.

The battle for Rupert Sheldrake's Wikipedia biography page rages on. As of this writing, a full two months after I started, the page has finally softened up a bit and is less slanderous. An attempt was recently made to haul all of the ideologues into arbitration and toss them all out on their ear, but it failed to gain enough traction to go to arbitration.

The debate that both Sheldrake and Hancock proposed never happened. TED never responded; their anonymous science board was silent; the loudest skeptics, Jerry Coyne, PZ Myers and Kylie Sturgess, who first called for the removal of Sheldrake's video, never responded and neither did anyone else in the skeptical community. These scientists and pundits, who collectively demanded the head of Rupert Sheldrake et al.; whose counsel Chris Anderson and the rest of TED depended on to get the science right, left that media organization looking idiotic and reactionary. TED's crime was in believing that these self-assured skeptics knew what they were talking about.

Some of them were professors and scientists after all. Yet, when this incredibly noisy skeptical lynch mob was faced with the prospect of having to get down the to the facts and prove what they had claimed, all you could hear was the light chirping of crickets.

The Dutch have a saying: „De honden blaffen, maar de karavaan trekt verder." The dogs bark, but the caravan moves on.

CHAPTER TWENTY

ONCE MORE
INTO THE BREECH

The controversy went on even after this book was published. On April 2, 2014, parapsychology advocate Paul Revis organized a very civilized protest (they called it a rebuttal) at TED headquarters in New York and presented Chris Anderson personally with a petition signed by over 250 PhD's and MD's protesting TED's actions as well as over 350 people without advanced degrees.

It was a Wednesday and it was held in the middle of the day and it had rained earlier so about 12 people showed up. Paul Revis explained his reasons for organizing it.

> I started Set Science Free because I'm very passionate about the nature of reality and understanding the nature of reality. There is a large body of research within the scientific community that is dismissed sight unseen by scientists around the world. This is the key. This research is essentially overlooked because of dogmatic assumption. This is a major oversight that has gone on too long and must be confronted in order for science to progress. Ultimately, I'd like to see all scientific research introduced as part of the standard educational curriculum. Psi research is one example of this. This TED campaign is the first step in a larger movement to make that happen. This isn't just about

psi research or quantum mechanics; this is about all research within the scientific community. Everyone has dogmatic views and we all need to look beyond that individually and institutionally.

The whole thing was very civilized to the point that the TED office was notified a week in advance that this was happening. This approach paid off when Chris Anderson made a point of coming downstairs to talk to the protesters.

The mainstream press did not show up and did not cover the event. Considering how little coverage the controversy had generated even at its height, this wasn't at all surprising.

The protest had two demands:

1. Reinstate Rupert Sheldrake's Talk "The Science Delusion" into the main database of searchable talks on TED.com. Desegregate it and display it equally, among other talks, as it does not lack any quality or qualifying factors that other talks have demonstrated. The caliber of scientific research behind Sheldrake's talk is solid, and he should not be rejected purely due to (what we believe are) paradigmatic differences based in the dogmas of various scientists, vs. any actual scientific justification.

2. Publish the names of all members of TED's anonymous scientific board. Members of scientific boards and scientific journals must be public without exception because they are accountable to their peers and to their readers. The anonymity of TED's scientific board lends credence to the idea that its scientists may be biased against good science that leads to conclusions which do not fit neatly into the common scientific paradigm. If TED's scientific board members were not anonymous, they would presumably make themselves known, such that they could be engaged in an honest intellectual challenge such as the debate that has stirred around Sheldrake's lecture.

The whole protest/rebuttal did not last very long and did not come to any satisfying conclusions. Anderson stuck to the same belief system he had relied upon the entire time. I wrote at the time:

Perhaps because of the cordial atmosphere, Chris Anderson, curator and owner of TED, came down to talk with the protesters and graciously accepted the petition. He then spent about fifteen minutes getting into the whole parapsychology discussion with Paul Revis and Richard Perl. While nothing was decided, Chris Anderson did say that he supported their right to protest, but that his science advisors and the scientific community at large maintained that psychic ability is not accepted by mainstream science and that until it is, he regards the topic as too fringe for TED. (Or words to that effect. I don't have his exact words and can't directly quote him.)

And that was pretty much the end of it. As far as I know, that was the last event of any significance related directly to the controversy. To the best of my knowledge there haven't been any large controversies surrounding parapsychology in the intervening years where the public has gotten involved.

TED appears to have lost the tremendous buzz around their brand shortly after the controversy ended. TED talks stopped being the "IN" thing, they stopped being promoted by the *Huffington Post* and generally faded into the background somewhat. Very occasionally a TED talk will make the rounds, but it doesn't seem to have the gravitas that it once did.

Whether this was a direct result of the controversy I cannot say. I did not read anywhere that people were abandoning TED because of it. Rather, this was expressed as a disappointment of the shallow nature of TED talks, which is a natural and completely understandable outcome of a talk which is only 20 minutes long at most. Were these things somehow intertwined? Did the controversy take the shine off TED talks and then people found other things wrong with them? It's not a question that will ever have a definitive answer. Here's what I do know.

While the controversy never really made it into the mainstream press, it still travelled far and wide and boosted recognition of Rupert Sheldrake considerably. One of the videos of that talk has been viewed over 3.7 million times. Graham Hancock has an astounding 2.2 million views. Both videos come with a massive number of comments, almost universally critical of the banning. That's a LOT of bad press for TED talks. In addition, Joe Rogan's podcast with Graham Hancock has almost 6 million views. I don't have any polls or statistics to back this up, but my impression was that because the controversy was strictly on line, it tended to reach a younger, more connected audience that's less likely to rely on or care about mainstream sources. Losing the millennials is not good for your future.

TED not only wasn't doomed by this but has grown at a decent pace and this is reflected in their nonprofit financials for 2017 which showed $85,667,678 in income. For comparison in 2015 they had $66,194,730 in income. That's not terribly surprising because TED makes a unique and valuable product that reaches far beyond the confines of a single science controversy. The money comes chiefly from contributions and a lot of contributions are in the form of hefty membership fees, starting at $5,000. That demographic is going to be older and less sensitive to the controversy or perhaps not even aware of it. In any case they have survived this one mistake and are arguably thriving.

Taking a break

I took a break from all the controversy and dealing with skeptics and also stopped posting to my blog. It had run its course and it was time to move on. Blogs used to be a fairly important source of information on a wide variety of topics, but they don't seem to be used as much now. There was also very little that I had interest in posting anymore and I had started to veer off into other topics.

My wife commented that I seemed happier once I got away from all of it, which is not surprising at all. Dealing with immature angry skeptics is emotionally draining and it's easy to get caught in the stupid one-upmanship that always seems to happen. I needed to get away from that.

I spent a year exploring stand-up comedy and going out at night to do 5-and 10-minute gigs. I really didn't know what to do with myself. Eventually I gave that up as the late hours were too much and I wasn't really connecting with the audience. Although I have a blue-collar job, I'm not really a blue-collar guy.

Parapsychology has continued its slow march forward with the latest drama centering around the "Feeling the Future" studies. As I said before, since the studies really couldn't be criticized on methodology or statistics, the skeptics chose, instead, to question all of psychology. The last article is from about a year ago. I'm not quite sure where that's all going, but skeptics are very serious about not accepting Bem's research.

Eventually, I settled myself back in front of the computer and encountered a question and answer site called Quora and felt drawn to put in a correct answer about parapsychology after encountering several bad ones. After some puttering around, I realized that I wasn't getting ganged up on and kicked off the site. Nothing happened.

This was unique on a universally accessible social media site. Getting on community moderated sites with a subject like parapsychology is just asking for trouble. When the moderators and other skeptics gang up on you, it's time to leave if they don't just kick you out.

But this site used a computer algorithm and some humans within the company and did not have any community moderators. People with minority opinions were free to express themselves and everyone had to abide by the rules, which amount to Be Nice, Be Respectful. The rules are applied equally to everyone. They also have a real name policy.

The site has its share of creeps, blowhards, trolls and immature idiots, and women get trolled way too much with creepy messages from disposable accounts, but they do not overwhelm the good content. It's actually a very pleasant site if you play by the rules.

On Quora I had my very first chance to go head to head with skeptics on parapsychology questions. No one could stop me. And the outcome was pretty much what I expected—better actually. The skeptics would say "there is no evidence" and in my answer I would provide evidence. Over time, the skeptics began to lose credibility and their answers on these subjects drew less and less interest. There is no substitute for knowing what you're talking about.

Currently, I have a feed on Quora[195] where I post scientific psi research and it has been steadily collecting followers. About ten thousand to date. Parapsychology has a chance at respectability if it's allowed to share information. The sheer weight of evidence can overcome the steady noise of skepticism over time if people are given the opportunity to learn of it.

Another interesting thing that's happened is that skeptics are interacting more, and the general public is getting a feel for how these people think. They can see the difference between what skeptics think they know and what they actually do know. And they can see how intolerant skeptics can be when confronted with new information.

They can be really touchy when presented with evidence that suggests that they're wrong. To be fair, no one likes to be proven wrong and I dislike it as much as anybody. The need to be right can be very powerful. The question, however, isn't whether we emotionally react, but what we do after that. A person who can never concede is much different from one who can, eventually, even if they both feel the same about being wrong.

When I first started posting on Quora, I was attacked relentlessly by skeptics and I responded rudely. This got me reported for violating policy, so I stopped doing that. And the zealot skeptics on the site had to gradually change their story to accommodate the fact that someone had showed up who was making them look bad. Instead of "no evidence" they were forced to concede the existence of evidence, but hastily claimed that it was very poor.

The fact that they had to make any concessions at all is telling. Even more interesting to me was that on Quora I have the ability to delete comments on what I write. At first, I avoided this, remembering the backlash that has occurred in the past, but gradually I became bolder and now I just delete comments that are factually incorrect. Skeptics can write their own answers if they choose.

CHAPTER TWENTY-ONE

WHENCEFORTH
FROM HERE?

If you've been paying attention while reading this book, you'll see that convincing skeptics with evidence is a non-starter. It will never happen and they'll continue to deny the existence of psychic ability all the way to their graves no matter how much scientific evidence they're confronted with. Their emotional resistance is simply too strong.

Whatever the path to acceptance is for parapsychology, it will not come about because the weight of evidence caused skeptics to change their minds. Rather, it will be because enough unbiased people were exposed to the subject to overwhelm the skeptics.

In this way, it's like other social areas where there are long-standing barriers that for whatever reason won't go away. We're not getting rid of misogyny or racism anytime soon. People know it's wrong not to treat women and minorities as equals, but they do it anyway. We all know how difficult it is to change this behavior to the point that we have had to create laws to enforce what should be common decency.

You can convince only people who are already predisposed to consider evidence and examine the facts impartially. This isn't everybody and it sometimes isn't the people who, we imagine, would do this. I have seen people with a high school education or less, sort out intellectually challenging issues with more clarity than some people with advanced degrees. They have no reputation to protect, so they are free to examine evidence and reach conclusions that would cause academics professional trouble.

Resistance to change is typically cultural and emotional. In this way, the reluctance to embrace a non-materialistic view of the universe is no different. Evidence piles up but does little to change the culture of denial.

I gave up arguing with skeptics because it is a fool's errand. The methods of skepticism are ultimately the methods of marketing, not science. They repeat their message over and over, attempting to suppress opposing points of view, which they disagree with, and attack and trivialize any positive information that reaches the mass media. They typically focus most of their attention on information that rises in the public awareness and ignore info. that doesn't.

When faced with this sort of an attack, the only sane response is to use the same tactics as a counterbalance. Rupert Sheldrake understands this all too well and it is the reason behind the website: Skeptical About Skeptics.

If the scientific field of parapsychology is ever to get beyond Fringe Hell, there must be people constantly repeating positive messages over and over again in social media and providing enough evidence to show that the skeptics are wrong.

I've discovered something encouraging, though. Setting aside the batshit crazy that is American politics, most other areas tend towards truth over time. That is to say, in order for lies, half-truths and obfuscation to succeed, they need to be constantly fed into the public sphere, but, as the truth takes hold, it generally can't be removed and slowly begins to take the oxygen away from the lies.

In the world of social media, the lies start suffering from lack of attention as more and more people recognize them for what they are. Algorithms notice this and begin to share that information less and a sort of death spiral begins.

I've begun to see this on Quora, where the number of skeptics willing to trot out their well-worn lies has diminished and their ability to attract views and upvotes as well. Meanwhile, people are curious about psychic ability and if someone knowledgeable answers, those things tend to get viewed more often, which leads to upvotes and more sharing by algorithms.

It's slow, but noticeable. What makes this slow is that there are very few people interested in plugging away on social media to promote parapsychology.

The skeptics are driven by their internal zealotry; others? Not so much. And, unless you are driven by zealotry, it's hard to repeat the same messages over and over again without any end in sight. It's boring and, more importantly, time consuming. It's very easy to say something is wrong or doesn't exist, but it takes a lot of explaining to counteract that.

This has become somewhat easier over the years as more information has come on line, such as the psi encyclopedia and various YouTube video podcasts, such as New Thinking Allowed, but all of this stuff still requires explanations.

Marketing is about getting your message out there and repeating it ad nauseum until people tend to see it as the truth. It's a psychological trick and it totally works.

It's also about making sure your message stays on top and in front of any criticism. Since most media sources already tend towards giving skeptics this edge, it's very difficult for any positive information about parapsychology to prevail. The media are essentially doing the skeptic's marketing for them.

To counteract massive negative marketing, you need massive positive marketing. And, as luck would have it, I have an example.

It turns out that in the world of finance there are short-sellers who borrow stocks in order to sell them at their current price on the agreement that they will buy them back at a later date and return them to the lender. If the stock goes down, they pocket the difference. If the stock goes up, they lose money.

Got that? In order to drive a stock down and make money, short sellers sometimes resort to anonymous smear campaigns using social media and paid stories in prominent media outlets. It should be completely illegal, but it's not. It's a grey area of law.

The practice is widespread enough to have attracted the attention of law academics.[196]

> In recent years, anonymous online hit pieces against public companies have become an increasingly common and effective form of short activism. Given their success in driving down stock prices, anonymous online short campaigns are likely here to stay.

The example I'm going to use is the well-known young car company, Tesla, which exclusively makes electric vehicles. The short selling attacks began right around the time Tesla began mass producing their all electric sedan, the Model 3, in the later part of 2017. I was a bit of a Tesla fanboy and was following news of their progress and writing answers on Quora about Tesla every now and again for fun, when negative stories—many of them wildly inaccurate—began to pop up in various national media stories.

The tone around Tesla changed almost immediately and, before long, I was dealing with relentless attacks on my writing and seeing an endless stream of very negative questions about the company and its cars. It was so much like the crazy hateful nonsense that surrounds parapsychology that I had strong feelings of déjà vu. It was a huge well-coordinated smear campaign far bigger than anything I'd seen in parapsychology. The joy of writing about something fun and interesting to me changed into taking a constantly defensive position where I was disputing lies and half-truths.

These negative stories can create a lot of stress for these companies and the president and CEO of Tesla, Elon Musk, was no exception. Although production ramped up as expected, and Tesla more or less met their numbers, sometimes faltering, sometimes doing better than expected, as one would anticipate for a company doing mass production of a completely new type of car for the first time, Musk made some missteps which made business headlines for weeks at a time.

It has a happy ending. The negative press did not carry the day and has done little to reduce demand for these cars. And the short sellers lost billions of dollars. I've informally polled people from time to time and I get a variety of responses from people being pro-Tesla, to indifference to being anti-Tesla.

I was following this at the peak of the attack on Quora, where things are usually dealt with in more depth, due to the nature of the platform and discovered at least one account that was there solely to smear Tesla, and one other that was probably 90% Tesla smears with some random stuff thrown in. It was easy to get the former account deleted by reporting it, but the latter did not cross whatever line Quora created and it stayed. In any case, people were clearly getting paid to attack Tesla anonymously through social media.

The attacks were the very definition of truthiness. Constant predictions of imminent bankruptcy, which have been going on for ten years; claims that the company is losing money on every car it makes, (false); making a big deal that it loses money every quarter, (it's capital intensive and they're heavily investing in the company's growth), its cars constantly catch fire, (nope, safer than gas cars in that respect), management is fleeing, (nope, just normal levels of turnover), autopilot kills people, (yes, but only if you ignore the oft repeated warnings that autopilot does not function in all situations and you have to be ready to control your vehicle at all times.), and so on.

In addition to this, there are personal attacks on anyone who comes out publicly in support of Tesla vehicles:

> But when a smear is in play, it doesn't stop with negative news stories. If smear professionals are at work (and I believe they are in this case), they go beyond negative stories to attack any person or story that presents a positive spin. A recent example is the story of the automotive journalist Dan Neil of The *Wall Street Journal*. Neil was viciously attacked by Twitter trolls who questioned his ethics after a glowing review of the new Tesla Model 3 Dual Motor Performance Model. It's important to note that personal attacks and character assassination are hallmarks of a coordinated smear campaign.[197]

What makes the Tesla story relevant here is Tesla has built up a fan base over the years of people who are knowledgeable about the car and the company. And when the anonymous short seller attacks began, this army of ordinary people got on social media and began a sort of informal positive media campaign on Tesla's behalf.[198]

It helped. Tesla's stock price would nosedive during a wave of negative articles and then bounce right back shortly thereafter. Even recently the stock price, which in one small period of time had a high of about $400, fluctuated by almost $200 *in a span of just 5 days*.[199]

While there are also positive stories about Tesla, they can't quite compete with the noise of negativity and it takes influencers to get on social media and talk about how flawed the negative stories are so that they have less impact. The influencers in this case aren't paid and write about other things, so their credibility is high enough to cause their readers to read the negative stories more critically. In Tesla's case there are enough of these people to somewhat offset the barrage of negativity. Because of this, Tesla Inc. survives.

Parapsychology faces a very similar type of attack, although at nowhere near the same scale and if people are being paid for it, there is no evidence of it. Still, there is the same misinformation and personal attacks that are associated with a coordinated smear campaign. (How coordinated it actually is, I cannot say, but the overall effect is similar.) What the Tesla experience shows is that it is very hard to overcome this but that a sizeable fan base with knowledgeable individuals can make a pretty big dent in the arena of public opinion.

Tesla is helped by the fact that their cars are on the road and that people can see them driving every day. (This varies a lot according to where you live. I see as many as 30 of their cars in a day where some people might see only one a week.)

Parapsychology is helped by the fact that a lot of people have psychic experiences. The leap, though, from having a psychic experience to defending the science of psychic ability, is a large one. First, one has to sort through all of the misinformation and then, ultimately, make up their minds about what the truth is, all while being personally attacked by trolls. There is a lot of ground to cover and much to learn with no obvious payoff for the effort except learning something new.

I don't think that most people have the stomach to advocate for parapsychology. Interacting with the public attracts the zealot skeptics who will turn the whole experience into a defensive one. You need a thick skin to do this and a lot of the joy is lost in dealing with hostile, angry people.

Whenceforth from here? My best guess is that things slowly go forward towards acceptance of psychic ability until some unknown tipping point is reached, and then things will move very quickly. Where that tipping point is, I cannot say, but I think it will be within my lifetime. It's easier than ever to smear people, but it's also easier to get the truth out there.

At some point there will be a critical mass of people who know that parapsychology is a real science and that there is substantial scientific evidence supporting psychic ability. When that critical mass is reached, the genie will no longer fit in the bottle.

ENDNOTES

If you have the print edition, I have provided a webpage with all the links for easy referencing. Google "The Weiler Psi" including the quotation marks. The title is: Psi Wars, 2nd Edition, supplemental materials for print edition

1   A straw man argument is a misrepresentation of an opponent's position through an unfair comparison. Example: "After Will said that we should put more money into health and education, Warren responded by saying that he was surprised that Will hates our country so much that he wants to leave it defenseless by cutting military spending."

2   Psychical Research in the Psychological Review, 1894–1900: A Bibliographical Note, Journal *of Scientific Exploration*, Vol. 23, No. 2, pp. 211–220, 2009

3   Joseph Jastrow, *Psychological Review,* 1900, p. 411

4   http://archived.parapsych.org/members/jb_rhine.html

5   https://www.theepochtimes.com/does-telepathy-conflict-with-science_1487352.html

6   https://web.archive.org/web/20080819235335/http://www.gatesofhorn.com/blog/the_religion_and_dogma_of_science

7   http://www.ted.com/pages/16

8   http://www.reddit.com/r/tedtalks/comments/1443ke/the_ted_name_is_being_dragged_through_the_mud_in/

9   http://www.naturalnews.com/031116_Dr_Andrew_Wakefield_British_Medical_Journal.html

10 http://www.centerforreikiresearch.org/RRSummariesHome.aspx

11 http://freethoughtblogs.com/pharyngula/2013/03/06/for-shame-tedx/

12 http://www.patheos.com/blogs/tokenskeptic/2013/03/remember-how-tedx-were-all-about-not-the-bad-science-pseudoscience-and-health-hoaxes/

13 http://whyevolutionistrue.wordpress.com/2013/03/06/tedx-talks-completely-discredited-rupert-sheldrake-speaks-argues-that-speed-of-light-is-dropping/

14 http://forum.mind-energy.net/

15 http://www.ted.com/conversations/16894/rupert_sheldrake_s_tedx_talk.html

16 Dean Radin, *The Conscious Universe*, p. 87

17 *Parapsychology and the Skeptics* by Chris Carter, p. 64

18 A Bayes Factor Meta-Analysis of Recent Extrasensory Perception Experiments: Comment on Storm, Tressoldi, and Di Risio (2010) Psychological Bulletin, 2013, Vol. 139, No. 1, 241–247

19 Testing the Storm et al. (2010) Meta-Analysis Using Bayesian and Frequentist Approaches: Reply to Rouder et al. (2013) Psychological Bulletin, 2013, Vol. 139, No. 1, 248–254

20 http://dbem.org/ResponsetoWagenmakers.pdf

21 http://www.sheldrake.org/Articles&Papers/papers/staring/schoolexp.html

22 https://www.sheldrake.org/research/sense-of-being-stared-at

23 http://www.sheldrake.org/Articles&Papers/papers/staring/pdf/JCSpaper1.pdf

24 Colwell, J, S. Schröder, and D. Sladen. 2000. The ability to detect unseen staring: A literature review and empirical tests. British Journal of Psychology 91: 71-85

25 Sheldrake and his Critics: The sense of being glared at, *Journal of Consciousness Studies*, Vol. 12, No. 6 (2005)

26 http://www.sheldrake.org/Articles&Papers/papers/staring/followup.html

27 *The Conscious Universe*, p. 153-155

28 Examining Psychokinesis: The Interaction of Human Intention With Random Number Generators—A Meta-Analysis, *Psychological Bulletin*, 2006, Vol. 132, No. 4, 497–523

29 Reexamining Psychokinesis: Comment on Bösch, Steinkamp, and Boller, *Psychological Bulletin*, Vol. 132, No. 4, 529–532 (2006)

30 A critique of the parapsychological random number generator meta-analyses of Radin and Nelson, Journal of Scientific Exploration 20(3) :402-419, September, 2006

31 https://www.csicop.org/specialarticles/show/
    response_to_alcocks_back_from_the_future_comments_on_bem

32 https://www.ejwagenmakers.com/2011/WagenmakersEtAl2011_JPSP.
    pdf

33 https://www.ncbi.nlm.nih.gov/pmc/articles/PMC3303812/

34 https://skeptiko.com/daryl-bem-responds-to-parapsychology-debunkers/

35 https://www.ncbi.nlm.nih.gov/pmc/articles/PMC4706048/

36 https://slate.com/health-and-science/2017/06/daryl-bem-proved-esp-is-
    real-showed-science-is-broken.html

37 http://weilerpsiblog.wordpress.com/2013/03/09/the-psi-wars-come-to-ted/

38 http://atheismexposed.tripod.com/dawkins_rebuttals.htm

39 http://www.atheismresearch.com/

40 http://www.gallup.com/poll/16915/three-four-americans-believe-
    paranormal.aspx

41 Richard Broughton, *Journal of Parapsychology*, 1991, pg. 10

42 L. David Leiter, The Pathology of Organized Skepticism, *Journal of Scientific
    Exploration*, vol. 16, no. 1, pg. 125-128, 2002

43 J.E. Kennedy, Journal *of Parapsychology*, 2005, Volume 69, pp. 263-292

44 http://www.myersbriggs.org/my-mbti-personality-type/mbti-basics/the-
    16-mbti-types.asp

45 J.E. Kennedy, *Journal of Parapsychology*, 2005, Volume 69, pp. 263-292

46 http://freethoughtblogs.com/pharyngula/2013/05/05/i-officially-divorce-
    myself-from-the-skeptic-movement/

47 http://www.quackwatch.com/

48 http://www.quackwatch.com/01QuackeryRelatedTopics/hfreedom.html

49 Brain functions are typically not confined to one side of the brain except
    through extreme brain damage, such as a severe stroke. The left/right
    dichotomy is more of an emphasis.

50 http://www.nytimes.com/2005/08/02/science/02deni.html?_r=0

51 http://thomassheridanarts.com/articles.php?article_id=82

52 https://web.archive.org/web/20130420234117/http://thomassheridanarts.
    com/articles.php?article_id=82

53 http://www.michaelnugent.com/2013/03/03/
    examples-of-nasty-pushback-against-some-feminists-on-the-internet/

54 http://www.slate.com/articles/double_x/doublex/2012/10/sexism_in_the_
    skeptic_community_i_spoke_out_then_came_the_rape_threats.html

55   http://www.skepticink.com/backgroundprobability/2012/11/14/
list-of-known-sexists/

56   http://blogs.scientificamerican.com/mind-guest-blog/2013/08/06/
im-sick-of-talking-about-sexual-harassment/

57   http://freethoughtblogs.com/pharyngula/2013/08/06/
no-it-could-never-happen-to-her/comment-page-1/

58   http://benjaminradford.com/wp-content/uploads/2015/06/Radford_
Stollznow-Joint-Statement-pic.jpg

59   http://freethoughtblogs.com/pharyngula/2013/08/07/carrie-poppy-tells-all/

60   http://freethoughtblogs.com/pharyngula/2013/08/08/what-do-you-do-
when-someone-pulls-the-pin-and-hands-you-a-grenade/

61   http://theothermccain.com/2013/08/08/bill-nye-the-science-guy-harasser/

62   http://online.wsj.com/article/SB115274744775305134.html

63   https://web.archive.org/web/20131111104227/http://radiofreethinker.
com/2013/08/02/the-candle-is-out/

64   http://www.themadskeptic.com/2012/07/modus-operandi-ad-hominem.html

65   Kerry S. Walters, Critical Thinking, Rationality and the Vulcanization of
Students, *Journal of Higher Education*, vol. 61, no. 4, (July/August 1990)

66   http://freethoughtblogs.com/pharyngula/2013/08/07/carrie-poppy-tells-all/

67   *The Conscious Universe*, by Dean Radin, p. 240

68   Parapsychology and the Skeptics, by Chris Carter, p. 83

69   *Randi's Prize*, by Robert McCluhan, p. 293-4

70   http://dailygrail.com/features/the-myth-of-james-randis-million-dollar-
challenge

71   http://michaelprescott.typepad.com/michael_prescotts_blog/2006/12/
the_challenge.html

72   http://weilerpsiblog.wordpress.com/randis-million-dollar-challenge/

73   https://www.sheldrake.org/reactions/
james-randi-a-conjurer-attempts-to-debunk-research-on-animals

74   *Randi's Prize*, by Robert McCluhan, p. 19

75   http://www.victorzammit.com/articles/lawyerebutsrandi.html

76   *The Heretics*, by Will Storr, p. 368

77   http://www.skepticalinvestigations.org/Mediaskeptics/index.
html#JamesRandi

78   http://forums.randi.org/showthread.php?t=73944

79   ibid.

80 http://web.archive.org/web/20120719085154/http://www.stevevolk.com/archives/952

81 Verified through a reliable source who has worked on several MDC applications.

82 http://forums.randi.org/showthread.php?s=192df0a489b90c99a0350e03d1fbfddc&t=119896&page=5

83 http://forums.randi.org/archive/index.php/t-34848.html

84 http://en.wikipedia.org/wiki/James_Randi_Educational_Foundation

85 http://forums.randi.org/showthread.php?t=82062

86 http://forums.randi.org/showthread.php?t=119896&page=6

87 http://forums.randi.org/showthread.php?t=119896&page=12

88 http://forums.randi.org/showthread.php?t=115239

89 https://web.archive.org/web/20131219075033/http://www.scienceofhomeopathy.com/challenge.html

90 http://www.theblindcarefoundation.com/Randi-eng.html

91 http://www.imdb.com/title/tt1589787/

92 https://web.archive.org/web/20130906114155/http://www.cfpf.org.uk/articles/background/nicholls.html

93 http://forums.randi.org/showthread.php?t=119896&page=12

94 http://monkeywah.typepad.com/paranormalia/2009/05/patricia-putt-score-for-sceptics.html

95 http://en.wikipedia.org/wiki/James_Randi_Educational_Foundation#One_Million_Dollar_Paranormal_Challenge

96 https://web.archive.org/web/20130225052551/https://en.wikipedia.org/wiki/Derek_Ogilvie

97 Wiseman, R. & Schlitz, M. (1998). Experimenter effects and the remote detection of staring. Journal of Parapsychology, 61(3), 197-208.

98 https://www.theguardian.com/science/2009/may/12/psychic-claims-james-randi-paranormal

99 https://web.archive.org/web/20120425211637/https://www.drgaryschwartz.com/THE-EXPERIMENTS-TRILOGY.html

100 http://www.discord.org/~lippard/rawlins-starbaby.txt

101 http://www.skepticalinvestigations.org/Observeskeptics/CSICOP/30yearswar_2.html

102 http://www.planetos.info/marchron.html

103 *The Journal of the American Society for Psychical Research*, Volume 86, No. 1, January 1992, pp. 19-63

[104]   https://web.archive.org/web/20090407032017/http://www.unconventional-wisdom.com/WAW/PHACT-FSGP.html

[105]   http://cura.free.fr/xv/14starbb.html

[106]   http://cura.free.fr/xv/14starbb.html

[107]   http://www.sheldrake.org/Articles&Papers/papers/animals/comment.html

[108]   "Heads I Win, Tails You Lose." Or, How Richard Wiseman Nullifies Positive Results, and What to Do about It: A Response to Wiseman's (2010) Critique of Parapsychology, *Journal of the Society for Psychical Research* 74: 156-167 (2010)

[109]   http://www.csicop.org/si/show/research_on_the_feeling_of_being_stared_at/

[110]   http://www.criticandokardec.com.br/CSICOP_vs_Natasha_Demkina.htm

[111]   http://www.huffingtonpost.com/2013/05/09/sylvia-brownes-amanda-perry-psychic_n_3240157.html

[112]   http://www.skepdic.com/tm.html

[113]   http://skepticsontm.blogspot.com/2009/03/review-skeptics-dictionary.html

[114]   http://www.skepdic.com/barron.html

[115]   http://www.jonbarron.org/article/rebutting-skeptic

[116]   http://www.bradburyac.mistral.co.uk/nlpfax27.htm

[117]   ttps://web.archive.org/web/20150311201011/http://www.missionatlantis.com/atlantis-articles/atlantis-grades.php

[118]   http://whatstheharm.net/

[119]   http://whatstheharm.net/hivaidsdenial.html

[120]   https://web.archive.org/web/20131222025119/https://www.fda.gov/Drugs/DevelopmentApprovalProcess/DevelopmentResources/DrugInteractionsLabeling/ucm114848.htm

[121]   https://web.archive.org/web/20131203022303/http://www.cancure.org/medical_errors.htm

[122]   http://www.canadafreepress.com/index.php/article/51525

[123]   http://plato.stanford.edu/entries/qm-copenhagen/

[124]   Dean Radin, *PHYSICS ESSAYS* 25, 2 (2012) p. 169-170

[125]   http://quantumenigma.com/nutshell/

[126]   http://www.robertlanzabiocentrism.com/biocentrism/

[127]   http://www.deepdyve.com/lp/american-association-of-physics-teachers/the-scandal-of-quantum-mechanics-RP6nCKGI2D

128 http://quantumenigma.com/controversy/

129 http://www.time.com/time/magazine/article/0,9171,1580394,00.html#ixzz2VjzfOIdF

130 http://www.skeptiko.com/217-gary-marcus-near-death-experience/

131 http://en.wikipedia.org/wiki/History_of_Wikipedia

132 https://www.bloomberg.com/news/articles/2010-02-18/google-and-wikipedia-separated-at-birth

133 https://web.archive.org/web/20121204172016/http://trafficplanet.com/topic/4299-how-google-really-works/

134 https://web.archive.org/web/20131219221734/http://www.intelligentpositioning.com/blog/2012/02/wikipedia-page-one-of-google-uk-for-99-of-searches/

135 http://www.bruceclay.com/blog/2007/02/the-lisas-problem-with-wikipedia-explained/

136 https://en.wikipedia.org/w/index.php?title=Talk:Energy_Catalyzer&oldid=424578443

137

138 http://wikipediocracy.com/2015/08/16/a-compendium-of-wikipedia-criticism/

139 http://econlog.econlib.org/archives/2012/05/the_problem_wit_6.html

140 http://doubletap.cs.umd.edu/WikipediaStudy/

141 https://web.archive.org/web/20131012044755/news.techeye.net/internet/wackypedia-admits-pagan-purge

142 https://en.wikipedia.org/wiki/Wikipedia:Identifying_and_using_primary_and_secondary_sources

143 http://chronicle.com/article/The-Undue-Weight-of-Truth-on/130704/

144 http://badsciencewikipedia.wordpress.com/2013/11/15/someone-beat-me-to-it-said-it-all-three-years-ago/

145 https://corporate.britannica.com/britannica_nature_response.pdf

146 https://web.archive.org/web/20120808165127/http://felipeortega.net/sites/default/files/thesis-jfelipe.pdf

147 http://deanradin.blogspot.com/2007/04/trouble-with-wiki.html

148 https://newslog.cyberjournal.org/climategate-the-corruption-of-wikipedia/

149 http://en.wikipedia.org/wiki/Wikipedia:WikiProject_Skepticism/Participants

150 http://www.chirobase.org/

[151] http://en.wikipedia.org/wiki/Parapsychology

[152] http://en.wikipedia.org/wiki/Special:Contributions/Nvdvn

[153] http://dailygrail.com/Skepticism/2011/5/Wikipedia-and-Fringe-Topics

[154] http://monkeywah.typepad.com/paranormalia/2013/03/guerrilla-skeptics.html

[155] https://www.youtube.com/watch?v=5FuJT9mp0jw

[156] http://guerrillaskepticismonwikipedia.blogspot.ca/2011/08/more-very-very-basic-editing-pet.html

[157] https://en.wikipedia.org/w/index.php?title=Pet_psychic&oldid=446932963

[158] https://en.wikipedia.org/wiki/List_of_skeptics_and_skeptical_organizations

[159] https://en.wikipedia.org/w/index.php?title=Talk:Rupert_Sheldrake&oldid=576744263#TEDx_talk

[160] On every Wikipedia page, just to the right of the Wikipedia logo are two tabs. One is marked "article". That's what you see when you go to a Wikipedia page. The other is marked "talk". If you click on that tab you are sent to a web page where editors discuss that article and work out editing conflicts.

[161] https://en.wikipedia.org/w/index.php?title=User_talk:Barney_the_barney_barney&oldid=577848953#Craig_Weiler

[162] From an email to the author

[163] https://en.wikipedia.org/w/index.php?title=Wikipedia:Administrators%27_noticeboard/Incidents&oldid=577289131#Craig_Weiler

[164] http://wikipediocracy.com/2013/07/08/how-to-ban-a-pov-you-dislike-in-9-easy-steps/

[165] There are many links on this blog post which can be followed at: http://weilerpsiblog.wordpress.com/2013/10/29/wikipedia-the-only-way-to-win-is-not-to-play/

[166] https://www.theatlantic.com/technology/archive/2015/10/how-wikipedia-is-hostile-to-women/411619/

[167] http://thewikipedian.net/category/future-of-wikipedia/

[168] http://whyevolutionistrue.wordpress.com/2013/03/22/oy-vey-tedx-continues-the-woo-now-with-more-self-help/

[169] http://whyevolutionistrue.wordpress.com/2013/03/30/ted-revokes-license-for-tedx-west-hollywood-event/

[170] http://www.kurzweilai.net/ted-removes-tedxwesthollywood-license-speakers-failed-to-gain-scientific-acceptance

171 http://www.huffingtonpost.com/deepak-chopra/dear-ted-is-it-bad-scienc_b_3104049.html

172 http://blog.ted.com/2013/04/01/a-note-to-the-ted-community-on-the-withdrawal-of-the-tedxwesthollywood-license/

173 http://www.ted.com/conversations/17348/discuss_the_note_to_the_ted_co.html

174 http://www.ted.com/profiles/1784880

175 http://www.ted.com/profiles/1747635

176 http://archived.parapsych.org/faq_file3.html

177 https://web.archive.org/web/20111004114553/http://www.ianbaker.org/news/beyond/

178 http://www.pflyceum.org/124.html

179 *Social Studies of Science,* vol.18, no. 3. Pg. 560. 1988

180 Jessica Utts, Replication and Meta-Analysis in Parapsychology, *Statistical Science,* vol. 6,no. 4, 1991, pgs. 363-364

181 https://web.archive.org/web/20130601094715/http://news.discovery.com/human/psychology/controversial-esp-study-fails-yet-again-120912.htm

182 Cleve Backster, *Primary Perception, Biocommunication with Plants, Living Foods, and Human Cells*, White Rose Millennium Press, 2003, Pg. 65

183 http://deanradin.blogspot.com/2010/04/psi-taboo-in-action.html

184 https://web.archive.org/web/20131224153235/http://www.timeshighereducation.co.uk/411401.article

185 William F. Bengston, *Journal of Scientific Exploration*, vol. 14, no. 3. pp. 353-364, 2000

186 https://newsvoice.se/2007/07/parapsychology-the-forbidden-research/

187 ibid

188 http://www.popsci.com/science/article/2013-09/why-were-shutting-our-comments

189 http://www.reachinglight.com/infographic-uk-filter-block-esoteric-content-worldwide-implications/

190 http://www.newrepublic.com/article/115533/rupert-sheldrake-fools-bbc-deepak-chopra

191 http://www.huffingtonpost.com/jimmy-soni/why-is-huffpost-ending-an_b_3817979.html

192 http://www.cnn.com/2013/09/24/tech/social-media/youtube-comment-upgrade/index.html

193 http://www.huffingtonpost.com/deepak-copra/dear-ted-is-it-bad-scienc_b_3104049.html

194 http://www.kickstarter.com/projects/1757859390/reality-sandwich-20

195 https://www.quora.com/q/parapsychology

196 https://corpgov.law.harvard.edu/2017/11/27/
short-activism-the-rise-in-anonymous-online-short-attacks/

197 https://insideevs.com/news/338572/
the-relentlessly-negative-tesla-smear-campaign-is-accelerating/

198 https://forums.tesla.com/en_AU/node/140211

199 https://cleantechnica.com/2019/05/24/
how-wild-useless-are-tesla-analyst-forecasts-morgan-stanley-edition/

ABOUT THE AUTHOR

Craig Weiler is a parapsychology journalist, speaker and host of the popular blog "The Weiler Psi" on the science of parapsychology, the skepticism and the psychics. A graduate of U.C. Berkeley, Craig runs a small successful construction business.

Craig has had an eclectic mix of interests over the years including acting, filmmaking, painting and writing and also built his own house.

Craig began his spiritual path during the New Age movement, teaching and practicing psychic healing, but found that it wasn't a good enough business. He does not follow any particular teachings, rather he explores a very westernized mixture of science and spirituality.

He lives on the San Francisco Peninsula with his wife and too many cats.

INDEX

A

Alcock, James, xi
Alvarado, Carlos, 4
Alvarez, José Luis, 81
Anderson, Chris, 9, 21, 72-74, 101, 108, 129-132, 180, 191, 193, 217-221, 223, 225-227
Armstrong, Karen, 218
Atkins, Anthony, 41
Atkins, Peter, 25

B

Backster, Cleve, 185-186
Baker, Ian, 41, 184
Banks, Joseph, viii
Barnum, P.T., 3
Barres, Barbara, 65
Barres, Ben, 65
Barrett, Stephen, 60
Barone, Lisa, 135
Barron, Jon, 97
Bell, John, 113, 115
Bem, Daryl, 44, 46-47, 185, 228
Bengston, William, 186
Benneth, John, 87

Berry, Amanda, 95
Blackmore, Susan, 80-81, 93, 187
Bohm, David, 115
Bohr, Niels, 115
Bolte Taylor, Jill, 10, 119
Bono, 9
Bradbury, Andy, 97
Browne, Sylvia, 76, 94-95
Bruno, Giordano, 220
Burns, Jean, 42

C

Cardeña, Etzel, xi
Carroll, Robert Todd, 96
Carroll, Sean, 70, 103
Carter, Chris, 38, 77, 119
Carter, Jimmy, 190
Chalmers, David, 117
Chopra, Deepak, vi, 14, 141, 155, 178, 217-223
Clowe, Ethan, 65
Coyne, Jerry, 14, 23-25, 50, 101-102, 104, 163, 178, 193, 197, 203-204, 222-223

D

Dalton, Kathy, 38
Dawkins, Richard, 56, 64, 218
Delanoy, Deborah, 25
d'Espagnat, Bernard, 115
Dossey, Larry, 169, 176-177, 181, 189-191, 213, 216

E

Edward, John, 76-77
Einstein, Albert, 115, 191
Eisenstein, Charles, 218
Erhard, Werner, 141

F

Fenwick, Peter, 25
Feynman, Richard, 115
French, Chris, ix, 38, 46, 152

G

Gabriel, Peter, 9
Galileo, 203, 219
Gates, Bill, 9, 221
Gauquelin, Michel, 91, 93
Gehry, Frank, 9
Geller, Uri, 77
Gerbic, Susan, 143-144
Goertzel, Ben, 31, 218
Goodall, Jane, 9
Gordin, Michael, 11
Gore, Al, 9
Graham, Billy, 9
Greyson, Bruce, 120
Grothe, D. J., 64, 76, 95-96

H

Hameroff, Stuart, 217
Hammid, Hella, 191
Hancock, Graham, 13, 70-72, 102, 105, 111, 118, 125-126, 129-131, 133, 163, 165, 171, 173-174, 180-181, 189, 191-194, 227
Harris, Sam, 64, 218
Hearst, Patricia, 190
Hebb, Donald, 6
Heisenberg, Werner, 115
Henderson, David, 136
Higgins, Henry, 66
His Holiness the Karmapa, 218
Hoffman, Bill, 25
Honorton, Charles, 5, 37
Hoopes, John, 179
Hough, Michael, xii
Huffington, Arianna, 117
Humphrey, Nicholas, 187
Hyman, Ray, 37, 80-81, 94, 142, 144, 157, 185

J

Jahn, Robert, 191
Jastrow, Joseph, 4
Joan of Arc, 219
Jones, Quincy, 9
Jordan, Ken, 179 182
Jordan, Pascual, 115
Josephson, Brian, 21, 94, 135, 178, 186
Jung, Carl, 4

K

Kafatos, Menas C., 217
Kafka, Franz, 130
Koestler, Arthur, 187
Krippner, Stanley, 38, 157
Kuhn, Thomas, 220
Kurz, Paul, 92-93
Kurzweil, Ray, 178
Kuttner, Fred, 114-116

L

Lanza, Robert, 115-116
Lasagna, Louis, 92
Leiter, L. David, 58
Lennox, Annie, 9
Lewin, Leonard, 92
Lomax, Abd ul-Rahman, 154
Lott, John, 136
Lulova, Natalya, 88

M

Marcus, Gary, 120
Marks, Harry, 9, 11, 40-41, 94, 178
Martin, Rod Jr, 98, 115
May, Ed, 56
McCarthy, Jenny, 143
McKenna, Terence, 31
McKinley Ball, Tom, 97
McLuhan, Robert, 5, 77, 142
McManus, Emily, 14, 23, 33, 50
Messer-Kruse, Timothy, 137
Metcalfe, David, 218
Milton, Julie, 38, 94
Morris, Robert, 14, 187
Myers, F.W.H., 4
Myers, PZ, 14, 24, 32, 50, 59, 64, 223

N

Nichols, Sam, 88
Nickell, Joe, 95-96, 144
Noble, Kathleen D., 221
Nugent, Michael
Nugent, Paul, 63, 176
Nye, Bill, 64

O

O'Brien, Chris, 178
Ogilvie, Derek, 88
Ortega, Filipe, 139

P

Palmer, John, 184
Parnia, Sam, 120
Pell, Claiborne, 185
Pena, Deyvi, 76, 81
Penrose, Roger, 191
Pinker, Steve, 64, 118
Poppy, Carry, 64
Prescott, Michael, 78
Putt, Patricia, 88-89

Q

Queen, Richard, 190

R

Radford, Ben, 64, 95-96, 144, 185
Radin, Dean, 37-38, 42-44, 52, 77,
    113, 139, 183-184, 186, 196
Randi, James, xi, 5, 19, 21, 64, 68, 75-
    83, 85-90, 95, 157
Rauf, Feisal Abdul, 218
Rawlings, Dennis, 91, 93
Reber, Arthur, xi
Rees, Martin, 115
Rhine, Joseph Banks, vii-viii, 5-6,
    199
Rhine, Louisa, viii
Ricard, Matthieu, 218
Robinson, Sir Ken, 10
Roe, Chris, xi, xiii
Rose, Steve, 153
Rosenblum, Bruce, 114-116
Rubery, Philip, 26

S

Saylor, C. P., 104
Schlitz, Marilyn, 42, 176-177, 181
Schmidt, Helmut, 43
Schub, M. H., 43-44
Schwartz, Gary, 89, 156

Sebald, Hans, 92
Sheldrake, Rupert, v-vi, x-xi, 13-15,
   22-33, 39-42, 46-47, 50, 52-53, 59,
   69-73, 79-80, 93-94, 101-105, 107-
   109, 111, 123, 125-129, 131, 133,
   141, 143-147, 151, 153-155, 159-160,
   163, 167, 173-177, 180-181, 189,
   191, 193, 196-197, 203-204, 206,
   220-223, 226-227, 232
Shermer, Michae, 64l
Smith, Alison, 86
Stein, Lara, 11, 166
Steindl-Rast, David, 218
Stollznow, Karen, 64, 144
Storm, Lance, 37
Storr, Will, 80
Sturgess, Kylie, 14, 24, 223

T

Talbot, Michael, 115
Targ, Russell, x
Taylor, Greg, 78, 128, 142
Taylor, Jill Bolte, 119
Taylor, Suzanne, 1, 163, 168, 174,
   176, 211-212
Theise, Neil, 217
Tice, Troy, 25
Tressoldi, Patrizio E, 37
Truzzi, Marcello, 67, 91
Tsakiris, Alex, 119-120

V

Valentini, Antony, 186
van Kampen, Nico, 116
van Lommel, Pim, 120
Van Praagh, James, 76
Von Neumann, John, 115

W

Warren, Rick, 218
Watson, Rebecca, 63-64
Watt, Caroline, ix
Wigner, Eugene, 115
Wilczek, Frank, 117
Williamson, Marianne, 171, 176, 216
Wilson, Robert Anton, 92
Winfrey, Oprah, 177
Wiseman, Richard, 38, 46-47, 89,
   93-94, 144, 187
Wurman, Saul, 9

Z

Zammit, Victor, 80
Ziborov, Pavel, 83, 85, 87-88

CPSIA information can be obtained
at www.ICGtesting.com
Printed in the USA
LVHW110732130720
660355LV00009B/446